This Book Includes:

Empath,

How to Analyze People,

Dark Psychology Secrets.

Learn How to Master Your Emotions, Improve Your Self-Confidence and Social Skills

Diana Brain

Table of Contents

EMPATH

HOW TO ANALYZE PEOPLE

DARK PSYCHOLOGY SECRETS

Empath

A Simple Guide for Empaths and Highly Sensitive People to Develop Your Gift and Thrive the Sense of Self, Raising Psychological and Spiritual Healing

Diana Brain

Introduction

Welcome to your journey into the world of empathy. If you are here, it is because you are keen on learning more about what empathy is and how it can be developed. The following words encourages us to love one another: "thou shall love thy neighbor as yourself." However, as we grow, we tend to change our natural tendency due to the harsh blows we get from the world. It is at this period that we start mistrusting other people, and we even become self-protective. We may start having attitudes that separate us from the others due to the perception that they are different from us. This itself tendency has some serious consequences, not only to us and our health, but also to the well-being of those who we neglect. We have the ability to hate or kill when the connection we have to other people is lost. We forget the importance behind seeing others as ourselves; hence not living according to the world's greatest teachings, can keep us from experiencing true empathy.

Most people have found challenges differentiating empathy (feeling with someone) from pity (the feeling of being sorry for someone), especially since the researchers who have handled this topic have ended up mudding the waters with a myriad of definitions.

Empathy is described as the ability for one to identify and comprehend another person's feelings and circumstances. This is a true definition of being shoulder to shoulder, heart to heart, eye to eye, and toe to toe with Someone else. Through empathy, we can attain the knowledge of our friends' experience through the direct individual awareness of the experience they are undergoing. Empathy is said to penetrate much deeper than reason, and this helps us to get knowledge through our senses and heart and not through our mind. Very pure and deep information about others manages to emerge via an empathetic connection.

In other words, it involves one's ability to perceive the feelings of other people (and recognize the emotions that we possess), to think what the underlying cause for someone else's feelings could be and showing concern to their situations. Compassionate action has always shown to be the most logical response once empathy is activated. Empathy has something to do with various parts of the brain which are responsible for the connection of one person with another and motivating one to show care. Pain pathways in our brains light up if we see someone cut themselves accidentally with a knife and crying in pain, but we feel the pain at a lesser degree. That can be said to be the emotional part of empathy, which is at times referred to as emotional resonance in which it is quite often ignored by many doctors despite going against their instincts.

Our sophisticated neurological system gives us the room to observe other individuals undergo pain, and it, in return, it gives us a small taste of the pain so to trigger action to help them.

However, relying on emotional resonance alone is not practical. In one way or the other, it gets much too strong for the people who are similar to us, and this might affect us greatly from achieving our goals. Notably, empathy possesses a cognitive component, and when it clearly set in our mind, we are able to understand the unique feelings of our friends, partners, and enemies. The ability to separate the feelings that belong to us from those of others allows us to calm any discomfort that we might be having, as we are vigilant on what our counterparts might be going through.

Empathy can also be defined as the inner motivation that forces us to respond and show our urge to care about the welfare of other people. Indeed, the amount of concern is said to vary from one person to another with different environmental factors influencing them. The influencers include how attractive the person going through a hard time is to you, the person's social class, whether you have gone through a similar situation yourself, if you feel that their suffering is a random act, or whether they deserve it as a result of their bad acts. In addition, the social status that you are in, meaning that if you are a richer person, you will notice the suffering of other people much less often. This suggests that while empathy is a built-in biological response to suffering, we still need to work on it if we want to develop it for use in everyday situations.

Chapter 1: The Nature of Empathy

Clinical psychologists have over and over again tried to define the "skill" of empathy in a bid to recognize it in the interactions of counseling. According to Carl Rogers, empathy can only occur only when a therapist views the patient with unconditional positive regard and also when they pay attention to what the patient tends to say, showing sensitivity in their feedback offered after a session. This would lead to a psychological sense of healing.

In reference to one of the works by Carl Rogers, in which he described empathy as a skill which can be confidently taught, he emphasizes that empathy is not so much a skill, but a way of being. On the other hand, Jewish theologian, Martin Buber came up with a different narrative which ended up influencing the shift in the understanding of the empathy process. In Buber's work, he focused on the description of "I-Thou" relationship to the humans' health and hence described dialogue to be central to this relationship.

A dialogue involves two people embarking on a conversation in order to exchange ideas and information. When real communication takes place, the two parties find themselves connected closely or even being aligned in a moment of shared meaning. Rogers, on the other hand, described a dialogue as being identical to achieving empathy. In his argument, Rogers poses that we cannot trigger cross-communication to happen; we can only allow it to happen. In his argument, the process should only happen, at will, with the person listening carefully and mirroring his or her words and feelings. Buber maintains that cognitive processes can't lead to psychological healing taking place as it can't be controlled by an individual but takes place as a result of a conversation between two people happening spontaneously.

Another scholar who sought to define this was Edith Stein. She is phenomenologist and student of Edmund Husserl. In her dissertation entitled, "On the Problem of Empathy", she described empathy as a far more complex process. In this book, she has outlined how empathy emerges from the inter-subjective processes of the mind. This occurrence can be seen in three stages given to us "non-primordially," or after the fact, somewhat like a post-event realization. She gives further examples of events that occur when we are unaware of something, for instance, falling in love with someone. We might want to be in love with a person we have known for so long but are not requited in our feelings. Yet, the other person may begin to develop feelings over time without noticing them. In this event, there is nothing actually triggering such feelings consciously. They are main a consequence of a subconscious process in which we are becoming more and more interconnected with the other person.

Processes Most Often Confused with Empathy

The interactions mostly mistaken as empathy include pity, sympathy, kindness, and identification. Each of them will be discussed according to the phenomenological literature available to us.

Max Schleler has shed some light on the discussion of sympathy by identifying various versions of the main process. According to Schleler, sympathy is an associated feeling. By this, he means that two people can have the same feelings and the same ideas about an event happening around them — for instance, the feeling after your favorite team lost a match or because of frustrating weather. The moment you feel joyful with the other person over their success, then you are in sympathy with them. Therefore, it means that sympathy entails standing side by side with someone, that is, sharing a common feeling over an event that is taking place at the moment or in the past. During this time, you won't experience any crossover feelings, but the sympathy you experience will be much stronger than just being an agreement with the person.

Pity has been discussed and described as a form of sympathy; a kind of sympathetic sorrow, but the mutual, shared nature of sympathy is replaced with a position of superiority. The moment you pity another person it means that you feel very sorry for them (perhaps subconsciously).

The identification is said to be an interpersonal process as it orients or self-aligns itself to the other person very closely. For instance, a mentor, a group of political party members within a region such as country club can result in having a strong emotional tie. The moment you get to identify with a group or a person, you tend to adopt their values, priorities, mannerisms, and even dress code. The process of identification becomes much easier and successive when it is not focused on a person's unique identity and nor does it enable the process of searching for one's place in the world. Notably, cult behavior in a group can develop if an individual's ego takes over individuals or the group as a whole.

Self-transposal has, in most cases, been thought to be empathy. This is the process whereby an individual thinks and feels in a similar position of another person. This is exactly the way Rogers, in his works, defined empathy to be. Empathy is said to be much more complex than the act of thinking and having the same feelings as another individual.

To sum up pity, sympathy, identification, and self-transposal are not precisely understood and hence the reason why they are often confused with empathy. All of them are similar to one another thus leading to the possibility of them being described as a one-stage, inter-subjective process which can take place without being triggered. We can't make empathy happen, but we give it a chance to occur only when we provide room for it to happen.

What is Empathy?

Empathy is an extremely reactive emotional response. Empaths do not have the same characteristics that allow other people to block feelings of identification. This is one of the characteristics that distinguish empaths from the rest of the world. Personally, being an empath, I can state that we do take in both positive and negative situations surrounding us, may it be in our jobs, home, school, social life or any other area. Every empath tends to be extra sensitive, and this can be same as holding the hand of a person with fifty fingers instead of a normal hand. The true definition of how empaths react is that of super responders.

From previous research, it has been found that over 20 percent of the population is affected by sensitivity. From this research, we can surmise that the degree of sensitivity does indeed vary from one person to another.

Empaths have often been labeled as "overly sensitive" and can be told to "get a thicker skin." Children and adults at are greatly shamed by society for their sensitivity instead of being acknowledged as caring individuals. When shamed, they wish to get retreat from this world when they are overwhelmed. They have felt like giving themselves, but still, the fact remains that they aren't able to do so. As an empath, I can sense the earth's secrets and also get to know my passions beyond my wildest dreams. However, my empathic abilities haven't always felt this incredible to me.

The fact is that empaths have a strength that is wonderful to develop. This strength includes intuition, depth, compassion, and a profound connection to others and the universe. This world requires your gift and hence the reason why it's important and to bring the warrior spirit out always.

What is a warrior empath?

A warrior empath can be defined by the following characteristics: strength, care, attention and protectiveness. Since empathic people understand themselves to the core, they can practice self-care. They have the toolkit of strategies to be practiced daily, or at least regularly, in a bid to remain strong and thrive in any situation. With the use of these strategies, one will be at a point of not absorbing other people's stress.

Empaths with strategic, energy-saving tools are unstoppable. To support my warrior spirit, I use these five strategies each day. I will outline these in my book. Give them a try and see how your energy and clarity improve.

Warrior Empath Toolkit

Express gratitude: it is key for one to kick off the day with gratefulness affirmation and not only to focus on the things to be done throughout the day. Gratitude brings about positive energy, keeps the person on their toes and ready to act rather than wasting the energy catastrophizing about the future.

Meditate: it is recommended to put into practice the three-minute meditation day in, and day out. This meditation should be centered on the heart energy allowing the release of fear. Short meditations help in bringing one back to the center of power when there is a feeling sensory overload. Meditation plays a key role in stopping the accumulation of stress in the body.

Strengthen your intuition: It is always important to trust your intuition in order to allow positive people in your inner circle. Elimination of energy vampires is crucial whenever possible. Intuition will tell you when your energy has increased or decreased around someone. It is highly advisable that one keeps company with those people who give off positive energy that can allow you to thrive. Moreover, set boundaries with those who will drain your positive energy.

Love yourself: We are all wonderfully made, hence the need to love ourselves at all times. Let your daily mantra be "I embrace my sensitivities. I can be vulnerable and strong at the same time."

The empath's journey can be said to be the journey of a lifetime. One has to be grateful for all that the world brings such as the exquisite experience of joy and passion. This gives you the ability to see the bigger picture on deeper levels. An empathetic person gets to be connected with the poetry, beauty, and energy found in life. With compassion, one can give a helping hand to other needy friends. One cannot be callous, coldhearted or shut off from others' need. A sensitive person resolves to be very caring, aware, and vulnerable.

Embracing the warrior spirit helps the empathetic person be able to improve their relationships with themselves as well as others. Celebrate your progress every time you listen to your intuition and assert your empathic needs; this can help you center yourself amid chaos. One can live this life fully without having to deny oneself anything to make others comfortable. It is highly encouraged that we all love ourselves today, and every day, without any conflicts or hesitations. We have to be in control of our advances and be happy about them.

Growing Up as An Empath

I find it hard to fit in today's society. When I was growing up, I used to feel like an alien here on earth waiting to be taken to my place in the stars. Nowadays, I can still recall when I sat in my front yard gazing at the sky wishing a spaceship would come down and take me home. Since I was born a single child, I would spend so much time alone. I barely had anyone to relate to or share my sensitivity with. Neither my neighbors, family members, nor children in my area were like me.

Little did I know that my entire community and its surroundings had a subtle energy field enveloping their bodies; a radiant light penetrating from about an inch of distance to about a foot. Studies have shown that if we are in the midst of other people, the energy of others does overlap with ours. As a child, I could pick out all those intense sensations, even without a clue of what they were, or how to interpret them. In those times, I would become highly anxious and grow tired when in crowds. All in all, I wanted to run away, escape, and be alone.

Due to this, I found myself getting involved with drugs in a bid to block my sensitivities even though this is not the least bit recommendable. When everything cooled down, I would later go out to parties, go to the nearest shopping mall with other friends, something which made me feel quite good and relieved.

I would fight my therapist the entire time. However, this angel in a human body was the one person who helped me understand that I needed to grasp my sensitivity and how to deal with it in an effective manner. It was at this point when I began to mend and acknowledge my empathetic nature. Since I was so alarmed by my empathetic and instinctive encounters at such a young age, some portion of my development as a doctor and a person has led me to figure out how to grasp these capacities.

The Empath Experience

Let's have a close evaluation of empathetic experiences. We will need to have a self-evaluation; also, we will need to evaluate our loved ones, friends, and relatives who would qualify as an empath.

We will need to understand the difference that lies between ordinary empathy and just being a true empath. For ordinary empathy, we get to have our hearts go out to another person being faced with a serious or disturbing situation. Also, with this kind of empathy, one can be happy for others in the time of their joy. As an empath, we sharply sense our friend's energy, emotions, and physical symptoms in our being as a consequence of not having the filters that many people possess. As an empath, we always face sorrow, happiness, pain and joy. We have heightened sensitiveness to others' tone of voice and body language. The empath can hear that which has not been spoken by reading nonverbal communications and also interpreting silence. As an empath, I first feel things, and then I think; this is opposite of how others behave in our over intellectualized society. This is the reason as to why empaths are different from the people who have built up their defenses as a result of their upbringing.

Empaths share several of the characteristics which are highlighted by therapist Elaine Aron in the concept of "Highly Sensitive People", or HSPs. A portion of the attributes that empaths possess as a part of their core being, include the need for alone time, affectability to light, sound, and smell, in addition to reluctance for huge gatherings.

Notably, highly sensitive people take longer to settle their minds after a long day as their system of transmission from higher stimulation to lower takes further time to work. Empaths also share a great deal of personal love for nature and environments that offer peace, quiet and serenity. In addition, people under this category further the experience of sensitive people to a greater extent. As empaths, we can sense subtle energy, which is called Shakti, or prana, in Eastern healing traditions. Moreover, we absorb this energy into our bodies. This type of person consistently does this, and it is this type of capacity, that gives us room to experience the energies that surround us in both superficial and deeper ways.

Empaths tend to internalize pain, feelings, and other physical sensations of other people. Research has proven that these types of people have challenges while trying to distinguish other people's discomfort from theirs. As an empath, I always have a profound spiritual and intuitive experience, which is, in most cases, linked to my highly sensitive nature.

Empaths can speak with nature, animals, and inner self. However, being a very sensitive individual and an empath are not necessarily the same thing; while you can be both, deciding whether you are an empath is more a question of your choice to embrace the role rather than checking off a number of boxes on a quiz.

Chapter 2: General Types of Empaths

Main types of Empaths

1. Emotional Empaths

This type of empath quickly picks up on the emotions of the other people. Emotional empaths tend to be a sponge for the feelings of others, such as sadness and happiness. If you are in this group, then it's quite easy for you to pick up the emotions of other people and be at a point in which you feel as if it is you undergoing such feelings. These empaths will find themselves having a deep identification with others in their bodies. For instance, this kind of person can be very sad when in the company of a sad friend. This group of empaths needs to learn and understand the differences that exist between their emotions, and those of other people. It is through this that they will be able to give positive assistance to others without having negative situations drain the empath.

2. Physical Empaths

Empaths in this group can pick up on the energy from people's bodies. They keenly understand what ails others. Most people under this category end up being healers either in the conventional medical profession or in other related fields such as psychology. They always feel awareness when they are treating a patient. They can also see the blockages that exist in the person's energy field. Physical empaths have a strong feeling to treat others who need it. Research has shown that people under this category can pick up other people's symptoms and as if they were experiencing them in their own bodies. This act of taking on someone else's illness can lead to one having or experiencing serious health issues in the long run. People with serious chronic diseases such as fibromyalgia or autoimmune diseases might find it helpful to strengthen their personal energy. In particular, it is good for one to take training in treating the symptoms of conditions. People can be energized by other people's sense of wellbeing.

3. Geomantic Empath

This type of empathy has also been referred to as a spatial or environmental empathy. People under this group have a fine attunement to their surroundings and the context in which they find themselves in. In a way, they are in tune with the bigger picture around them. So, instead of focusing on individuals, they are able to pick up on the feelings of a collective group of individuals. This is one of the reasons behind most empath's reluctance to attend large group gatherings such as sporting events or concerts. If the vibe given off by the group is more negative than positive, this will cause the empath to become both physically and emotionally affected by the circumstances.

4. Intellectual Empaths

People found in this group experience extraordinary perception such as heightened intuition, receiving messages in their dreams, telepathy, communicating with animals and plants. They are also known to have the ability to contact the spiritual realm. These people have difficulty when it comes to communicating with traditional language. This is evident in the way that these empaths often say, "I can't find the words to express what I'm feeling". At times, they use language and phrases that match those of other people. For them, building rapport and mirroring behaviors don't give them a hard time since it just happens automatically.

5. Intuitive Empath

These empaths have the innate sense of understanding or simply "knowing". They can know something which is not physically seen, or they can also sense something that is just about to take place. It is also true that they have dreams that are pre-cognitive. This means that such dreams happen in the days following their dream. They possess a strong ability to detect when an individual is telling a lie, and they are keen about other individuals' obvious or clandestine expectations. Those with this gift reverberate to other realms as they read the vitality of others effectively. This is firmly established by the clairvoyant empath who can anticipate someone else's feelings and intentions.

6. Animal Empaths

Animal empaths are the dog and horse whisperers of the world. They can tell the feelings of an individual animal, its experience, and needs. They don't just love the creatures they associate with; they may incline toward interacting with animals more than humans! What's more, animals feel equally drawn towards an empath human.

7. Plant Empaths

These are the people who possess very strong connections with nature, mostly with the trees and plants in the surrounding environment. They are people who can be said to have a green thumb. They are skilled gardeners and growers who would prefer being around nature. Plants generally thrive in their presence and care. They also have a high understanding of matters pertaining to the proper care of flowers. They possess a keen understanding of the uses of plants and their functions. They can separate the edible plants from others. Furthermore, they can assess what needs to be done to the environment so as to achieve ecological balance and sustainability.

8. Environmental Empaths

These people are also known as the geomantic empaths, and they are well known for their ability to foresee what is about to happen in the physical space or what has already happened. Similarly, geomantic empaths can 'read' a physical object. If they have entered into a new space, such as a room, they will be mindful of what had happened just before entering that environment. They also can glean information from a person by simply holding a personal object.

9. Spiritual Empaths

These people are said to have a direct connection to different realms. They have the ability to connect with the deceased or other spiritual human beings based on their system of beliefs. They will feel the physical and emotional sensations emanating from their communication with the spiritual world. It is said that spiritual empaths have the same connection with the spiritual realm as they do with the physical world.

10. Heyoka

According to the tradition of native Americans, a Heyoka is a type of sacred individual who is capable of joking around; a sort of spiritual jester. They are said to be disrupters but not in a negative manner. They are able to move from physical and spiritual worlds and are able to act as a psychic medium in order to communicate between both worlds. These people are said to behave like mirrors, in which they reflect the feelings of other people and go to the extent of showing them what they will need to see in themselves or the vice versa.

The Process of Becoming an Empath

There are various factors that cause one to become an empath. From an early age, we understand that some of individuals do enter the world with various sensitivities. They have quite a temperament. These can be quite evident the moment a person comes out of the womb. These children are highly receptive to light, contact, and smell, temperature, environment, and sound. Likewise, from what I've seen with my patients and workshop members, some sensitivity might be hereditarily transmitted. It is argued that these traits can come from either their father's or mother's genes.

However, how the child is brought up plays a key role. If a child is neglected or abused at the very early stages of life, then it is clear that they will have issues as adults. During my time in a health clinic, I managed to treat people who experienced early trauma; this included physical and emotional abuse. Other empaths were brought up by depressed, alcoholic, or narcissistic parents, and this highly affected the life of that child even at the adult stage of their lives.

Being raised under such situations and circumstances can potentially wear down the health of the child. Such conditions have adverse effects to such children, thus making them feel unseen by their families and also invisible to the greater world around them especially because it doesn't value sensitive people very highly. However, empaths cannot handle rough times, such as when they are going through a stressful period, in the same way others do. Therefore, it can be concluded that we are diverse in this regard. A toxic environment, for example, being around a furious individual, large groups, clamoring people, or bright lights, can unsettle us on the grounds of sensory overload as our threshold for stimuli is rather low.

The main reasons that have been known to trigger empaths are:

Reason 1: Temperament

As discussed earlier, babies who enter the world with much more sensitivity than others are said to belong in this category. Their sensitivity to the following factors may lead them to develop their empathetic abilities, among them, being sensitive to light, touch, movement, sound, and crowds.

Reason 2: Genetics

While I was growing up, I came to learn that empathy has much to do with genetics as empathetic abilities can highly be transmitted through families.

Reason 3: Trauma

Children who face abuse and neglect at the early stages of life may find that their empathetic abilities stagnate due to inadequate emotional development. This can lead to inadequate formation of the child's personality leading them to become adults with profound issues thereby increasing their overall sensitivities for others due to the fact that they have "been there".

Reason 4: Supportive Parenting

Supportive parents have a key role to play in helping the child acknowledge and honor their gifts. Parents act as a powerful role model for their children, but in particular, to the sensitive kids.

Please bear in mind that all sensitive people are prone to healing. It is good to note that all cases of trauma can be healed. This includes those who have been through early childhood trauma, child abuse, or being brought up by narcissistic parents. The key point is that being positive, and learning how to embrace your sensitiveness, is quite important. This will call for the selection of very healthy people around you, and also setting healthy boundaries. Also, it is highly advisable that you consider taking medication and centering techniques in a bid to help strengthen your core; this is to help you become both strong and sensitive.

Understanding yourself as an empath or one you know

If you think you are an empath, or have somebody in your life who is, you will realize that it isn't generally simple to be one. Being sensitive to other individuals' feelings, vitality, and nature can be hard. It is important for empaths to develop their gifts as they get older. That way, they can create the abilities which are useful when taking care of themselves. Also, keeping their very own space and limits are essential. There might be times when an empath needs to step away from their empathetic, mystical, or otherworldly side. Finding a means to not assimilate, or take on, other individuals' "stuff" will help with recapturing the feeling of individuality and self-identity within themselves. On the other hand, being an empath should be viewed as a blessing which is to be utilized wisely throughout everyday life.

What is next for you as an empath?

From the above explanation, you will understand the type of empath you are; all you need is to be smart about it. You do not need to learn everything there is to know at once. But it is important to recognize your abilities as an empath sooner rather than later. You will need to understand that it is important to have the necessary skills to manage empathy. Anyone can call themselves an empath but only a chosen few actually live it.

So, how can you develop your empathetic skills? If you are a novice, it is of the utmost importance that you find yourself a trainer who will offer you more than just a few coping mechanisms. It is good that you stay away from any trainer who tends to treat you like a fragile crystal figurine. A trainer should be able to coach you to strengthen yourself and give you the skills you need so that you can support your natural sensitivity.

Empaths have beautiful and diversely nuanced sensitiveness. It is also true that one can be one or more of empath types described earlier. Still, there are two other types of empaths which aren't widely discussed, which include: food empaths (who are sensitive to the vitality of sustenance) and relationship/sexual empaths (who are receptive to their partners' and companions' temperaments, erotic nature, and physical wellbeing). If you are busy learning about your talents, you will discover that they can not only enrich yourself but also to touch others positively.

Styles of Relating: Introverted and Extroverted Empaths

Our neurodiversity plays a key role in making us different. In our society, we need to understand that some people we interact with have an extroverted nature and therefore require a higher level of social and environmental stimulation to keep them leveled and feeling energized.

Others may become diagnosed with conditions such as ADHD due to their overactive nature. They express a very clear talent in matters of creativity, but most notably, they have challenges when it comes to concentrating in environments that require a higher degree of focus.

On the other hand, we have the empaths, highly sensitive people, who are considered to be introverts. They are very similar to extroverts in that they enjoy the company of others. These kinds of empaths are easily stimulated by happenings around them, but this is where the differences between empath types arise. An introvert empath needs time away from the hustle and bustle of daily life in order to recharge and reflect.

It is good to understand that the physical, intuitive, and emotional empaths have a different style of socializing. They interact quite differently with the world around them. It is argued that most empaths are introverted, but still, some are extroverted while others are a combination of both natures. If you are an introvert, like me, you will need to understand that we are minimal when it comes to socializing, that is, we talk less. When we attend meetings, we tend to leave a bit earlier than the rest and spend much of the time silent, taking in our surroundings.

Introverted empaths may even make sure to arrive in their own cars in a bid to not feel trapped or feel as they have to depend on others for a ride. Personally, I refer my close circle of friends, and most times, I love staying away from the parties or gatherings. I generally prefer to engage in deep and meaningful talks as opposed to making pointless small talk since meaningless chatter is not conducive to connecting with people. The good thing is that all my friends understand my way of life. So, they never get offended when I ask to leave an event earlier than they do.

Empaths, who are extroverts, are said to be increasingly verbal and outgoing when mingling and appreciate the exchange with others more than introverted empaths do. Likewise, they can remain longer in social circumstances without getting depleted or overstimulated.

Overly sensitive empaths can quickly become tired in large social settings such as meetings, concerts, sporting events and clubs. While they may be having a good time, sensory overload eventually takes over. The reason for this is that they feel the energy of both the crowds and the individuals. After a certain amount of time, this can become quite exhausting, especially if the atmosphere isn't a positive one.

So why do people become empaths? Is it due to their temperament? Genetics? Trauma? Neglectful or supportive parents?

The fact of the matter is that become an empath is the result of innate abilities and proper nurturing. It should be noted that we all have the capacity for empathy. The difference with more naturally inclined people is that they have an easier time developing their abilities. Nevertheless, anyone can develop these skills. The starting point is to become in tune with your sensitivities. It is important to pay close attention to what others feel and, essentially, putting yourself in their place especially when they hurt you or even attack you.

Chapter 3: The Science of Empathy

Recent scientific findings have explained empathetic experience. I find them absolutely fascinating. But before dedicated research, it was believed that people who claimed to have the ability to feel the emotional, physical, and mental state of their close friends or people, were simply "nice" or "kind". The idea that one can feel the pain of another human being sounds more like fantasy than fact. Scientific backing on this issue has also grown over time. Most researchers argue that they understand more and more about the neurology behind the concept of empathy in general.

From recently conducted research, it has been revealed that empaths do exist, estimating that between 1 to 2 percent of the population reports not having some kind of empathetic experience.

Synesthesia

From recent findings, it has been established that there is an extraordinary condition referred to as mirror-touch synesthesia. This is a neurological condition under which various senses end up being paired in the brain. A good example of this is when one identifies colors after hearing a piece of music or when "tasting" words.

Individuals who have been known to experience synesthesia include Isaac Newton, Billy Joel, and Itzhak Perlman. In addition, with mirror-touch synesthesia, individuals feel the emotions and impressions of others in their own bodies, as though these feelings were their own. This is a magnificent neurological explanation of an empath's physiological functioning.

Synesthesia is said to occur when normally distinct senses are blurred together. By this, I mean that there are people who can hear colors, taste words, and see sounds. When one has mirror-touch synesthesia, touch and sight overlap to the extent that when an individual with synesthesia sees another person laying their hands on their face, they feel the same sensation on their face as if they were the ones being touched.

In the case of mirror-pain synesthesia, it is quite common for many people to feel this to some extent. A great example of this happens when someone is scratching all over, so the empath starts feeling pain, itchiness, all over their body as well. From my personal research, I have found that, about 30 percent of people I have come into contact with undergoes, or experiences, this kind of synesthesia. Being able to feel the feelings of others is quite a rare experience indeed.

Also, I found out that most of the people who have a mirror synesthesia happen to be unaware that they have it. While carrying out research, I took a keen interest in the issues that surround the potential blurring of senses into a single one. I have personally been through this when focusing on the pain of others. So, to understand this concept better, I sought to truly empathize with others, that is, really put myself in their shoes without actually being in them. So, I fully concentrated on the other person, rather than myself, so as to empathize with them in a myriad of other situations. I realized that people with the ability to empathize may experience difficulty when it comes to controlling their feelings around others as this is not the type of skill you can just turn on or off.

Furthermore, there could be an infinite number of mental, emotional, and physical repercussions. For instance, mirror-touch sensitive people have reported feeling overwhelmed on a consistent basis throughout their lives. As an empath and a psychiatrist, I am highly fascinated by how the phenomenon of empathy works in our society. Empathy is the only medicine that the world is in dire need of at the moment.

Increased Dopamine Sensitivity

Research involving dopamine, which is a neurotransmitter, has linked the prevalence of dopamine and increased activity of the neurons as a response to pressure and stimuli in the environment. We have come to understand that dopamine is a critical chemical messenger to the brain. As a result, it is believed that dopamine has many functions. Dopamine is involved in matters of motivation, reward, memory, attention, and the regulation of the body movements.

To understand dopamine better, we need to know that when it is released in large quantities, it creates a feeling of pleasure, and reward motivating the person to repeat an action, or a certain behavior. A person would be less motivated and experience lower levels of enthusiasm for the same things that most people would find exciting, if the person has low levels of dopamine.

Research has found that introverts have a higher level of sensitivity to dopamine in comparison to extroverts. Empaths who are introverts require less dopamine in order to feel happy. This is a clear definition of why they tend to be more content with spending their time while alone, doing reading and meditating, or any other type of activity that shies away from large interactions of people. This type of person also needs less to no external stimulation from parties or intense gatherings. As a matter of fact, extroverted folks (empaths or not), are said to highly crave for dopamine rushes. That is why they need to get it from intense events and emotions. It is said that they can hardly get enough of it.

Ways to Increase Dopamine Levels

- o Eating Lots of Proteins

Proteins are made of amino acids which are small building blocks of the body. One amino acid is known as tyrosine and has a key role to play in the production of dopamine. These types of blocks can be harnessed form foods like turkey, eggs, beef, soy, dairy, and legumes.

o   Consuming Less Saturated Fats

Saturated fats are mostly found in animal fats, butter, palm oil, full-fat dairy, and coconut oil. These can highly disrupt dopamine from signaling the brain when it is produced in large quantities. Notably, research on this effect has been conducted on rats with was quite intriguing results.

o   Consumption of Probiotics

The gut and brain are closely linked. Therefore, it has been argued by scientists that some of the bacteria living in the human gut is able to produce dopamine thus having full capacity to impact both mood and behavior. Researchers have concluded that the production of dopamine plays a key role when it comes to how probiotics improve one's mood. Still, more research is required in order to expound clearly on how significant this effect can be.

o   The Consumption of Velvet Beans

This type of bean is also known as the *mucuna pruriens,* and has high levels of L-dopa, which is the precursor to dopamine. Studies have revealed that the consumption of these beans contribute significantly towards the improvement of dopamine levels in one's body. Higher levels of dopamine reduce the risk of being afflicted by Parkinson's disease; this disease is associated with low levels of dopamine.

- o Getting regular exercise

A person who does frequent exercise is believed to have improved endorphin levels and mood. Changes in moods can be noticed after as little as 10 minutes of exercise while the greatest improvements can be seen after 20 minutes of continuous exercise. The latest research has shown that exercise can boost and improve dopamine levels in the human brain. This is the reason why we are encouraged to get regular exercise.

- o Enough Sleep

Dopamine creates a feeling of alertness and being awake when it is released in the brain. According to an animal study, dopamine is released in the early morning and at huge amounts. Generally, this occurs around the time when one is almost awake, and it is at its lowest during the times when one is getting ready to sleep. When you lack sleep, the natural rhythm is disrupted. Also, when one stays up at night, dopamine receptors in the brain are reduced significantly thereby limiting cognitive functions.

- o Listening to Music

Listening to music is known to stimulate the levels of dopamine released in one's brain. One study has revealed that increased listening of music plays a role in boosting the reward and pleasure areas of our medulla. This area is believed to be very rich in dopamine receptors. It has been found that there is a 9 percent boost in dopamine when a person is listening to relaxing or soothing music over a brief period of time.

- o   Meditation

This is the act under which a person clears the mind, focuses on inward, and lets thoughts float by without judging them. Meditation can be done while seated, standing, or when walking. It is closely associated with mental and physical health. Research into meditation has found that such benefits are due to the increased dopamine levels in the person's brain.

From the above explanation, it can be concluded that dopamine is quite an important brain chemical. As a result, it can influence our mood, feelings, rewards, and motivation. It exerts control over the regulation of our body's movements as well. A person who takes in a balanced diet with the required amounts of vitamins, proteins, minerals, probiotics, and the required amounts of saturated fats can have their bodies produce the much-needed dopamine levels in order to regulate movement.

People with low dopamine level should consider consuming natural food sources containing L-dopa such as fava beans so that their dopamine levels are restored to normal. Other factors that one can't brush away include getting enough sleep, enough exposure to the sun, doing exercise, listening to music, and spending much time in meditation in order to boost the levels of dopamine in the brain. A healthy lifestyle and balanced diet can play a significant role in assisting you to increase your body's natural production of dopamine while stabilizing your body's overall performance.

Emotional Contagion

The findings from research have concluded that we can enhance our understanding as empaths through the phenomenon of emotional contagion. Scientists have come to understand that people do pick up the emotions of those around them. For instance, a crying infant will set off a wave of crying babies in a hospital ward. A worker who happens to express anxiety in a crowded workplace can end up spreading the same feeling to the other workers located in the same area. People tend to catch other people's feelings quite easily when in larger groups.

The ability for one to be able to synchronize moods with other people is quite important for a healthy relationship. How can this improve our understanding of empathy? We need to have people with positive motives in our lives, as this will keep us far away from being pulled down by negativity. If a very serious challenge is facing one of our friends, then we have a mandate to play a positive role in solving the matter. As friends, we should take a special precaution to ground and center ourselves.

At this point, we might infer that there is a divide between empathy and emotional contagion. But the fact of the matter is that emotional contagion is closely linked to empathy. Emotional contagion is part of the greater puzzle known as empathy. One might find a challenge if one fails to differentiate the two of them, as they both have a very specific meaning and purpose. Despite them being very closely related, one has to note that they are two different concepts. To break it down, and make it easier to digest, we can go over their definitions.

Empathy: As discussed earlier, empathy is the ability of an individual to not only share in, but also understand another person's emotions and feelings; this is often known as putting oneself in the other person's shoes. To put it another way, to experience what someone else is going through.

Emotional contagion: This is the ability a person possesses in order to catch and feel emotions of others as they are felt in the environment surrounding the individual. In other words, it can be said that it is a process in which a group of people, or an individual person influences the behavior or emotions of the others in a group of people through conscious or unconscious induction of emotional states leading to changes in attitude and behavior.

Therefore, empathy is the ability to actually put yourself in the actually place that another person is in while emotional contagion is the act in which your personal attitudes and feelings are influenced by those of others around you. So, you are not actually feeling what they are feeling; you are simply influenced by the feelings of others.

On the other hand, emotional contagion is more of an automated process and not a conscious one which relies heavily on non-verbal communication. This can include emails, calls, forums, and chats. People in this group may experience a 'social virus' that urges them to mimic the facial expressions, postures, vocal expressions, and physical behaviors of the people surrounding them. Ultimately, they are merely copying the behavioral patterns of those around them. Often, it is a subconscious response that seeks to win the approval or others.

Chapter 4: The Process of Empathy

The process of empathy has six very distinct phases and are said to overlap each other. They can be a bit confusing at times when trying to differentiate them. However, it is good to note that all six phases can be grouped into two categories. The first category is the cognitive level, while the other is the emotional level. Within the scope of the cognitive level, the three major phases include the theory of the mind, cognitive empathy, and perspective-taking. For the emotional level, we have Identification, true empathy, and emotional contagion.

In this section, we are going to discuss each facet of the empathetic process in detail. I will also analyze why each phase is considered unique from the others.

The Cognitive Level

a) Theory of the Mind

The Theory of the Mind is said to be the ability of an individual to attribute mental states, including the intents, beliefs, pretensions, desires, knowledge and the likes either in oneself or those of others. It is also the ability to understand the beliefs, intentions, and desires of others which are different from yours. In research conducted by Simon Baron, he described the theory of the mind as "being able to infer the full range of mental states such as beliefs, desires, imaginations, intentions, emotions, and so on.

b) Perspective Taking

This has been defined as the ability of one to see things from a point of view that is very different than that of one's own. We will be able to find a different number of traits that fit this description.

To begin with, we must first acknowledge the fact that we all have varying perspectives on the same situations and phenomena. So, even if we "agree", it is very likely that we will all have a different perception. This leads to a type of relativism in what we tend to perceive as "reality". As a result, we cannot assume that everyone completely agrees with us especially is the object in questions does not have a clearly defined aspect. For example, love has a plethora of definitions. So, even if there is a consensus on what feeling love entails, there is not clear consensus on a definition of the word. Hence, the perception of love is very personal to every individual. Ultimately, attaining consensus can be a monumental task.

c) Cognitive Empathy

This term can be defined as having awareness of the needs of others. As such, it is one thing to empathize with others, that is, to feel what others feel, and it is another completely different thing to be aware of what others need. Consider this situation: you are in the care of a sick person. This person is going through pain and discomfort on both a physical and emotional level. So, you empathize with them. You feel that they feel. This can happen at a subconscious level in which there is a connection, but the empath is not fully aware of this connection. As a result, empathy takes place, but both parties are not conscious of what is actually occurring.

When cognitive empathy takes place, the empath is fully aware of what they are feeling and will use that to "sense" what the other person is feeling. After a while, the caregiver knows when the other person is in pain or is feeling depressed as a result of their illness.

The Emotional Level

d) Identification

Identification occurs on a deeper, emotion level. While the cognitive level creates a level of awareness in the empath, the emotional level creates the actual feeling and sensation of empathy. This is a gut-level reaction that occurs any time there is an empathetic reaction. Consequently, the empath is able to absorb what others are feeling. The end result of this situation is the empath imbibing their surroundings. This is one of the fundamental reasons why empaths tend to become overwhelmed when faced with large groups of people especially in situations of despair and suffering. Imagine yourself, as a finely tuned empath, working as a relief worker in the zone of a natural disaster. The feelings of the affected people will certainly cause you to feel a great sense of despondency. This can lead to a great sense of loss and suffering, as well.

e) True Empathy

True empathy happens when a person, not just an empath, is able to truly put themselves in the position of someone else. This usually happens when the empath has been through the same, or similar situation. For instance, the empath will pick up on feelings of sadness from someone else as a result of the loss of a loved on. This is empathy. However, true empathy will occur when the empath has also been through the loss of a loved one. This maximizes the empath's ability to fully immerse themselves in the emotions of others.

f) Emotional Contagion

As stated earlier, this is when a person, basically anyone, ins influenced by the circumstances surrounding them. For instance, when a person goes to a sporting event, they may be influenced by the reaction of the crowd even if they have little interest in the sporting even itself. Yet, it is the reaction of the collective group of individuals that leads to an emotional response in the individual attending the event.

Also, emotional contagion is very common in the workplace. When the environment in a place of work is tense, this rubs off on even the most of cheerful employees. This is why psychologists strive to understand what motivates employees and what can lead to creating a positive atmosphere within the workspace. While the link between positive workspace atmospheres and high levels of productivity is clear, what is not fully understood is what drives workers as a collective group. Of course, we have a clear understanding of what motivates individuals, but not as a collective group. As such, if a person works in a toxic environment, it is quite probable that they will end up become influenced by this environment to the extent that it affects their life outside of work, as well.

Emotional Contagion vs. Empathy

So, the debate rages on: are emotional contagion and empathy the same thing? The short is answer is no. Emotional contagion is a part of a greater system known as empathy.

Now, the long answer is that emotional contagion is simply a perception of someone else's feelings based on their environment whereas as empathy is the process by which the individual is transported to the same state of others.

Let's consider this example: a caregiver is tending to a terminally ill patient. It is obvious that the patient is suffering. Emotional contagion would occur when the caregiver is affected by the patient's despondent state, but the caregiver would really care less if the patient died the next day. In fact, they would be glad if they did. This callous and inhuman attitude highlights how emotional contagion is not necessarily the same as empathy.

An empathetic caregiver is not only noticeably affected by the suffering of the patient but is actually in pain along with the patient. Then, when the patient finally passes away, the empathetic caregiver would most like become shattered at the loss. This is one of the reasons why the health care profession takes such an emotional toll on doctors, nurses, caregivers and paramedics.

The Mirror Neuron System

Mirror neurons are a specific class of visuomotor neurons, initially found in territory F5 of the monkey premotor cortex, that release both when the monkey completes a specific activity and when it watches another individual (monkey or human) completing a comparable activity. These cells empower each one to reflect feelings, to sympathize with someone else's torment, dread, or euphoria. Since empaths are thought to have hyperresponsive mirror neurons, we profoundly reverberate with other individuals' sentiments.

Furthermore, the mirror neurons have been said to be triggered by external events. For instance, when our spouse gets hurt, we also feel this kind of pain. When we have a happy friend, the same feelings rub off on us, making us happy. As a result, mirror neurons provide us with physiological evidence that allows us to explain the reasons behind empathy. Research has also shown that individuals who have brain lesions in the parts of the brain which house mirror neurons tend to feel a lack of empathy. This is one of the tell-tale signs of psychopathic behavior. Since psychopaths are unable to feel empathy, they have no trouble inflicting pain on their victims. As a result, they are able to commit unspeakable acts without feeling any kind of remorse.

Evidence of this system in the humans emanates from neuroimaging studies and noninvasive neurophysiological investigations. Neuroimaging further brought about an understanding of the two main networks that exists with the mirror properties: one resides in the parietal lobe together with the premotor cortex and the caudal part of the inferior frontal gyrus. The other is formed by the insula and the anterior medial frontal cortex (limbic mirror system). In this type of system, there is the involvement of the recognition of behaviors that can be said to be highly effective.

Mirror-Neuron System and Communication

Gestural Communication

The mirror neurons represent a neural premise of the systems that make the immediate linkage between the message sender and the beneficiary. One study has suggested that the mirror neuron framework speaks to the neurophysiological component from which language developed. Its functioning is comprised of the way that it shows a neurophysiological instrument that makes a typical (equality prerequisite), nonarbitrary, semantic connection between imparting people.

Electromagnetic Fields

Scientists in this field have concluded that the brain and heart have a role to play in this study, considering that they highly generate electromagnetic fields. HeartMath Institute made it clear that these are the fields that are in charge to the role of transmitting information about the humans' thoughts together with the emotions. We get to understand that empathy as well, can be overwhelmed as it is sensitive to the input. Notably, empaths have proved to have a strong physical and emotional response when there are changes in the electromagnetic fields of both the sun and earth. Happening on the earth and sun have a significant effect on the empaths state of mind and energy.

What Areas of Life Does Empathy Affect?

Human beings present empathy in their day to day activities in various ways. They include:

a) Health

As a specialist, most of the empaths who visit my office as patients have the feeling of being overwhelmed, downright exhausted and fatigued due to the fact they have no idea on how to go about with their situation of being sensitive. After some time with them, I get to understand that they have previously been diagnosed with agoraphobia, fibromyalgia, chronic fatigue, migraines, allergies, chronic pain, and adrenal fatigue (a form of burnout). I also realize they at times experience depression, anxiety, or panic attacks.

b) Addictions

A study has revealed that most of the empaths become addicts to alcohol, sex, food, drugs, shopping, or other behaviors as they seek to numb their sensitivities. Another common activity is overeating. Most of the empaths resort to using food to ground themselves. As a result, they can easily gain a lot of weight since using food to insulate themselves gives them a sense of protection from negative energy.

c) Relationships, Love, and Sex.

Empaths are said to experience anxiety, illness, or depression as a result of getting involved with toxic partners, either knowingly or unknowingly. These people have proven that they give their hearts quite easily to narcissists and other people who will never be there for them. They are quick to love, and they love deeply expecting the same in return, of which in most cases it never comes to pass. In the process of loving, they also get to absorb their partners stress and emotions such as depression or anger. These feelings can be exacerbated during times of vulnerability or stress in one, or both partners.

Empaths have distinctive requirements in order for a relationship to work. Empaths need a great deal of alone time. They will often need separate beds or even rooms. Empaths get overstimulated with "an excessive amount of fellowship" and need to legitimately convey this to their partners. Empaths are regularly pulled in to "inaccessible individuals" who don't give them a chance to "detox" from constant closeness and interaction. It's conceivable to have adoring, sound connections if empaths can characterize and express their exceptional needs, which in turn, as respected and met by the other party.

Generally, they have the dire need of understanding on how to have a healthy relationship and not being overloaded in the process and also be taught on how they can be able to set boundaries when they are interacting or in a relationship with the toxic people.

d) Parenting

Child-rearing, at times proves, to be a very challenging task for the empaths as they often get overwhelmed by having in mind the intense demands of children. They tend to be absorbed by their empathy leading to feelings of pain and even fear. Empathetic parents need to study and understand how they can prevent themselves from being affected by their children's demands. Participating in such training will also help the parents understand how they can help their children nurture their gifts they have so to thrive.

e) Work

Empaths can feel depleted by energy vampires in their work environment. Yet, they may be unable to determine how to define limits in order to protect themselves. There is a need for empaths to learn and understand how to replenish themselves in the workplace and how to cope with an environment that may be excessively stimulating or offers little to no privacy.

f) Extraordinary Perceptual Abilities

Since empaths have a heightened sensitivity, this can lead them to develop extraordinary perceptual abilities. This can come in the form of being a "human lie detector" or simply being able to see things others cannot. When properly tuned, this ability can lead empaths to become extremely successful at interacting with others.

Chapter 5: The Importance of Empathy to Humans

Empathy plays a key role in the ability of our society to function, promoting our needs, sharing experiences, and desires among one another. Our neural networks are set up to connect with the neural systems of others to both see and comprehend their feelings, and to separate them from our own. This makes it feasible for people to live with each other without always battling or feeling taken over by someone else.

Empathy is vital as it helps us be able to comprehend and understand the feelings others, and what they are going through, so that we can be able to respond appropriately to the situation at hand. To a greater extent, empathy has been associated with the social behaviors. There is plenty of research supporting this argument. Thus, the higher the degree of empathy a person feels, the more they tend to help others. Notably, an empath is also able to control actions or even go to the extent of curtailing immoral behavior. For example, someone who sees a car accident and is overwhelmed by emotions upon witnessing the victims in severe pain, might be far more inclined to help the victims or call for help.

Additionally, having strong empathetic feelings can also lead to negative effects. When a person demonstrates strong feelings toward people or causes, negative emotions may be stirred in others as a result of their insecurities. A good example of this can be seen in the way charlatans such as so-called fortune tellers exploit the insecurities of individuals. As a result, they may be able to trick empaths into actually believing that the end of the world is upon us and so forth.

Interestingly, people with a more pronounced psychopathic trait are said to show a more pragmatic response to events where there are moral dilemmas, for instance, the "footbridge dilemma". In this thought experiment, the conductor of a runaway train has to make a choice: since the train has no breaks it is heading toward five people crossing the tracks. Alternatively, the conductor may switch tracks and hit only one. Thus, the dilemma lies in whether you choose to kill one or kill all five people crossing the street. Hence, a pragmatic approach would lead to killing the least number of people whereas an empathetic approach would lead to killing none, if possible.

Measuring Empathy

Quite often, a self-report questionnaire is used in measuring empathy. This is in the likes of the Interpersonal Reactivity Index (IRI) or the Questionnaire for Cognitive and Affective Empathy (QCAE). In the process of measuring empathy, the person is asked to indicate how much they accept the statements that are set to help measure the different types of empathy that one might be having.

One will find statements like "It affects me very much when one of my friends is upset," which QCAE test uses to measure the effect of empathy. QCAE plays a key role in the identification of cognitive empathy by the use of statements the likes of "I try to look at everybody's side of a disagreement before I make a decision."

With the use of this method, it was discovered that people scoring higher on affective empathy have more grey matter. Grey matter is said to be a collection of nerve cells in the anterior insula, which is an area of the brain.

This zone is regularly associated with directing positive and negative feelings by coordinating external stimuli – for example, seeing an auto crash - with instinctive and programmed sensations. Likewise, individuals utilizing this strategy gauging compassion have found that high scorers of sympathy had a progressively dark issue in the dorsomedial prefrontal cortex.

The activation of this particular area takes place when there are more cognitive processes; this includes the Theory of the Mind. As stated earlier, this theory calls for the individual to understand the beliefs, intentions and motivations that drive them. As a result, the individual is then able to fully immerse themselves in the mindset of others.

Can Humans Lack Empathy?

Several cases have proven that not all humans have empathy. For instance, walking down Minnesota, you bump into a homeless person shivering in the cold, you will notice that few people will express sympathy, or any kind of compassion for the homeless person. There are many cases in which passersby express outright hostility towards such people. So, what could be the cause of expressing what seems to be selective empathy? Various elements come to mind: how we see the other individual, how we characterize their actions, what we attribute their misfortunes to, and our very own past encounters and desires. These all become an integral factor in our ability to express or repress empathy.

Furthermore, the two main things that contribute to experiencing empathy are socialization and genetics. And while the "nature vs. nurture" debate is far from being conclusively settled, the fact of the matter is that our preconceived notions tend to influence the way we act and react when confronted with a situation that requires us to express compassion in a fellow human being.

Here are the top reasons why we sometimes lack empathy:

a) We fall victim to cognitive biases

In this factor, our cognitive biases, that is, our judgments, lead us to pin the misfortunes on an individual on themselves. We tend to attribute their pain and suffering to their own shortcomings as opposed to being compassionate and attempting to aid the victim whenever possible. These biases can be the result of societal and cultural perceptions.

b) We dehumanize victims

Quite often, we tend to view victims as people who are different from us. For example, the common "that will never happen to me" concept creates a barrier that separates us from our fellows. In this regard, we not only dehumanize the victim, but we don't necessarily assume that they are in pain and suffering. This is generally the case when victims are viewed as number and statistics rather the flesh and blood beings who suffer and experience sorrow.

c) We blame victims

This is one of the most common responses when analyzing someone's misfortunes. We tend to see them as victims of their own consequences. And while there are cases in which that is true, the fact of the matter is that a true empath does not care how a person got to be in the situation they are in. All they care about is how to help the victim feel better or even solve the issue they are in.

True empaths are capable of filtering out logic and reason insofar as assigning blame and responsibility and looking at the reality of what others are experiencing. So, even if it is the victim's fault, it doesn't matter. What matters is that the person needs help. That means that the rest can be sorted out later on.

Moreover, blaming a person's misfortunes on themselves tends to take away any responsibility from others. That is, if the victim is responsible for their lot, then they should be the ones to solve their problem. As such, why are they asking for help if they were the ones who caused the problem in the first place? Such attitudes create a significant barrier for empathy.

Can Empathy Be Selective?

Previous research has found that humans tend to be more empathetic with members that belong to their social or ethnic group, such as in the case of immigrants. For instance, one researcher looked into the cerebrums of Chinese and Caucasian individuals while they watched recordings of individuals from their own ethnic group in distress. They likewise watched individuals from the other ethnic group in a similar situation.

In the case study, it was found that anterior cingulate cortex, which is a brain area that is always active if one perceives scenes of distress, was far more active when seeing members of their own ethnic group in distress as opposed to seeing members of the other.

A separate study has also found that brain areas involved in empathy are quite less active when we are watching people undergoing pain as a result of their own reckless actions. An example of this is when an individual is performing a stunt that goes wrong. Since we attribute this negative consequence to their own actions, we tend not to view the individual as a victim.

It is good to note that in such times, we don't generally feel empathy for the people who are directly responsible for their own actions. In fact, the brain reacts very differently when we see people suffering from what we perceive to be an injustice. However, if we feel that their pain is justified, the brain basically nullifies and feelings of empathy.

These perceptions also extend to ethnic and social groups. We see the suffering of people from varying social groups in a very different light. For example, the poor have little to no empathy for the rich; the rich may view the poor as solely responsible for their lot. Thus, empathy tends to become skewed in one direction or another.

Consequently, it is encouraged to practice empathy regardless of social class or ethnicity. While this is hard to do, it is a skill which can be practiced and developed over time. Nevertheless, the true empath will not find it difficult to identify with others.

Determining If You Are an Empath

Here is a simple test that can help you define if you are an empath or not. You can go through it, giving a simple "yes" or "no" answer to each question.

- Have I in any time been labeled as sensitive, introvert, or shy?

- Do I get anxious or overwhelmed frequently?

- Do fights, yelling, and arguments often make me ill?

- Do I often have the feeling that I don't fit in?

- Do I find myself being drained by the crowds, and by that then do I mostly need my time alone so to revive myself?

- Do odors, noise, or nonstop talkers get me overwhelmed?

- Do I have chemical sensitiveness or low tolerance for scratchy clothes?

- Do I prefer using my car when attending an event or going to a place so that I will be free to leave earlier?

- Do I use food as my source to escape from stress?

- Do I feel afraid of being suffocated by relationship intimacy?

- Do I easily startle?

- Do I have a strong reaction to medications or caffeine?

- Do I have a low threshold for pain?

- Do I tend to be socially isolated?

- Do I get to absorb the stress, symptoms, and emotions of the other people?

- Am I mostly overwhelmed by doing several things at a go, and do I always prefer handling one thing at a go?

- Do I replenish myself generally?

- Do I need a long time to recuperate after being with difficult people or energy vampires?

- Do I always feel being in a better place while in small cities than the big ones?

- Do I always prefer having one on one interaction and small groups and not the large gathering?

You can now try to know who you are by calculating your results.

- If you agreed to at least five of the questions, then you are partly an empath.

- If you agreed to at least ten questions, you are at a moderate level.

- If you agreed to eleven or fifteen questions, then you are a strong empath with strong tendencies.

- If you have agreed to more than fifteen questions, then it's without a doubt that you are a full-blown empath.

The determination of your degree of an empath is important as it will make it easy for you to clarify the types of needs and the type of strategy you will need to adapt in a bit to be able to meet them. With the determination, then you will be able to find a comfort zone in your life.

Are you unable to define yourself using the above questions? Then is a simpler explanation for you.

Chapter 6: The Traits of an Empath

Main Traits of an Empath

i. What do your friends say about you?

An empath is most likely to be called an emotional or moody person by their close friends and family. You will find that most people make fun of them quite often in addition to teasing them. As an empath, this makes you feel as if there is something wrong with your sensitivity. However, that's not the case, and it is at this time that you will need to learn your own ways to stabilize your energy.

ii. Are you a lone wolf?

How often do you opt to be alone? Could it be quite regularly? Studies have shown that the act of wanting to be alone is due to the natural effect of having taken in too much energy of your friends and relatives with whom you relate. When things get heavy for you, this is when you tend to be alone so that you can clean it. Otherwise, you easily get irritated, overwhelmed, and sad. You do this unconsciously without realizing that you're protecting yourself. But also, you can be able to give a judgment of yourself for not being so social or being an introvert.

iii. You feel like no one understands you.

When with your friends, you will tend to feel like an outsider and that nobody understands who you are. Many empaths have been said to feel like they are space aliens among humans. Even though people will barely understand you, you will need to be able to understand why they don't. Could this be your case?

Do you know why they don't understand you? It is because you tend to take in so many energies from them, traits, behaviors and thoughts to a point where it ends up mixing your personality. So, don't try to make them understand you but instead try to understand yourself first. Think about who you are (without the outside energy). You have to become your own best friend and walk yourself through the process of mastering your gift.

iv.   Are you experiencing many negative patterns?

This trait can be a slippery slope as everyone experiences family and social conditioning. This leads to creating patterns of behavior that are often painful. Being an empath myself, in addition to having worked with so many empaths, I have come to notice that this type of person tends to go through a severe negative family pattern.

Empaths find themselves taking on their family's problems so they can assist in solving or healing them. In the majority of cases, all this is done at an unconscious level.

However, there is no guarantee that they will actually be able to solve their family's issues simply due to the fact that they cannot control every single aspect of their family. Therefore, it might become frustrating to see that loved ones simply refuse to change.

On the other hand, it still stands that, in one way or the other, empaths help their loved ones become able to nurse their pain. Nevertheless, you will need to understand that the only way you can assist someone is by first healing yourself, and through that then the pattern becomes lighter for the others as well.

As an empath, you will need to understand that pain sharing only creates more suffering; this is something which has proven to be a challenge for so many people since we misinterpret healing ourselves first as being selfish. In fact, it's one of the least selfish things we can do.

v.   Your friends take you down quite often and easily?

Humans tend to be very cheerful when they meet their friends under happy and joyous circumstances. These meetings come rather effortlessly. Yet, you can tell that your friends might be weighing you down when you come away from meeting them in a sad and sorrowful state.

To understand this better, we can say you really were in a really good mood before meeting up, but things started changing once you began talking about your friend's negative experiences. Then, all over sudden you start feeling quite miserable by the end of the chat.

After the chat, you might find your friend tells you that they much feel much better after talking with you. Of course, the talk was intended to help them, but the situation is not the same for you since you have absorbed their negative energy. In this example, we are not saying that you should put a stop to meeting friends who are feeling down; it is not practical either. However, it is important to learn how to ground yourself after being charged with so much negative energy.

vi.   Do you easily get sick?

Do you find yourself getting ill quite often? You will then need to understand that you are an empath. Studies have revealed that the empaths often get sick especially after being around ill people. You can recreate similar conditions in your body after coming into contact with sick people. Or, you might even show symptoms mimicking their illness, only to become miraculously healed after a short while.

A person who has a "shadow illness", that is they are mimicking the symptoms of another person, and even if they go to the hospital, no sickness will be detected. This is quite true because you have just created the symptoms via the use of mind's power. I used to undergo the same when I was growing up. Anytime I heard that someone was suffering from a particular illness, I would develop such illness. I could even think that I have very poor health until the day I realized that this was happening unconsciously.

Since then, I'm very rarely ill and even less so since I have my own business as a coach. I'd still pick up other people's health issues when I was working in an open space. I have come to realize that many empaths have no idea that this happens. They seem to develop symptoms quite often despite eating healthy, living a balanced lifestyle, and getting regular exercise. By this, I don't mean that there are no real and severe illnesses out there, but being an empath, you need to beware of falling ill with no apparent cause.

vii.   You're interested in spirituality and healing.

Researchers have concluded that empaths can be excellent healers at the physical level, as well as, other types of healing such as emotional, spiritual and sexual. Therefore, you feel drawn to healing and reading about spiritual matters.

On the other hand, just a few end up being healers in their life as this involves taking in a great deal of the other person's energy. This can be quite a lot and, exhausting. You're also keen on self-help books, metaphysical studies, philosophy, and just about anything which can give you more answers about the purpose of life and yourself.

viii.   You need constant change.

Are you that person who gets bored easily and dislikes commitments and routines? Do you tend to feel that predictability and repetition of the same things are weighing you down? How about having issues in respecting the people who try to impose their will on you? A person who does this quite often may be made to feel guilty by being labeled as a selfish and troublesome person. Do you always have dreams of visiting new places and doing new things? This is thanks to your creativity and generally high levels of energy.

A person who is not aware of their nature could find day to day interactions with others being a source of stress to them. Empaths who are not aware of the abilities they possess might be inclined to start using alcohol, food, and drugs to overcome their emotional distress

Due to the positive impacts that the empaths bring, I tend to believe that they are the medicine that the world needs. They have a profound impact on humanity with their understanding and compassion. They possess the ability of learning and understanding their own talents and those of others. They realize that they may only enrich themselves but also the people around them. As an empath, you need to understand that it is an important skill to understand fully on how to be able to take charge of your sensitivities and also understand the specific strategies that you need to use in a bid to prevent sensory overload.

Advantages and Challenges of Being an Empath

Being empathic has inconceivable advantages, for example, more prominent instincts, sympathy, innovativeness, and a more profound association with other individuals. In any case, living in this condition of high sensitivity is also accompanied by difficulties. For example, ending up effectively overpowered, over-invigorated, depleted, or engrossed by the pressure and pessimism of others are just a few of the potential outcomes.

I do cherish being an empath so much. I thank God for the gift of sensitiveness bestowed on me. I have a strong liking to being intuitive, feeling the flow of the world's energy, getting to read people, and also being able to experience the rich feeling that life offers.

I came to realize that God has given us so many marvelous traits that we ought to use on our day to day lives. You will need to understand that God gave us a huge heart and wonderful instincts that allow us to be able to help our society day in day out and those who are less fortunate. Empaths are said to be both idealists and dreamers. Other character traits that define us include being creative, deep, passionate, compassionate, being in touch with our emotions, and always being able to see the bigger picture. Empaths can be friends with other people due to their ability to appreciate their feelings. They are quite spiritual and intuitive and always have a good level of energy. They have much appreciation for nature and feel it as their home. They resonate with nature, forests, plants, and gardens and have a deep love for the water.

Empaths get energized by the water, may it be warm or cold, taking a shower and especially if they live near it. They feel a solid bond with animals; you can find them talking to animals just as if they were human. With such a strong bond to animals, such people might end up being involved with the rescue of animals or animal communication.

Being an empath is a blessing as they are natural healers with the ability to gift healing energy to their friends via their hands, voice, or by playing a musical instrument.

Being an empath is an advantage given their heightened sense of smell. This allows them to enjoy food, flowers, beverages, essential oils, etc. An empath who works hard and manages to increase their sensitivity can even smell death or disease from a person or an animal. With such an ability, they can potentially save lives.

Empaths have the knack to sense danger before it hits; this is done by using their sixth sense. Isn't that amazing? Notably, empaths enjoy feeling greater highs than the other people who don't have the same level of sensitivity. This happens despite being prone to feeling down as a result of the energy they get from other people. Empaths have greater enthusiasm towards life; they experience joy and life itself with greater intensity. They are blessed as they are always kind, compassionate, caring, and understanding as compared to the other people who are not quite so sensitive.

Even though the people who are not empathetic feel guilty for not spending time with others, the case is quite different for the empaths as they love being alone as this is the time they need to balance and de-stress. Empaths use this time to recuperate; this makes them much more aware of themselves due to the time they spend alone.

As discussed earlier, empaths have high levels of creativity throughout their lives. This is not only in the artistic field but also in situations, experiences, and possibilities. They can see things in advance, at the point of conceptualizing art before it materializes. Many people might label this creativity of thought and processing as not being worthwhile; but don't worry, anything you do will be fruitful because you have put your heart into it.

Empaths enjoy the advantage of being able to read emotional cues. This makes them be able to understand other people better since they can understand what that person is feeling and how it will affect that person if their needs aren't met.

Due to their sensitiveness, they are said to be very good at capturing all kinds of nonverbal communication and indicators of physical needs and emotions. With this ability, they are said to have a knack for intuiting the unconscious mind as well as for being able to sense the needs of plants, animals, the human body and those that are unable to speak.

Empaths have the advantage of being able to understand the thoughts of people, their feelings and emotions, and this ability enables them to sense a lie when being told. They can easily understand when something is the matter despite the person insisting that they are fine but hurting on the inside. Because of our heightened awareness, we can see through the false facades people up.

Empaths have an advantage when it comes to loving as their degree of love is said to be on another level. It is believed that coming up with a mutual understanding in a relationship has proven itself to be a very hard thing. Empaths try as much as they can to explain their feelings to the other person but unfortunately, they don't understand their feelings in the same manner. It can take someone a lot of time for them to be able to place themselves in the shoes of the other person.

Through this, an empath can cultivate that high level of love and compassion which might be difficult for the other person to match despite the much time they might have at their disposal. With deeper levels of love, understanding and relating with people, understanding others becomes quite easy, even those you are most likely to disagree with.

Empaths enjoy the advantage of being very creative. This is part and parcel of all empaths; through their emotions, they can express their levels of creativity. Empaths can channel their feelings into a piece of art. If you are in the space that you need to be in, then your creations will touch other people around you.

Let's say, for instance, and you are a person who is unable to dance or paint; by embracing your creativity nonetheless, you will be able to learn so much more about yourself. I came to realize that I am so creative. This is when, I started embracing books. This has aided me in understanding so much about who I am, the meaning of life, and the patterns involved in life.

Empaths receive insights naturally. Every creation allows an empath to be much happier, and further allow pure essence to explore itself fully. This is why exercises such as meditation and mindfulness are key to developing an empath's sense of awareness and perception.

Another benefit enjoyed by empaths is the ability to find and understand their true self. This means that they are quite authentic and always speak from their hearts. In my career, I came to notice that so many people face challenges when it comes to this. This is clearly evident in the current generation; many people see authenticity as a norm. Most of my clients have expressed themselves to me, saying that they would find it quite hard to be themselves. We do build a substantial prison around us, within our society. You will need to make use of the facts to make sense of your surroundings. Empaths can connect to the deepest parts of themselves if they allow themselves to be free. Some of the activities that you can engage in when alone include writing journals, having a new hobby, and dancing. All of these activities enable you to realize your true self. The main point behind this is to help you explore the depths within you. After feeling comfortable about it, you can then share your authentic self with your friends.

Therefore, when having a conversation with someone, you should always express yourself comfortably, and don't shy from saying something if you feel the need to. It is always advisable to be polite to others and not utter statements that might leave them hurt. This becomes easier when you decide to freely share what is in your heart. Understandably, it is a sign of care and love when people speak their hearts out. And, if the truth from our hearts becomes offensive to the other person, then it indicates that their ego has interpreted the message as an attack. However, you have the responsibility to say what matters to you and do it lovingly and openly.

Empaths are said to be peacemakers. This is because they have the ability to make their outside surroundings be more like their inner self. This, in turn, leads them to be able to forego their needs and focus on the other person's needs. Generally, empaths are seen to be less violent, less aggressive, and they always tend to lean more about being a peacemaker than a troublemaker. They are always filled by an uncomfortable feeling at the moment they are in a surrounding filled with disharmony. If they find out that they in the middle of a confrontation, they will seek ways in which they can resolve the matter within the shortest time possible or avoid it altogether. When they use harsh words in defense, they tend to resent their lack of self-control. They will always opt to handle the matter and resolve it promptly. Have you ever been in a similar situation? How did you handle it?

Empaths' sensitivity is a gift and not a curse. These folks have the advantage of having creative thoughts, and through them, they can become something great. Therefore, before you start cursing your heightened awareness, you need to remember that some of these advantages you possess, and you will need to uncover them. It is high time you start focusing on the benefits and advantages that you possess as an empath as this will enable you to create a life in which you will be able to benefit greatly from your gifts rather than having them drain you.

Chapter 7: Common Challenges facing Empaths

Once you begin to deal with the challenges of being an empath and gain more coping skills, you will enjoy all the advantages. We have to accept the fact that being an empath in such a chaotic world will have you misunderstood quite often. An empath's ability to understand other people's hidden motives and emotions can be said to be eerily spot on.

These are the people who genuinely bring real meaning to the term "reading room." Empaths are not people who only skim the pages or read the Coles Notes. By this, it means that the moment you get into a room, you immediately get bombarded with all the data and information of all the room occupants. It might be hard for you to interpret the information given at the moment, but undeniably, you will be able to sense the underlying feelings and thoughts.

I can give an instance just to put this into perspective. An empath will be the first to detect a lie. They feel it right in their gut. They can tell when a genuine person is saying the truth. Notably, they always want to be around other empaths who have kindred spirits. Meanwhile, insensitive, abrasive personalities are said to drain empaths quite rapidly.

Despite the fact that empaths possess a beautiful and wise soul, they are still said to struggle in a bid to find their footing in the world. Empaths and HSPs often face day to day challenges, mostly due to the way they perceive energy, non-verbal communication, and emotions primarily contained in their surrounding environments.

The Most Common Challenges that Empaths Face

The most common challenges I've come to know with my patients and workshop participants include the following:

i.   They struggle with anxiety and depression

Anxiety, depression, and doubt have been known to cause strife in the life of empaths. I am not surprised by this especially when considering how they are singled out by our society and given all sorts of negative energy. Besides, most empaths have been brought up in unstable homes; places where emotional welfare is not generally protected. It is from this point that most empaths have resorted to addictions in a bid to be able to cope with the overwhelming emotional burden.

ii.   They attract narcissists and energy vampires

We will agree that being an empath hurts because it does. These people sense everything that every other person feels. They become greatly affected by other people's emotions. They can feel the loss and pain the other person is going through. They can feel their tears and the tone of their soul as a result of being hurt. But the average person doesn't understand what the empath goes through.

Empaths will act as an emotional sponge due to the fact that they attract all manners of emotions when they are at the bank, grocery store, office, everywhere, from the people surrounding them. They get to absorb the energy of the people with whom they come into contact.

Even though they have quite an active intuition, once in a while, they all fall into the trap of toxic people. This is the time when we give room to narcissists and other energy vampires to take advantage of our kind and compassionate nature. They find it hard to detach ourselves from such relationships. We are highly disadvantaged because we tend to let many people enter our lives, and when we do, we tend to give our all, of which the other person might take advantage of.

iii.   They feel too much but may not know why.

With so many emotions and information hitting them from all corners, it is quite easy for empaths to become confused. They may be unable to differentiate what issue belongs to them and what they collected along the way from other people. They are also at a disadvantage because of the fact that their moods become affected by the physical environment. A very lovely looking home might elevate their levels of anxiety due to inexplicable reasons and factors. Because these people spend a lot of time going through the subtleties around them, they end up spending a lot of time picking up energy and vibration that has nothing to do with outward appearances. There is a dire need for an empath to take time to center and be fully in their body and thoughts, as this is quite important. By doing this, they will be able to establish boundaries in their life.

iv. They may get stung by the people closest to them

One of the main things that empaths hate is to disappoint others. This is brought about by the fact that they always feel the emotions inside them. So, the thought of hurting another person is what makes their anxiety levels soar. They will feel quite guilty if they have to say no. It is for this reason that they might tend to have very soft boundaries; something which might be taken for granted by other people, hence hurting the empath.

Also, if a person is seeking help from an empath, and the situation is quite dire, the helplessness behind the plea will highly affect the empath triggering them to accept the request even if it would mean personal misfortune to themselves. For an empath to stop being taken advantage of, they will need to learn how to turn people away by saying no to requests that might cost them too much.

v.   They face challenges when winding down

Empaths go through a hard time as they try to transition themselves from high stimulation to solitude. Brains never stop buzzing after a very challenging and busy day at work. It is due to this that the empaths aren't able to focus easily. It is for this reason that empaths become sad or moody, or they feel a strange sensation after getting home from work, social events, or even a party despite it being filled with fun.

Have you been a victim of any of the above challenges? Then it is good to understand that nearly every empath has felt the same way. There is no need to be ashamed of your sensitivity. Your empathy offers much more positive than detrimental energy to the world; it brings you closer to the light more so when you get a handle on the skills needed to cope.

vi.   System Overload

Empaths are wired to notice everything happening around them; hence, they experience a lot until they get overwhelmed. Every empath should build up a tolerance because it's an important coping mechanism, and this helps them be able to be stay aware when their sensory perception is being overloaded. Due to their awareness, they need to have time for release and discharge.

Sometimes you can't tell if an emotion or sensation of bodily discomfort is your own or someone else's. Taking on other people's energy can cause a variety of physical and emotional symptoms in you, ranging from pain to anxiety. So, it is important to find an outlet in which you can discharge all of these energies.

vii. Challenges in relationships

Empaths face real challenges when in a relationship. Consider this scenario: there are times when an empath needs time to connect with their partner in both body and spirit. They need togetherness and intimacy. Then, there are times when they need time alone to reflect and recharge energies. This may pose a problem for the empath's partner especially if they are needy and require a great deal of attention.

viii. Becoming overstimulated

Empaths can quickly run out of gas when it comes to social interactions. This is due to the cumulative effect of everyone's individual and collective energies. Depending on the circumstances, this may result in the empath simply growing weary after a short period of time.

Failing to have enough time for oneself every day will lead to them to suffer from the toxic effects caused by being overstimulated and sensory overload.

ix.   They Feel things intensely

Empaths have a challenge when it comes to anything seemingly brutal or cruel. They actually can't be comfortable when watching a violent or upsetting movie be it about animals or humans being harmed because they will be badly hurt in the process. Empaths will be severely affected by graphic scenes of violence and suffering on TV such as in the news and other media.

x.   They experience emotional and social hangovers

If the empath associates with many people on a daily basis, then they might be quite overloaded by the end of the day. This is the main reason why empaths need time alone to recover and reflect.

xi.   They have a feeling of being isolated and lonely.

Because the world might appear to be quite overwhelming, you might find yourself keeping yourself distant and shying away from the rest. In the end, people may view you as standoffish. Like many empaths, you may be hyper vigilant, scanning your environment to ensure its safety. Others can perceive this as a signal to stay away. Some empaths prefer socializing online to keep others at a distance, so there's less of the tendency to absorb their discomfort and stress.

xii.   Experiencing emotional burnout

The fact that people flock to you to share their disturbing stories will surely be emotionally distressing. It felt as if I was wearing as sign saying "I can help you" ever since I was a small child. And this clearly explains why empaths will have to set boundaries in their life if they want to stop being drained.

xiii.   Coping with increased sensitivity to smell, light, smell, touch, sound, and temperature

Empaths, myself included, find loud noises and bright lights quite painful. They react with our bodies, penetrate and shock us profoundly. Every time an ambulance passes by, I have no option but to cover my ears. Could this be your case? What are your experiences when walking down a busy street with lots of cars and people making their way through? I have come to realize that I can't withstand the explosive blasts of fireworks. They startle me so much that I react similarly to a frightened dog.

Scientists have found that empaths have an enhanced startle response because they are super-responsive when it comes to sensory input. Empaths feel queasy if they are exposed to strong smells and chemicals, such as perfumes and exhaust gases. Could this be your case, too? Empaths are also susceptible to extreme temperatures and even dislike air-conditioned places. Scientists have proven that our bodies, as empaths, can also be depleted, or energized, when in intense weather, such as gusty winds, thunderstorms or snowfall. Empaths get very energized by a bright full moon whereas, other empaths may feel agitated by the same situation.

xiv.   Expressing needs in intimate relationships

Anyone sharing the same bed or same home with an empath will need to understand that they have specific needs. In most instances, it has been found that empaths prefer having their own space and bed in a bid for them to feel more comfortable. Therefore, if you are in a relationship with an empath, you need to understand such needs. So, get to know the reasons for these reactions.

Being an empath is not something that one should be thinking about getting rid of; embracing it is rather important as it is an integral part that forms who you are. An empath should seek ways to be more flexible, know how to flow, and be comfortable with their status rather than being against it. Having an understanding of oneself and how the external world perceives you is quite important to assist you in balancing. Part of this will be developing a daily practice that will strengthen your empathetic muscles and give you a sort of reset button.

xv. Empaths get overwhelmed by media

They never get to enjoy some of the products offered by television, movies, videos, news, and broadcast due to their sensitivity. Anything that seems violent or having emotional dramas with a lot of scenes that are shocking and prone to cause pain on children, adults, or animals can make an empath cry. This can, at times, make them feel as if they are ill or even start crying over and over again. You might struggle to seek ways you can comprehend such cruelty. You will even find it difficult to explain the scene to others, especially if it shows cruelty to humans, ignorance, lack of compassion, and closed-mindedness. At this point, you will find it hard to justify what you have watched due to the suffering you have seen and felt.

Special Challenges for Each Gender

An empath's sensitivities can be challenging in different ways for men and women, though, of course there is a lot in common.

For instance, male empaths are often ashamed of their sensitivities and reluctant to talk about them. They may feel they're not "masculine enough." Men have had to fight gender stereotypes and have been probably warned not to be a "crybaby" and to "act like a man." Boys are taught that "strong men don't cry," and sensitive boys can be bullied at school for being "sissies." Male empaths may not be attracted to football, soccer, or aggressive contact sports, and so they may be excluded and shamed by other boys.

Consequently, male empaths may repress their emotions and eventually even become emotionally unavailable. For all these reasons, they often suffer in silence, which can negatively impact their relationships, careers, and health. Highly sensitive celebrities include Abraham Lincoln, Albert Einstein, and Jim Carrey.

I find sensitive men incredibly attractive. I love Alanis Morrissette's song "In Praise of the Vulnerable Man." To become well balanced, men must own their sensitive sides. I'm not talking about overly feminized men who have not learned to embody the masculine but relatively balanced men who are strong enough to be sensitive and secure enough to be vulnerable. Such men have a high emotional IQ. They are not afraid of emotions, their own, or any else's. This makes them compassionate and attractive partners, friends, and leaders.

In contrast, female empaths in Western culture are given more permission to express their emotions and "female intuition," though by no means does our world embrace feminine power. Throughout much of history, the feminine has been squashed. Think of the inquisition during the Dark Ages or the Salem trials, where many sensitive people were convicted of witchcraft and subsequently executed. When I first started speaking about intuition to groups, I was afraid I would be harmed. But once I realized I was tuning in to the collective energy of women seers who had been suppressed over the ages, I discovered that today is a different time. It is much safer to express my voice now, so my discomfort has lifted.

Similarly, many of my female patients have been reluctant to express their sensitivities for fear of being misunderstood, judged, or abandoned. We must learn to be authentic in relationships about our empathetic needs. Also, for some women empaths, empathy can turn into codependency. They have such big hearts that they get caught up in caretaking roles, tending to others more than they tend to themselves. A female empath who is balanced knows how to set boundaries with her time and energy. She learns to give and receive in a balanced way, a powerful combination. Female empath celebrities include Nicole Kidman, Jewel (her song "Sensitive" is about empaths), Winona Ryder, Alanis Morrissette, and Princess Diana.

Dealing with the Challenges of Being an Empath

Empaths are born; they are not "created". They possess a genetic trait in their DNA which is passed through generations. This means that we cannot really "learn" how to be empath unless we are born one. Empaths don't commonly deal in "sympathy". To the empath, sympathy is a superficial emotion in which they barely feel sorry for someone. Therefore, sympathy is something that a non-empath would feel.

At this point in our discussion, we can see how being an empath is a double-edged sword. Therefore, empaths need to be handled very carefully lest we get seriously cut. For instance, caregivers and health care workers end up becoming seriously hurt by the effects of caring for patients. This is especially true when a patient passes away thereby leaving a gaping sense of loss.

Being an empath, you might have been accused of being too sensitive and maybe needed to lighten up. I believe that being an empath is a uniquely valuable gift. Empaths have the ability to experience a deeper inner life. They get the chance to understand how other people feel. However, as much as you try to absorb the surrounding joy, you might consume the stress in your surroundings as well. This is something which can leave you drained or overloaded in the end. Therefore, incorporating critical strategies into your daily life will enable you to have a more abundant life as you share your gifts with others.

Thus, for you to be able to maneuver, you will need to replenish yourself quite often in nature so to have a depletion feeling. Empaths in most cases will have a profound, spiritual experience in nature. You will have no option but to carve out time in which you will need to move out and refuel yourself. This can involve going to the lake, hikes, gardening, or any other activity involving water and nature.

To be able to cope with empathy and its challenges will also need you to practice meditation and yoga on a daily basis. These practices will be vital in helping you relax your emotions through the creation of a robust body connection. Yoga and meditation have been highly rated for their ability to achieve this. You should consider starting one of these practices, or both, as soon as possible. Preferably, you can retreat in your personal place or area of residence.

Have you ever thought about how you can channel your creative ability when feeling negative? Yes, you can use your creativity in unleashing the excessive negative emotions or energy that you might pick up from your surroundings or environment. So, what do you need to do? Just pick up a new and creative hobby like swimming, or you can also consider dedicating much of your time to concentrate on an existing one. Some of the things you can consider doing include drawing, painting, writing, singing, or dancing.

Are you aware that reading quite often as possible can help you manage your situation? It does. Just get a good book, and before you know it, you will have gotten yourself away from it all after losing yourself in that book. The act of reading has been considered as one of the most common hobbies shared by empaths, and therefore, it will be of great importance for you, too. This can be done for leisure or personal development. Undeniably, a book acts as a real excuse for one to use when undergoing that feeling of being overpowered by internal energies. Cracking a book open will help you release all that energy and feel replenished in the end.

Have you ever considered lighting a scented candle or incense in a bid to boost your mood? Yes, this is one of the most effective ideas to help you manage tour challenges. Empaths are quite sensitive to various sensations, and this includes smell. Incorporating scents into your environment will play a pivotal role in improving your mood and relaxation ability. Scents also help in countering any strong or unpleasant smells that distract or unsettle you.

You also need to understand that dedicating time to unwind each evening is highly encouraged, as it will help the mind settle after a very long and busy day. With ample time, you will be able to detach and unload your mind and emotions before heading to bed. Though this practice, you will be able to sleep much better and wake up feeling refreshed. You will need to shut down all the stimulating electronics a few hours before retiring to bed. Play some soft music, journal, meditate, read something interesting, grab a cup of tea, or consider taking a warm bath.

Protecting yourself from negative energy is quite essential at all times. So, how can you do this? Taking deep breaths several times daily will have you achieve this. You need to support your mental health. This can be achieved by taking time out of your busy day to check on your breathing. Ever thought of drawing in air from your nose and then holding it for a few seconds, and later release it via the mouth? How about you try it now and repeat it several times throughout the day. Too much stimulation from the surrounding world leads to stress and depression, and in some instances, addiction is the result. Deep breathing helps the mind to reset thereby easing stress and also do away with destructive habits.

Visualizing a shield that protects you in a high-stress environment is also very useful. Through such actions, your defense will be greatly increased before you start engaging with social situations that are quite draining or overwhelming. For you to be able to achieve this successfully, you will need to visualize the energy shield that is around you and protecting you from the bad energy. How about you close your eyes and then take in several deep breaths? While in the process, you will need to imagine a golden light, or bubble, that is radiating the breath you are taking. Retreating into the bubble of light will help you buffer yourself from emotional vampires or drainers energy.

Also, don't be afraid to question the reasons behind strong emotions. Rather than pushing away or ignoring any powerful emotions, try to understand what they mean and how you can fulfill the any underlying need. For instance, when you are feeling hungry, try to observe what is happening in your body and go about addressing it. Always pay attention to how the emotions you feel in your body. For instance, listen to the signals your body is sending you. It is always good to tell yourself, "It is okay to feel what I am feeling". This is showing compassion for yourself.

You will need to trust your gut when you are feeling a negative sensation. So, to be able to do this successfully, you will need to join people who bring joy and inspiration. You will always need to take enough time to reflect and analyze your intuition if you happen to get a hunch about someone or something. Empaths can easily find it hard to make their own decisions as they can be caught up in other people's energies. The moment you begin to trust your gut, you will enable you to stop giving the people with negative energy room and space to influence you. Boosting your intuition with meditations or having creative expressions is important.

As an empath, it is always recommended that you understand the limitations that you operate within and also the boundaries you will always need to set. For you to be able to overcome the challenges, learning to say NO is quite vital as it's a skill every empath needs. You might become so enmeshed with others that you give and give until you are empty. As an empath, you will need to learn the importance of identifying your personal limitations and be keen to express yourself in your relationships. For example, you might want to tell a friend that "I need you to respect my personal space. Please don't show up at my apartment, unannounced." It might just be that your friend is an energy drainer. Here is an example of how you could handle such a situation: "I would love to have lunch with you, but let's not spend the entire time dwelling on the negatives. If we can't keep it positive, I'll have to pass." It goes without saying that for one to set boundaries with their loved ones can be one of the hardest and most challenging things to do. However, you don't need to freak out about it; it is quite healthy for your emotions. Spending time with energizers rather than energy drainers is key. You will have to take an inventory on all the people you have welcomed in your life, seek to understand what kind of energy they leave to you, and then take time to determine if they stand in comparison to when they find in you and when they give you. By the time you part, are you left feeling anxious, demeaned, cranky, or irritable? Then you will need to stop such company with an immediate effect. Start spending time with the friends who, after leaving, leave you feeling positive, invigorated, both emotionally and mentally. If it's a must for you as an empath to be near emotional vampires or drainers, always consider practicing self-care before and after the encounter.

It is advisable that, as an empath, you can say yes to intimate gatherings. Research has proven empaths to be quite introverted. This is why empaths value quality over quantity when it comes to socializing. One might feel quite drained and overwhelmed by the larger groups, and therefore, it is advised that you consider one-on-one settings. There is always a need for empaths to leave things as they are and not fix them for others. As an empath, you will listen to someone's problems, but don't solve them as many tend to shoulder them as their own. Be aware of your tendency to do this and make a conscious effort to listen without internalizing the problem or trying to fix it. Try repeating this affirmation to yourself: "I can help by only using my ears to listen."

Empaths should always give their time to the most important cause. It is without speaking that you will discover the need to share your gifts safely, maybe via volunteering. Find that which moves you and identify how you can be involved effectively. You can consider calling your local politician to offer support. You can also consider doing charity work, donating some money to organizations or even going to work a few hours at a shelter on a weekly basis. When participating in volunteer work, you will be engaging all the emotions which are considered healthy.

Because the empaths often get caught by what is going around them, it is advised they consider having time for themselves and tune out. The critical inner voice is a very nasty coach that dwells in our heads waiting for something to come up so they can criticize us severely. Self-compassion is the simplest (yet most challenging) practice of self-care. The reason as to why this is known as a practice is because it is something that you will need time to get over. At the end of it all, we need to recognize the blessings and challenges that the empath has and goes through. In such an environment where people struggle to identify and express emotions, people with empathy can be seen to have superpowers.

Chapter 8: Thriving as an Empath: Skills to Prevent Overload

Our society can view empaths to as too sensitive and suggest them to tighten up. I encourage empathetic people to tighten up when they need to. But they should also develop more sensitiveness while staying centered within themselves. You need to realize that being an empath is considered a significant asset but only when you manage to understand how to manage it. Empaths are not crazy, hypochondriacs, weak, or neurotic. They are wonderful, and sensitive individuals who possess a gift. Still, all empaths need to have the right tools in order to cope with life.

One of the key things that you will need to learn and understand is on how to go about when you have sensory overload especially when you have so much intake within a short period of time. With so much collection from your surroundings, you can easily be left being feeling depressed, stressed, exhausted, anxious, or sick. Just like many, I do feel at times as if I have no on/off switch for my empathy. But this is not quite true. I will be taking you through on how you can take charge of your sensitivities without letting them give you that feeling of being a victim. The world can be your playground the moment you feel safe and protected.

For you to be able to gain a sense of safety, the realization of some factors contributing to empathy overload is quite important.

Realizing what triggers you, can help you respond efficiently to any situation. Do you understand what worsens your empathy symptoms? They include rushing, traffic, illness, fatigue, crowds, toxic people, loud environments, low blood sugar, overwork, arguments, chemical sensitivities, doing too much socializing and when you have the feeling of being trapped in a situation that is quite over-stimulating for instance, cruises or parties. A combination of the above situations can cause the condition of an empath to intensify significantly.

Therefore, you need to understand that when you have stress together with low blood sugar, you will feel quite exhausted and perhaps be overcome by a bad mood. You will also need to understand what makes it better for empathetic overloads. When undergoing sensory overload, I always consider slowing down everything and unplugging myself from all the stimulations that I might be having. When it persists, or rather it becomes quite intense, the feeling of a wilting flower engulfs me. That is the point when I feel illness taking over. I consider moving to a room that has no sound or light, to sleep, or meditate, and recalibrate to a lower level of stimulation.

Notably, having solitude for a weekend or an entire day is considered quite necessary when you feel that the sensory overload has been to the extreme. In such times, you can consider taking walks in nature and also limit trips out even if it is to take care of some errands. In addition, most empaths view things as all or nothing. By this, I mean that empaths consider that they have to give everything they have to give or retreat entirely for the safe haven of home. Your ability to moderate this radical stance is essential in allowing you to find balance and avoid suffering from extreme loneliness and isolation. Always be keen on your intuition; it will lead you to what is good and right for you. We all need to find the best manner in which to honor our needs. It is essential to understand that one-to-one contact can be one of the best ways to deal with people. This is due to the fact that groups can feel intense at times. A patient once told me, "I decompress when everyone is at sleep, which is at night when the world is at rest. That's the time when the invisible energetic buzz of the day calms down giving me time to relax and focus on myself."

In addition to this, I recommend that you consider shielding yourself. This is a fundamental skill that helps in lowering your ability to avoid being overloaded. Shielding has been found to be an easy and quick way for you to be able to offer yourself protection. Most of the empaths that have made use of shielding to protect themselves from toxic energy, allow room for the free flow of the positive energy around them. Therefore, using this skill regularly can be quite advisable. Any moment you realize that you are getting uncomfortable with someone, situation or a place, hold your shield up high. This method can be applied, for instance, when in a party, or airport, or you are feeling that you are communicating to an energy vampire such as in a room waiting for the doctor to attend to you. This tactic will indeed put you in a very safe bubble away from the factors that are draining you.

Coping with Empathetic Overload

As we have discussed throughout this book, overload can happen at any time, and it can happen very quickly. In fact, it can happen faster than you have the chance to figure out what's happened. That is why it is important to recognize the onset of the symptoms that may be afflicting you when you become overloaded.

One of the first symptoms you might encounter is a sudden headache. This type of headache is different from other types of headaches in the sense that it doesn't feel like a pounding pain running through your head. It feels more like there's a weight on top of your head, putting pressure on you. In a way, it feels as though there is something weighing you down. When this happens, it is best to practice the deep breathing exercises we have discussed earlier.

Another one of the symptoms your might feel when overload is upon you is a hollow feeling in the center of your chest. This hollowness is akin to feeling frightened or unsettled. Some empaths indicate that this type of feeling occurs when they are in the presence of someone they view as aggressive or even threatening. In such cases, shielding is definitely the right way to you. You can quickly imagine yourself being enveloped by a light that protects you while you are in the proximity of such people.

Perhaps the biggest issue with empathetic overload is dealing with energy vampires. These folks can suck your energies dry in a heartbeat. Some of the most skilled energy vampires can say something to make you feel terrible in a matter of seconds. These people know what buttons to push and when to push them. When they attempt to do so, it is often best to ignore them and move away. Often times, energy vampires seek confrontation since this is the time when they are able to extract the largest amount of energy from their victims.

It should be noted that avoiding a confrontation with an aggressive individual is by no means a sign of cowardice; in fact, it takes a lot more courage to stand up and back down from a challenge than it is to fall into the trap. The most skilled energy vampires will trick you into a confrontation so that they can emerge as the victims. Believe it or not, this type of behavior is extremely common.

If you are especially religious, saying a small prayer is always helpful. Religious empaths find short, but effective, prayers that they can recite when they begin to feel overwhelmed. Appealing to a higher power can have an immediate calming effect. So, I would encourage you to explore this option if you feel particularly compelled to do so. After all, embracing your religious faith is just another expression of your empathetic feelings.

That being said, here is another exercise which you can try to help you deal with empathetic overload.

- Take a few minutes to think that actually, you have taken in excessive energy.

- You will need to be viewing whatever is bugging you to be energy and depersonalize it. There is an option imagining it as a color that is in your body.

- Imagine having a root that connects into your mother earth through your legs.

- View all that energy taken on running down your body.

- Take a deep breath as you keep on releasing the energy.

- Due to the energy lost to the Mother Earth, you will need to be more aware and refrain from taking others' energy quickly.

- Now you can go ahead and picture golden light down from above your head.

- Allow yourself to be filled the entire body by the golden light through the top of the head.

- The golden light can flow down the roots, cleaning all the colors you had collected from the surroundings.

- The golden light will bring healing to both you and the Mother Earth.

- Give the Golden light space to flow from up the head to the roots and the Mother Earth.

- Now you can visualize the golden light vividly filling up the body and also expand out in a radius of approximately 5-foot.

- You can then allow the golden light to dissipate after saturating your entire circle.

- In conclusion, you can use the Recycling Angles to descend and pick what was released.

As you can see, visualization is a very powerful exercise. Please remember that one of the most powerful tools that an empath can put to use is their mind, that is, their imagination. You have a divine power which you can use to help you build your own reality around you.

Activities that can help you thrive as an empath

a) **Express Your Thoughts and Feelings**

Get into the habit of consciously expressing yourself when you feel something. It gives you the power to handle your emotions more effectively. This does not mean throwing a fit of rage, yelling at people or crying all the time. However, when you feel something, open up at least with people whom you can trust.

Do not get aggressive or act increasingly submissive. Gently stand up for your feelings without resorting to belittling or pulling down others. Assertiveness is taking charge of the situation and your emotions in a more constructive and calm manner, without doing things that will further damage the situation.

If you want to become more emotionally intelligent, start getting into the habit of taking control of the situation in a balanced and assertive manner without resorting to aggression or passivity. Present your stand in a clear, non-offensive and sure manner. You will eventually start becoming more confident, develop better negotiation/problem-solving skills and manage anxiety efficiently.

i) Identify Feelings without Judging Them

Tune into your deepest feelings and emotions without being judgmental about it. For instance, when you identify that you are experiencing pangs of jealousy towards another person, do not automatically term yourself or your feelings as bad or wrong.

Simply acknowledge that there is a feeling of jealousy and try to tackle it more positively.

ii) **Take Responsibility for Your Actions**

Accepting complete responsibility for your actions is one of the first steps towards developing higher emotional quotient. Emotionally intelligent people do not feel the need to shift responsibility on someone else, justify their wrongdoings or defend themselves aggressively. They shy away from putting the blame elsewhere and completely own up to the mistake.

You acquire the ability to control your emotions, manage negative feelings, develop more fruitful interpersonal relationships, wield better decisions and influencer your actions more positively. You are not relying on others or external circumstances for determining your emotions but taking charge of how you feel.

iii) **Use Generous Doses of Humor**

Sure, life is serious business. People get hurt, they pass away, tragedies happen, and many lose their livelihood. But whenever appropriate, use your humor to lighten the mood. After all, life is so much more bearable when you can have a laugh about trivial things. Unless you are talking about serious business, you can always help others life their spirits by providing a humorous tone to your interactions.

By looking at things from a more light-hearted perspective, you will learn to stop taking everything too seriously. In fact, when you look at things from a completely different point of view, you will also notice how your stress and anxiety will begin to curtail your emotions of empathetic overload. In fact, you can find the best way to turn a frown upside down. While I am not saying that you should make fun of people or the situations they are going through, being able to have a laugh, when appropriate, can go a long way toward diffusing potentially tense situations.

iv) **Master Empathizing with People**

Emotionally intelligent people are adept in the art of feeling other people's feelings. They place themselves in other people's shoes to understand the other person's perspective. When you develop empathy, you learn to consider every situation from other people's point of view too before coming to a decision that benefits everyone. This understanding paves the way for less conflict and greater stability in relationships. Connecting with others becomes effective and more fruitful when you learn to acknowledge the feelings of others.

The next time you find yourself getting angry with someone, stop in your tracks and try to understand why they may be compelled to behave the way they do. Is it related to their childhood experiences? Is it related to issues related to low self-confidence or self-esteem? Has an incident deeply impacted them? Try and pin down their behavior to underlying factors to gain a more holistic overview of the situation. This will help you handle the situation more intelligently rather than succumbing to impulses or thoughtless actions.

Chapter 9: Balancing Ways to protect yourself as an Empath

After years of specializing in the treatment of highly empathetic individuals, I have learned that one of the most obvious things that empaths lack is protection mechanisms. This is important to note since most empaths can't find a good way to keep the bad energies out and keeping the good energies from escaping.

Think about this way: imagine that it is winter, and you have the heat running in your home. Also, you have the window open. What does that mean? It means that the heat is escaping, and the cold air is rushing in. What that does is force you to turn the heat up so that you can reach your desired temperature. Over time, you will get a ridiculously high heating bill.

What is the solution to the problem?

Closing the window, of course!

Now, imagine that, if for some reason, you can't close the window. What do you do? You need to figure out how to close that window so you can keep the heat in and the cold air out. Well, the average empath doesn't have a clear idea of how to close that window. So, in this chapter, we will explore the possible ways in which you can close that window.

Shielding Visualization

We have talked at length about how shielding can help you build up your defenses so that you can keep the cold air at bay. One of the most important things to consider is making sure that you have your shields up when you need them to be up.

One of the most effective exercises that I have encountered is visualizing your shielding during meditation and quiet time. You can engage is this simple, but effective practice when you are taking a break from the world around you.

Here's how it works:

Start off by taking some time off from everything, including yourself. What that means is that if you are going through something, for example you are fixated on a problem, then let that go for a while and focus on your shielding.

Now, imagine situations that get you down. You can picture toxic people around you, or perhaps you can relive an incident that left you feeling particularly vulnerable. Then, picture your defenses going up. Visualize how your defenses protect you from these toxic individuals or hurtful situations.

Some of the empaths I have worked with have told me they see a light covering them. Other have told me they see themselves wrapped in an invisible blanket. As a matter of fact, the concept of a blanket seems fitting as it is commonly used by children as a defense mechanism when they feel vulnerable. Consequently, you too can use a blanket as a metaphor for your individual protection.

Personally, I have pictured a light wind, a small breeze if you will, that blows in with a comforting scent. This puff of air helps me to find protection and comfort when I need it most. Best of all, when I do my deep breathing exercises, it allows me to focus on what I need to do to relax. So, I can literally breath in the soothing wind. When I take this wind in, I can feel my lungs expand and take in all of the air that I need to survive. I now feel relieved and more confident in myself.

At the end of the day, the success of your visualization depends on what makes you feel protected. Picturing angels, saints and divine spirits all have been known to invoke feelings of protection and calm. Many folks who like to pray also visualize sacred images in their mind. This helps ground them because they are in contact with the divine forces that support their faith.

Ultimately, you can choose whatever makes you feel good so long as it is something which you can consistently rely on to help you feel better about yourself in the situation you are in. Other than that, please take the time to discard any negative ideas and thoughts; they will only serve to bring you down at the worst possible time.

Define and express the relationship needs you have

One of the hardest things that empaths are faced with is asserting their own, personal needs in a relationship. Often, empaths are engulfed by the needs of their significant other. In fact, a co-dependent relationship may emerge in which the recipient of the empath's attention and care becomes addicted, in a way, to the empath's care. What this does is create an unhealthy balance in which one of the parties gives and the other party takes. This can leave the empath drained and exhausted. When the empath is unable to assert their needs, they may end up resenting a person they once loved. They may still hold deep feelings for this person. Yet they may have been warped into a sense of resentment.

This is why the empath of the relationship needs to speak up and make their needs clear. When an empath is able to do this, their significant other will take note. If their partner is callous and shallow, they may brush off such demands. In this case, it might be best to consider ending the relationship especially if it has become unhealthy. Please bear in mind that your partner, spouse and/or significant other may be an energy vampire. That is why it is of the utmost importance to put yourself in a prominent position. Sadly, recipients of empathy don't understand that if they don't take care of their empath partner, they may lose the love and care that they have come to rely upon.

Always set energetic boundaries both at home and at work.

Setting boundaries is one of the most common issues in today's society. Most people have issues setting and respecting boundaries. In fact, it may be common for people to set their own boundaries only to walk all over them. For example, it is to common to see someone who is eager to go on a diet only to break it a couple of days later.

As an empath, you need to set your boundaries in such a way that people know you are accessible to them, but that you are not a limitless ATM machine where they can withdraw empathy from an unlimited amount. One of the easiest things you can do is set a schedule. People need to know that you are unavailable after a certain time. If they call or email after this time, then they will need to wait until you are back online.

Protect yourself from empathetic overload

We have discussed overload extensively throughout this book. Yet, there is still one item that is worth discussing: taking care of your physical health. In addition to getting enough sleep and regular exercise, having a balanced diet and taking in the proper nutritional ingredients that your body needs is essential toward building up your health.

Often, empaths neglect to take care of their physical body. This could be due to the hustle and bustle of daily life. Also, it can be the result of the demands that others have upon you. For example, a busy working mother may be left over with very little time for herself. The same goes for a working dad who is left with virtually no time to think about getting adequate nutrition.

Well, I have to say that this is one of the non-negotiable items that you must include in your daily life. You must take the necessary steps to ensure proper nutrition in your life. This could come in the way of a balanced diet and the consumption of a nutritional supplement. Please bear in mind that if your body is out of whack, your spirit will also find itself in an unsteady situation. Therefore, taking care of your body through proper nutrition is a must for all empaths.

I would recommend that you make an appointment with your doctor to go over your diet and see where you can improve. That way, your empathetic feelings can thrive in a healthy body. In doing so, positive energies will be met with as little resistance as possible. Before you know it, the positive energies that being to swirl around within you will help you achieve the best possible health condition you can imagine.

The power of prayer

Earlier, we talked about how prayer can be a useful means of helping you cope with stressful situations. Prayer is a very powerful tool which can help you connect with your spiritual being and the higher power in which you believe in.

The beauty of this exercise is that it isn't specific to any faith or religion. This is the type of exercise which anyone can do. Some religions have specific holy entities which are worshipped while others call upon saints and angels. Ultimately, what truly matters is your faith in the power that you believe in. This is what will make your prayer effective.

When you pray for protection, try to picture that mystical energy emanating from your supreme power. That power will then engulf you in such a way that you can then begin to feel their positive energy rushing through your body. As this energy builds up, your higher power is bestowing upon you the protection you seek.

If you like, you can choose to use a prayer specific to your religion, or you can make up your own prayer. Something along the lines of "oh divine power, bestow upon me your protective grace in this time of need". This short prayer encompasses the energy which you seek to attract. You are invoking the divine grace of the higher power that is closest to you. Before you know it, you will be wrapped in the divine energy that connects us all. This energy will then give you the fortitude to get through whatever situation you are in. Then, you will be able to go about your usual business with the confidence that you have the divine energy rushing through your veins.

Please bear in mind that you have the divine power inside of you as we speak. By using the power of prayer, you are seeking to release that energy in order to protect yourself and those you love. At the end of the day, this is one of the most powerful forces in the universe.

Chapter 10: The Scientific Connection between Sleep, Kindness, and Empathy

The topic of empathy tends to get shoved into a corner, often being dismissed as quackery and pseudo-science. Those who express themselves in this manner do so because they don't understand the underlying scientific logic found within empathy. While empaths may not have the necessary scientific and academic training to explain why they feel what they do, they do have the keen insight and understanding of what is going on inside their heads and hearts. That is why we will devote this chapter to furthering our understanding of empathy in scientific terms. We hope that this will dispel any confusion or uncertainty you may have regarding this wonderful gift that we have been blessed to receive. So, sit tight and let's get down to some serious academic and scientific business.

According to Inna Khazan Ph.D., a faculty member at the Harvard Medical School wrote that if one doesn't get enough shuteye "then we have high chances of having problems when it comes to emotion regulation and therefore, we feel irritable and anxious." On the other hand, compassion is said to be associated with the nervous system under the parasympathetic system. According to Doctor Khazan, we will always find it hard to show kindness not only to others but also to ourselves when we don't get enough sleep and rest.

According to a study by Eti Ben, Ph.D., a neuroscientist at UC Berkeley's Center, a person who is sleep deprived will always have lower levels of empathy. "Concern for people requires an understanding of what they want or feel, and we now have preliminary evidence that regions of the brain dealing with that understanding are impaired by sleep loss, and thus meaning the basis of empathy is lost" reads his book. Sleep in most cases has been referred to as something that highly takes us away from our social activity, but the truth is that "Sleep is a glue that biologically and psychologically binds us together as a species'" Ben states. It helps us to connect or reconnect with partners, friends, colleagues, and even strangers.

Therefore, getting enough sleep is critical in ensuring that you can replenish your empathetic energy especially when you are in need of some self-care. Here are some tips which can help you improve your overall sleep.

a) Cease from the mindless scrolling

Try figuring out why you have been not able to sleep, and then ask yourself if whatever it was is worth the consequences. According to Khazan, you will need to think about the content you are consuming. If you find yourself mindlessly scrolling through social media, then you might question just how beneficial this material is to you. If you can't find a solid reason for content being useful, then you might want to reconsider spending time on social media.

b) Try a simple breathing exercise

According to Khazan, doing heart rate variability (HRV) biofeedback will be able to train your heart rates to go up and down as much as you want. The changes in heart rates are associated with a higher level of health and resilience. She states that this technique will help you catch up sleep before you know it. It also helps in the regulation of emotions of which it includes the ability for one to be more compassionate and empathic. Try shifting your breath down to your stomach/belly. To be successful in this, inhale for three to four seconds, then release slowly for six seconds, do it repeatedly for ten minutes.

c) Meditate

Just like you have tried breathing, meditation is essential and can help you when it comes to relaxing. You can do this also through the help of applications such as Headspace and Calm as they will offer the specific meditations that will help you in drifting off.

d) Keep the phone out of your bedroom

While you may justify the presence of your phone next to your bedside claiming that it is your alarm clock, the fact of the matter is that a phone next to the bed represents the temptation to check it every chance you get. When you go about checking your phone right before bed, you are stimulating your brain. When this happens, you may end up crashing your sleep mechanism. If this were to happen, you might find yourself dead tired, but unable to sleep.

e) Check-in with your fatigue

You know your body better than anyone else. You can recognize when you are tired and when you can still hang in there. Of course, some folks have a higher tolerance for sleep deprivation while others have a need for longer periods of sleep and rest. As an empath, you will mostly likely require higher amounts of sleep. This is why you must make sleep a priority. If you need 8 hours, then get you 8 hours. If you happen to need more, then try your best to get it in whenever you can. At the end of the day, you must learn to identify the fatigue you are feeling.

Why the World Needs an Empathetic Revolution

There are times when we are faced with an overwhelming situation. For example, you see people suffering halfway across the world. So, even if you really wanted to help, there's not a whole lot that you can do. Still, that doesn't stop you from feeling terrible at what is happening. At this point, some empaths choose to just tune out entirely. According to psychiatrist and researcher Helen Riess, author of the new book "The Empathy Effect" this is the wrong approach to take. The fact that you tune out is a disservice to yourself because you are negating your own feelings. Over time, you may end up become insensitive to such circumstances.

Riess has focused her research on health and how empathy plays a key role. Earlier, we talked about how health care workers have a greater tendency to be empathetic as compared to other types of individuals. After a while, health care workers may be tempted to tune out from their feelings especially if they are working with people who are seriously ill. Tuning out becomes a defense mechanism especially if the input of emotions is overwhelming. However, the negative effects on the empath may lead them to become jaded and even cynical. While these attitudes may seem like they are extreme, the fact of the matter is that tuning out to the needs of others may prove to be the "easy way out".

So, this raises the question, what should we when confronted with overwhelming situations? If there is literally nothing you can do about it, then you can offer your positive energy to the world. Think about it. If we, as individuals, offer out positive energy to the world, then the cumulative effect of thousands, or even millions, of people emanating positive energy will have a profoundly positive effect on the world.

The world needs empathy especially in the wake of such violent and inhumane acts that take place on a daily basis. There are acts of violence committed on innocent people all over the word. Honestly, there is very little we can do, as individuals, to stop people from suffering in every corner of the world. But that doesn't mean that we can't set off a revolution. This revolution is intended to blast negative energy from the world around us and permeate our reality with positive energy that can bring about a change.

Then again, there are little things that we can do on a daily and consistent basis to improve the world around us. Showing empathy at all times is something which requires a lot of courage, but it is something which you can do whenever possible. Clear signs of empathy may be helping someone cross the street, being kind to animals, and taking care of nature. Taking care of nature is something which we often neglect to do. So, it is certainly worth taking into consideration as a part of your daily habits.

Empaths are emotional safe havens for the people around them. They are sought for their warmth and compassion. True empaths, while having their own beliefs and ideals, will shy away from judging people. For example, if you, as an empath, see that someone is ill, even if it was their fault, you will do what you can to offer comfort and support. After all, there will be a time when you can call them out for their behavior. But until that time comes, you can use your powers to do what you can to help whoever is in need.

The world needs more empaths who can listen. We often get caught up in a society where everyone wants to say something, but no one wants to listen. Sure, everyone has a voice, and a right to be heard, but the true empath will always listen first; this is a sign of respect and compassion for the other individual with whom you are interacting.

One of the most interesting character traits of empaths is their idealistic and dreamy nature. In many ways, this nature makes is a bit tough for empaths to deal with the world since empaths believe in justice and equality. That is why facing the harsh realities of life can cause empaths to feel hopeless and even despondent.

The world needs empathy for nature. Nature encompasses a great deal of our surroundings, yet we don't always take the time to connect. Often, connecting with nature can happen on very subtle levels. For instance, if you literally take the time to stop and smell the roses, you will find that it is easy to find that vital link with the natural world around us. Also, connecting with nature can be a question of walking in the park or going hiking in the mountains. Moreover, connecting with nature can be achieve through contact with animals. Most empaths are known to have pets around them. Given the fact that empaths build deep emotional connections, don't be surprised if an empath treats a pet as if it were a regular person. Empaths usually make excellent gardeners and have very little trouble striking a balance between themselves and their ties to nature.

As an empath, it is recommended that you take time to connect with Mother Earth. This can be done both on land and in water. Often, taking the time to visit a lake or stream can help you find that balance. Other times, going to the beach can help you reconnect with the power of the ocean. Ultimately, the main thing to keep in mind is that you are one with the planet.

Can Empathy Be Taught?

At various points in this book, we have indicated that empaths are born and not "created". While that is true, the fact of the matter is that empathy is a skill that anyone can develop. However, there is one catch to this: the individual must want to develop the skills. This isn't the type of skill which can be taught like driving or using a computer. If the individual doesn't feel keen on learning empathy, they will have a hard time connecting with people on a deep and meaningful level.

Most of the time, feelings of compassion grab hold of the average individual. They are overcome by sadness and even guilt at the sight of certain events. Most of the time, this is the result of a specific event which triggers a personal response in the individual.

Consider this example:

A person who was the victim of child abuse will automatically feel empathy for anyone else who has been through a similar situation. And while this person's exterior may be rough and seemingly expressionless, deep down, they feel vulnerable and can easily identify with the suffering of the other person.

As you can see, being a sensitive person doesn't necessarily mean cooing at the sight of cute kittens or crying when you see the sunset. Being a sensitive person means having feelings and actually engaging in the emotions of others. Unless you are somehow callous and emotionless, it will be virtually impossible for you to go through life without experiencing deep feelings of identification with a person or cause.

Now, it should be noted that companies have caught on to making sensitivity training mandatory in the workplace. However, the jury is still out on the effectiveness of this type of training.

Sensitivity training is generally centered around building sympathy among co-workers. This includes understanding the needs of others and figuring out the best way in which everyone can be made comfortable in the workplace. However, this isn't always an easy task. The fact of the matter is that we all have specific needs and demands. As such, it might be hard to accommodate everyone under the same roof. Then, there are times when the needs of one individual, or a small group of individuals, may end up conflicting with the needs of the entire group.

For instance, if a company offers meals as part of their benefits package, the company may find itself in a bind if they happen to employ a small number of employees who are vegan. In this example, the company would have to go to great lengths to build a vegan menu so that these employees can be adequately represented. While the sensitivity playbook would call for the company to be aware of the needs of vegan dieters, the fact of the matter is that such changes to the menu may lead to a disruption of the dynamic within the company.

In this example, an empath wouldn't mind the extra effort needed to accommodate vegan dieters. If anything, an empath would approve of their life choice, that is, foregoing the consumption of animal products. On the contrary, someone who is not an empath would find it hard to understand why there is any need to modify the cafeteria menu just to suit the tastes of a small group of people.

The fact is that being an empath leads you to places where very few people are able to go. What this means is that you need to focus your energies on those causes and circumstances in which you actually feel like you have the opportunity to make a contribution. In the example of the cafeteria menu, you might be making the biggest contribution of all by avoiding conflict.

Over the years, I have seen how folks who are rather insensitive open up when given the chance to do so in a safe environment. By "safe" I mean environments in which people can feel safe from being singled out or even made fun of for expressing the sensitivity. This is what I believe should be the core of sensitivity training: creating an environment in which everyone is free to express their emotions without the fear of reject or ridicule.

If a company is really keen on creating such an environment, they may be keen on implementing policies in which co-workers are aware of the need to express themselves in a constructive manner. This can lead to improving communication and fostering camaraderie. Best of all, a toxic environment can go from being that, toxic, to improving significantly.

In one personal experience, I saw how a group of co-workers went from a cold and silent workplace to a very open and communicative one. The reason for their standoffishness was the fact that there were unresolved issues among the group. There had been argument and quarrels that were never properly dealt with. The end result was a crack that grew into a gaping chasm.

The solution to this situation was not easy. In fact, it took quite a bit of work to get the group to finally open up about what had been bothering them. I won't lie, there was some drama involved. There was some shouting and a few tears. In the end, the group realized that they had been fighting over rather insignificant matters. While the argument at the time wasn't that big of a deal, each individual let it become a big deal... at least to them.

The training we underwent was rather straightforward. We had each person speak their mind. Then, I asked everyone to pick one colleague and describe how they felt this colleague felt. We learned that they weren't far off in their perception. The problem was that they had never consciously put themselves in their colleague's place. When they did so, they realized where their colleagues were coming from and how their personal attitude might rub other colleagues the wrong way.

Now, I won't say that everything is alright and there are no more conflicts. Yes, this group of individuals still have their quarrels and arguments every once in a while. However, the huge difference is that they are not equipped with tools that have enabled them to think about others first, and then think about themselves. This allows them to diffuse situations before they get out of hand.

So, when you learn to understand how others feel, you can avoid hurting them needlessly. This leads to a crucial insight: if you don't hurt the people around you, they will be more likely to be helpful and supportive thereby creating a positive influence on you. What that means is that if you strive to help others feel better around you, their positive energy will rub off on you. In contrast, if you make others miserable, chances are they will make you feel pretty lousy, too.

At the end of the day, anyone can further their empathetic skills. Even if they are not born true empaths, they can still develop a great deal of sensitivity to the world around them. Yet, true empaths, the people who can seemingly change a person's life with their mere presence, are born with a heightened sense of awareness. Nevertheless, they need to be trained and oriented in such a way that they are able to harness their gifts and provide them to the world in the best possible manner.

Chapter 11: The Power of Grounding and Earthing

For empaths, grounding is all about finding stability and connection. In fact, grounding works essentially the same way it does with electricity. You see, when an electrical connection is set up, there is a part of the connection that is set to the ground, literally. What grounding does in an electrical circuit is dissipate excess current. Therefore, when there is a surge, the additional current will find a place to go and dissipate harmlessly. When there is no such outlet, then the circuit become overloaded and blow up.

Can you see the parallel?

That is why grounding is crucial for empaths. Connecting with Mother Nature is one of the most effective ways in which you can become grounded in your day to day life. When you take the necessary steps to ground yourself, then you can go about the process of centering.

A centered person is one that does not swing in one direction or another. A centered person is able to strike a balance between positive and negative energies. Sure, there are times when the individual will swing to one direction or another. But what proper grounding allows the individual to do, is regain the proper balance in their life. So, if they become overloaded with negative energy, they will be able to dissipate that energy. By the same token, if they become overloaded with positive energy, they will allow that to flow naturally. And yes, there is such a thing as having too much positive energy. That is why you need to let it flow that naturally so that it can reach others who need it, too.

Grounding and Earthing Visualization

When you feel overwhelmed and intensely overloaded, having a place to retreat is one of the best ways in which you can deal with the situation. You can find a quiet spot, a stream, a part, the woods, anywhere where nature is predominant. In that manner, you can find the proper way to balance your energy load. Some folks love to meditate in a forest or sit by the water. Others love being surrounded by flowers. Others still enjoy the company of pets.

Now, if you happen to find yourself in a situation in which you are not close to nature (for example in the middle of traffic on a busy highway), you can use visualization to help you. So, you can visualize yourself in that special place that you love to retreat to. In fact, you don't need to be physically present in such a location to connect with Mother Earth; you can do it anywhere, even if it is in the middle of the concrete jungle.

The reason for this is due to the fac that our planet radiates energy. After all, it is a living being. So, we can pick up that energy and synch it with our own. Likewise, we can give off our own energy and synch it with nature. That allows a free flow of energy which can then lead to a greater, overall sensation of oneness with the planet. This is a type of symbiosis which can not only heal negative energies, but also balance the mind and the body. So, if you are keen on connecting with nature, don't worry, you can do it anywhere you are so long as you open up your heart and blend in with the energies of the world, and the universe for that matter.

The Blessing of Being an Empath

By now, I don't have to tell you that being an empath is a gift. But it is also a blessing. Very few people have this wonderful ability. Many lack empathy because they choose to immerse themselves in the trivialities of daily life. They allow themselves to become consumed mindless chatter that abounds in the world.

In fact, your average social media news feed is a collection of pointless interactions intermingled with very interesting and sometimes inspiring content. Yet, those who choose to embrace the chatter, allow this disruptive noise to take over their senses.

Moreover, I have met empaths who willingly succumb to the distractors around them in an attempt to deal with their overload. This is nothing more than a coping mechanism. Sadly, it leads to the empath dulling their senses in an unhealthy fashion. Ultimately, this can cause the empath to suffer emotionally. In some cases, empaths suffer from anxiety. In others, they go into full-blown depression.

The fact of the matter is that being an empath is not easy. Even though we are blessed with this wonderful gift, we feel cursed at times. That is why my message to you is to first, and foremost, embrace your gifts. Your sensitivities are a sign that you are evolving along with the rest of the universe. You are becoming in tune with creation around you. You are tapping into the life force that has been created around us. When you are able to synch into everything and everyone around you, you will find that there are wonderful experiences to be had.

Now, here is something important to remember: you don't have to carry the weight on your shoulders. Even though it might feel like you are, the best way in which you can help others is to help them help themselves. What that means is that helping others cope with their feelings, cope with their stress and cope with their own challenges will help them radiate more positive energy. This will help you deal with less negativity and more positivity. At the end of the day, this is part of your journey as an empath. When you help others, you also fulfill your own life's purpose.

At least, that's what I have been trying to do ever since I accepted myself for who I am.

Conclusion

Thank you for purchasing this book. I hope you enjoyed reading it and were able to learn the finer details of empathy, general types of empaths, and many more interesting topics. I also hope it offered you plenty of functional tips, practical ideas, and wisdom about thriving as an empath as well as balancing ways to protect yourself as an empath.

The best part is empathy can be developed through regular practice, training, and application. Improving your emotional intelligence is a continuous and dynamic process that only helps you enhance your empathic skills with time. Besides, learning how to deal with your emotions can really help you know how to deal with the challenges that most empaths face.

The next step is to go out there and use all the proven strategies mentioned in this book. You cannot know how to deal with challenges overnight just by reading about it. Implement the techniques mentioned in the book in your daily life to witness finer results!

You will gradually change from an empathy incompetent individual who struggles with his or her and other people's emotions to an empathy evolved and adept person, who will enjoy better interpersonal relationships and professional success in life.

How to Analyze People

*The Simple Guide to Speed Reading
People Using Human Behavior
Psychology and Body Language Analysis
to Defend Yourself from Mind Control,
Manipulation, and Deception*

Diana Brain

Introduction

Most people wish they could quickly analyze the body language of another person to ascertain the honesty of the person, but it is not that easy. Even for trained psychologists and psychiatrists, analyzing a person is a complex task even though it appears straightforward. Human behaviors are complex, and this implies that we can only approximate the profile and intent of an individual rather than precisely modeling the person and the associated behavior. However, there is a reassuring source of analyzing people, and this is body language. Body language is diverse and includes gestures, facial expressions, posture, tone of voice, and distance in communication. The other aspect of body language is that it is largely happening at the subconscious level of the mind making it difficult to rehearse all aspects of nonverbal communication uniformly.

Against this backdrop, this book offers a simple guide to reading people. The book avoids landing the reader to techniques of analyzing people because it is important to anchor the reader on a brief introduction to human behavior psychology and the benefit of analyzing a person. The reader will learn that we do not just read people for the sake of fun of it but for us to establish the truth-value in their actions and words. The book will walk the reader through ways of becoming an analyst of people as well as tackling what constitutes nonverbal communication. Under nonverbal communication, we explored eye signals, facial expressions, nonverbal of legs and feet, and paralinguistic, among others. After walking the reader systematically through the basics of body language, the author introduced mind control and means of defending oneself against it, manipulation and handling manipulators, as well as detecting lying and deception.

Chapter 1: Introduction to Human Behavior Psychology

Human behavior is complex and dynamic, and this implies that the behavior of an individual depends on multiple factors, including the environment, genetics, instance, level of education, and age, among others. When human behavior is analyzed from a psychological perspective, human behavior entails the entire spectrum of emotional and physical behaviors that human beings participate in such as biological, social and intellectual actions as well as how they are influenced by culture, attitudes, rapport, ethics, and genetics among other factors. In this manner, human behavior is a complex interaction of emotion, actions, and cognition.

Relatedly, since actions capture everything that can be seen, then actions are a behavior component. For instance, actions can be captured via eyes or physiological sensors. An action refers to the transition from one state to another. These actions occur at different time instances such as muscular activation to sleep, sweat gland activity, or food consumption. Regarding cognition as behavior, cognition outlines mental images and thoughts that one carries and can be both verbal and nonverbal. Verbal cognition may include statements such as "I have to wash my clothes," and on the other hand, a nonverbal cognition may include the imagination of how the project will look after reworking on it. Therefore, the skills and knowledge by understanding how to deploy tools in a beneficial manner, such as vocalizing songs constitute cognitions.

Additionally, emotions can be seen as behavior and are considered as a comparatively short conscious experience defined by intense mental activity and a feeling that is not impacted by either knowledge or reasoning. As expected, emotions manifest from a positive to negative scoring scale. Enhanced arousal can trigger other aspects of physiology that are reflective of emotional processing, such as heightened respiration rate. As such, emotions can only be inferred indirectly, much like cognition via monitoring facial expressions and monitoring arousal, among others.

Psychological View of Behavior

The investment model concerns viewing human behavior in the form of work effort directed toward creating change. For instance, if Richard goes to watch a movie at the local theater, then the act of going to the movie is a form of investment. In this manner, the need to elicit the desired outcome motivates specific human behavior. If Richard gets to meet fellow fans and feels happy, then this can be regarded as the return of this investment. Akin to any other form of investment, human behavior occurs when one takes into account the cost-benefit-analysis of the desired outcome. For the case of Richard, he has to consider time, calories, risks, and opportunity costs of going to watch the match at the local stadium.

It can be argued that the motivation to invest our actions in a specific behavior seems to emanate from evolutionary influences that make us prioritize food, sex, territory, food, and higher social status over other states of affairs. It also appears that particular behavioral traits, like temperaments and dispositions. For example, extroverted individuals find stimulating social situations more contending compared to introverted people. The learning history of a person influences the investment value system against this backdrop. An illustration of this concept is where an individual that liked the first season of TV series "Blind Spot" is likely that the individual is likely to be eager to see the second season of the particular TV series.

Another illustration of the human behavior investment model is where one is seated on the couch watching the news when an advert of a cookie activates in the person the desire to pour a glass of milk. The individual had a long day and is feeling worn out. In the mind of the individual, he or she calculates the cost-benefit-analysis of having to get up and pour oneself a glass of milk. In the end, the urge to go get a glass of milk from the fridge wins.

However, a quick look in the refrigerator shows that no milk makes you take a glance at the dustbin where the person notices that the empty milk container. Then, the individual feels upset because his target goal has been interrupted and the person entertains the thought of walking to the store to get the milk, but the cost-benefit-analysis indicates that the person will spend significant time and effort to get the milk and so drops the idea. In the end, the individual settles on a glass of orange juice with mild feelings of annoyance.

As such, the investment model for understanding human behavior views behaviors in the form of work effort committed to realizing a particular outcome. The human behavior costs in the form of time and energy computed in the form of benefits and costs. Human behavior is largely a cost-benefit analysis according to the investment model of animal behavior. For instance, most animal documentaries on the behavior of animals can help you realize how inherently animals make the cost-benefit analysis. Take the case of wildebeests in African savanna plains that need to drink water and cross the river that is infested with hungry crocodiles. In this context, water and grass are scarce, and wildebeests desperately need water and grass. At the same time, the wildebeests have to watch out for marauding crocodiles lurking under the surface of water ready to devour the wildebeests. Eventually, wildebeests have to invoke an investment model of behavior to maximize the possibility of living, drinking water, and crossing the river to graze. Under this model, most wildebeests cautiously approach the river, ensuring that they near the riverbank when drinking water that would enable them to retract sporadically at the slightest hint of danger.

Correspondingly, human behavior is a form of commerce with the environment. The human being actions are primed to maximize benefits from the environment. The mind is a critical component of behavior as it stores a history of what has desired outcomes as well as computing the cost-benefit analysis before one act. It can be argued that the investment model of behavior affirms the assumption that human behavior is conscious and well thought. Additionally, actions lead to lost opportunities, and one has to pursue an action that best maximizes the intended outcomes. For example, if an animal spends time defending a territory, it will miss out on finding food.

The behavior of human beings can be considered from the understanding that human beings are social animals. Human behavior happens in the context of a social matrix. A social influence entails the actions that influence the investment of another person. For instance, when Richard was going to the movie, did he ask his girlfriend out or did the girlfriend ask him out. In most cases, social influence processes involve cooperation and whether the transactions move people closer or make them drift apart. Social influence also manifests as a resource. As a resource, social influence concerns the capacity to move other people in alignment with our interests. Social influence in this context refers to the levels of social and respect value other people show us and the degree to which they listen, care about our well-being, and are willing to sacrifice for us. For instance, if Richard is attracted to his girlfriend, and he agrees to go to the movie with her, then, this is an indicator of social influence as a resource. The girlfriend breaking up with Richard is a potent indication of a loss of social influence.

By the same measure, social influence is marked by the amount of attention from other people. In line with this understanding, the actions of a person will seek to attract attention from people or sustain the attention of people. Probably, you have colleagues or public figures that consistently act to attract and sustain admiration from other people. At a personal level, one is likely to act in a manner that invites admiration from colleagues, friends, and other people. The behavior and likely behavior of an individual is likely to optimize admiration from others.

Additionally, within the social influence model of human behavior, individuals are likely to act in a manner that invites more positive emotions than negative emotions from others. In a way, the need to attract more positive emotions from others is related to attracting admiration from others, but it is highly related to emotional intelligence. One can only enhance the likelihood of getting a positive emotional reaction from others if he or she has requisite emotional intelligence levels. Through emotional intelligence, one learns to show empathy and pay attention to how others are feeling. Against this backdrop, human behavior is likely to be reactive of how others are feeling, or it is likely to be highly considerate of others for the motivation of attracting positive emotions from them.

Equally important is the degree to which others will sacrifice their interests for the sake of another person as a mark of social influence. People with strong social influence will have tens to thousands of people willing to sacrifice their interests for the sake of the person. The behavior of the individual with great social influence is likely to take into account that there are tens to thousands of people who are willing to forego their interests for the sake of the influential figure. On the other hand, the followers of the influential people are likely to take the actions of the individual as guidance or message of how one should act and live.

In most cases, human behavior requires justifications by legitimizing it. For instance, when you shout at someone, there are chances that one will qualify the behavior by stating that they were upset. In reaching justification, one assesses the behavior and the ideal outcome. For instance, the ideal outcome may have been attracting admiration from others, but one ended up embarrassing themselves in public. Expectedly, the individual will feel angry for not only failing to attain ideal reaction from the audience but also degrading the status quo. In this state, the individual will justify subsequent undesired behavior by drawing attention to the disappointment he or she got earlier on.

Using Richard and the movie example, Richard may have felt justified to make his girlfriend tag along to the movie and allow the girlfriend to show romance because of this what lovers do. The justification of his behavior and the girlfriend's behavior emanates from observation and learned patterns of what lovers do and not necessarily, of how each of them individually feels. Justification of behavior can be simply that is what others do, and so the individual is obliged to emulate the same. Try watching court proceedings for you to realize how people place significant value of justification for their behavior.

Relatedly at the organizational level, organizations have invested significantly in assessing human behavior during recruitment stages and as well as assessing workers. Human behavior is complex, and organizations seek to have the best bet in recruiting and retaining predictable workers. Most of the personality tests administered during hiring and appraisal processes are meant to help profile workers and have a predictable look at how each of the workers may behave. There have been attempts to determine a formula for human behavior as a simple system, but it has been satisfactorily concluded that human behavior is dynamic.

Chapter 2: Why to Analyze a Person?

The primary role of analyzing people is to establish the truth status of their words, actions, and body language. Verbal communication is likely to mislead where an individual indicates that he or she is fine when truly the person is feeling upset. The other critical role in analyzing a person is to attain effective parenting. Parents will attest that in most cases, what the child says, and what he or she is feeling may sharply contradict. Any person handling children will conclude that it is important to analyze the kids lest the person sits with a sick child, a depressed child, or a disturbed child thinking that the child is fine. In relationships, analyzing people is important to score their honesty about themselves and another entity.

In detail, we analyze people to gauge the level of respect they have for themselves and others. In most cases, we need to determine how much a person respects himself or herself as well as others. Relying on verbal communication cues alone will not reveal much about levels of self-respect one has, including the respect that the person has for other people. Fortunately, analyzing the body language will reveal convincingly the levels of self-respect and respect for others that an individual has. For instance, your dressing and personal grooming may indicate how much you value oneself. On the other hand, your facial expressions and posture will reveal much about how you regard other people, especially during a conversation.

Through the analysis of a person, we can predict their spending habits. Another major reason for studying people is to predict their spending manners. For instance, when looking for a partner, it is necessary to profile their likely spending patterns. Through analysis of their body language when luxury items and services are, mentioned, one can predict how the person is likely to spend his or her cash. Additionally, the analysis of body language can indicate any signs of addictions that the person has. For instance, through an analysis of body language, we can get mild hints of substance abuse, alcoholism, shopping addiction, or signs of obsessive-compulsive disorder. From this analysis of body language, one can predict the spending habits of a fiancée, kin, or employee with remarkable accuracy.

Additionally, the analysis of people helps understand their patience levels. Being patient is a desirable trait, and like most desirable traits, we are likely to force it to manifest to enhance our success chances. For instance, when looking for a date, the target person is expected to push the attributes of being patient when he or she is not. It is only through reading body language that we can make an early prediction of the levels of patience that the person has. As indicated earlier on, the primary role of learning body language is because people tend to rehearse vocal communication, but it is a daunting task to uniformly rehearse tone of voice, the pitch of voice, gestures, postures, and eye contact to ensure consistency. Learning about the patience levels of an individual can help people around the target person relate better with him or her.

Again, the analysis of a person can reveal their hobby or how they spend their leisure time. In all social interactions, including workplace interactions, it is vital to determine the leisure preferences of the target person. A manager or supervisor in an organization will be interested in learning the actual leisure preferences of an employee with the understanding that during interviews people belt out answers that will enhance chances of being absorbed by the employer. Through analysis of the body language and incorporating verbal communication, it is possible to determine the leisure preferences of a candidate employee. In relationships, one needs to understand the partner wholesale, including their leisure preferences, to help create a middle ground with your individual leisure preferences.

Furthermore, a study of people can indicate their health status. As we will learn, our physiological condition influences the kind of emotions we express and how we express, including our physical behaviors. For instance, if feeling intense pain, then one is likely to frown, sigh, and sit in a non-upright position in an attempt to cope or mask the pain. Similarly, if one is feeling dizzy, then he or she is likely to appear sleepy, disconnected, and frail. In healthcare settings, the body language constitutes part of diagnosis where the eye stare and movements of limbs are taken into consideration among other aspects of physical examination. Against this backdrop, analyzing a person can help reveal the underlying health status.

Equally important is that the assessment of people can help one determine their confidence levels. The level of confidence one has is important in determining how much the person will feel comfortable. In a team setting, the team leader will need to read the confidence levels of each member to determine how to delegate duties with each person feeling comfortable. If the confidence levels of an individual are low, then the individual is likely to be highly sensitive even to the mildest form of humor. In such a case, it will help to take into consideration the sensitivity of the target person when communicating informally. In personal relationships, it will help to help boost the confidence levels of the target individual while being sensitive when communicating and acting.

Another role of analyzing people is to determine their levels of composure. Even though it is akin to patience, but composure is the quality to remain restraint and calm even when a provoking message is being passed. It is one of the most desired quality but hard to manifest in individuals. Being composed does not imply that one mask or hides his/her true feelings, but rather, it is the quality of carefully processing negative emotions without letting emotions overwhelm you. When you comprehend the levels of composure of the target person, then you are likely to understand when to pause the communication or ease tension rather than guiding the target person to an explosion of emotions.

Finally, the analysis of people can improve their social experience. Overall, we are likely to analyze people to help us improve our social experience. We are likely to analyze potential friends to help us admit to only those people that best align with our wishes. Without analyzing people, we are likely to admit just any person as a friend and lose them shortly after that may make you think that you are the problem or that you are difficult. Additionally, studying people will help determine their true-life status and help you become more sensitive and understanding about their feelings, even their verbal communication speaks the contrary. At the household level, reading the body language of your partner will help you become more understanding and responsive to their needs.

Chapter 3: Becoming an Analyst of People

As suggested, studying people is not reserved for psychiatrists but any other person even though psychiatrists are best positioned to analyze people. Analyzing people requires understanding their verbal and nonverbal cues. When studying people, you should try to remain objective and open to new information. Nearly each one of us has some form of personal biases and stereotypes that blocks our ability to understand another person correctly. When reading an individual, it is crucial to reconcile that information against the profession and cultural demands on the target person. Some environments may force an individual to exhibit particular behavior that is not necessarily part of their real one. For instance, working as a call center agent may force one to sound composed and patient when in real life, the person acts the contrary.

Start by analyzing the body language cues of the target person you are trying to read. Body language provides the most authoritative emotional and physiological status of an individual. It is difficult to rehearse all forms of body language, and this makes body language critical in understanding a person. Verbal communication can be faked through rehearsal and experience, and this can give misleading stand. When examining body language, analyze the different types of body language as a set. For instance, analyze facial expressions, body posture, pitch, tonal variation, touch and eye contact, as a related but different manifestation of communication and emotional status. For instance, when tired, one is likely to stretch their arms and rest them on the left and right tops of adjacent chairs, sit in a slumped position, stare at the ceiling, and drop their heads. Analyzing only one aspect of body language can mislead one to come up with a conclusion correctly.

Additionally, it would be best if you lent attention to appearance. The first impression counts, but it can also be misleading. In formal contexts, the appearance of an individual is critical to communicate the professionalism of the person and the organizational state of the mind of that individual. For example, an individual with an unbuttoned shirt indicates he hurried or is casual with the audience and the message. Wearing formal attire that is buttoned and tucked in suggests prior preparation and seriousness that the person lends to the occasion. Having unkempt hair may indicate a rebellious mind, and this might be common among African professors in Africa, for instance. In most settings, having unkempt hair suggests that one lacks the discipline to prepare for the formal context or the person is overworked and is busy. Lack of expected grooming may indicate an individual battling with life challenges or feeling uncared for.

It is also important that one should take note of the posture of the person. Posture communicates a lot about the involvement of an individual in a conversation. Having an upright posture suggests eagerness and active participation in what is being communicated. If one cups their face in the arms and lets the face rest on both thighs, then it suggests that one is feeling exhausted or has deviated from the conversation completely. Having crossed arms suggests defensiveness or deep thought. One sitting in a slumped position suggests that he/she is tired and not participating in the ongoing conversation. Leaning on the wall or any object suggests casualness that the person is lending to an ongoing conversation. If at home, sitting with crossed legs suggests that one is completely relaxed. However, the same posture at the workplace suggests that one is feeling tensed and at the same time concentrating.

Furthermore, observe the physical movements in terms of distance and gestures. The distance between you and the target individual is communicating communicates about the level of respect and assurance that the individual perceives. A social distance is the safest bet when communicating, and it suggests high levels of professionalism or respect between the participants. Human beings tend to be territorial as exhibited by the manner that they guard their distance. Any invasion of the personal distance will make the individual defensive and unease with the interaction.

For this reason, when an individual shows discomfort when the distance between communicators is regarded as social or public, then the individual may have other issues bothering him or her. Social and public distances should make one feel fully comfortable. Allowing a person close enough or into the personal distance suggests that the individual feels secure and familiar with the other person. Through reading, the distance between the communicators will give a hint on the respect, security, and familiarity between the individuals as well the likely profession of the individuals.

Correspondingly, then try to read facial expressions as deep frown lines indicate worry or over-thinking. Facial expressions are among the visible and critical forms of body language and tell more about the true emotional status of an individual. For instance, twitching the mouth suggests that an individual is not listening and is showing disdain to the speaker. A frozen face indicates that the person is shell-shocked, and this can happen when making a presentation of health and diseases or when releasing results of an examination. A smiling face with the smile not being prolonged communicates that one is happy and following the conversation. A prolonged smile suggests sarcasm.

If one continually licks, the lips may indicate that one is lying or that one is feeling disconnected from the conversation.

Relatedly, try to create a baseline for what merits as normal behavior. As you will discover, people have distinct mannerisms that may be misleading to analyze them as part of the communication process. For instance, some individuals will start a conversation by looking down or at the wall before turning to the audience. Mildly, mannerisms are like a ritual that one must activate before they make a delivery. Additionally, each person uniquely expresses the possible spectra of body language. By establishing a baseline of what is normal behavior, one gets to identify and analyze deviations from the standardized normal behavior accurately. Against this understanding, one will not erratically score a speaker that shuffles first if that is part of his behavior when speaking to an audience.

Furthermore, pay attention to inconsistencies between the established baseline that you have created and the individual's gestures and words. Once you have created a baseline, then examine for any deviations from this baseline. For instance, if one speaks in a high-pitched voice that is uncharacteristically of the individual, then the person may be feeling irritated. If one normally walks across the stage when speaking but the individual chooses to speak from a fixed position during the current speech, then the person is exhibiting a deviation that may suggest that the individual is having self-awareness or is feeling unease with the current audience. If an individual speaks fast, but usually the person speaks with a natural flow, then the person is in a hurry or has not prepared for the task.

Correspondingly, view gestures as clusters to elicit a meaning of what the person is communicating or trying to hide. When speaking a person, will express different gestures and dwelling on the current gesture may make you arrive at a misleading conclusion. Instead, one should view the gestures as clusters and interpret what they imply. For instance, if a speaker throws the hands randomly in the air, raises one of their feet, stamps the floor and shakes his or her hands, then all of these could suggest a speaker that is feeling irked and disappointed by the audience or the message. As such, different aspects of body language should be interpreted as a unit rather than in isolation.

Then compare and contrast. For one to fully read the target person, try comparing the body language of the person against the entire group or audience. For instance, if one appears bored and other people appear bored, then you should conclude the tiredness of the person is largely due to the actions of the speaker for speaking longer than necessary. In other terms, the body language of the target person is not isolated. However, if you make a comparison, and it happens that the target person's body language deviated from the rest, then you should profile the actions of the individual accordingly. Making a comparison and contrast helps arrive at a fair judgment of the target person.

By the same measure, try to make the individual react to your intentional communication. Another way of managing to read a person is to initiate communication and watch their reaction. For instance, establishing eye contact and evaluating the reciprocation of the target person can help tell more about their confidence and activeness in participating in the interaction. When an individual ignores your attempts to initiate communication, the person could be concentrating on other things, or the person feels insecure. Initiating communication is critical where it is difficult to profile a person, and one wants to convincingly read the person.

Go further and try to identify the strong voice. A strong voice suggests the confidence and authority of the speaker. If the speaker lacks a strong voice, then he or she is new to what is being presented or has stage fright. However, having a strong voice that is not natural suggests a spirited attempt to appear in charge and confident. A strong voice should be natural if the individual is feeling composed and confident in what he or she is talking about.

Relatedly, observe how the individual walks. When speaking to a target person, he or she will walk across the stage or make movements around the site where the conversation is happening.

From the manner of walking, we can read a lot about the individual. Frequently walking up and down while speaking to an audience may indicate panic or spirited attempt to appear in control. Speaking while walking slowly across the stage from one end to the other end indicates that one is comfortable speaking to the audience. If a member of the audience poses a question, and one walks towards the individual, then it suggests interest in clarifying what the individual is asking.

It might be necessary to scout for personality cues. Fortunately, all people have identifiable personalities, but these can be difficult to read for a person not trained in a psychologist. However, through observation, one will get cues on the personality of the individual. For instance, an outgoing person is likely to show a warm smile and laugh at jokes. A socially warm person is likely to want to make personal connections when speaking, such as mentioning a particular person in the audience. Reserved individuals are likely to use fewer words in their communication and appear scared or frozen on stage when speaking.

Additionally, one should listen to intuition, as it is often valid. Gut feelings are often correct, and when reading a person, you should give credence to your gut feeling about the person. When reading a person and you get a feeling that the person is socially warm, you should entertain this profiling while analyzing the body language of the person. While considering gut feeling, you should classify it under subjective analysis, as it is not based on observable traits and behaviors but an inner feeling.

Expectedly, watch the eye contact. Creating eye contact suggests eagerness and confidence in engaging the audience. Avoiding eye contact suggests stage fright and shyness as well as lack confidence in what one is talking about. A sustained look is a stare, and it is intended to intimidate, or it may suggest absentmindedness of the individual. If one continuously blinks eyes while looking at a target person suggests a flirting behavior. An eye contact that gradually drops to the chest and thigh of the individual suggests a deviation of thoughts from the conversation.

Additionally, pay attention to touch. The way a person shakes hands speaks a lot about their confidence and formality. A firm handshake that is brief indicates confidence and professionalism. A weak handshake that is brief indicates that one is feeling unease. On the other hand, a prolonged handshake, whether weak or strong, suggests that the person is trying to flirt with you, especially if it is between opposite sexes. Touching someone on the head may suggest rudeness and should be avoided.

Finally, listen to the tone of voice and laughter. Laughing may suggest happiness or sarcasm. Americans are good at manifesting sarcastic laughter, and it is attained by varying the tones of the laughter. The tone of the voice tells if the person is feeling confident and authoritative or not. Overall, a tonal variation implies that the individual is speaking naturally and convincingly. A flat tone indicates a lack of self-confidence and unfamiliarity with the conversation or audience and should be avoided.

Chapter 4: Nonverbal Communication

For this discussion, nonverbal communication is akin to body language. Let us start with facial expressions that affirm that the human face is highly expressive and communicates countless emotions even without vocalizing anything. A great aspect of nonverbal communication is that it is largely standard as the facial expression for anger, happiness, and fear is similar across different cultures. Like most aspects of nonverbal communication, one has little control over the source and manifestation of facial expression, making it a critical aspect of evaluating the honesty of communication. From facial expressions, we can determine how one is feeling.

Beginning with body movement and posture, how one stands, sits, holds their head or walks affects how others perceive one. For instance, your posture communicates much about your attentiveness and eagerness when listening to a speech. Your posture also communicates our emotional status. If one is angry, then he or she is unlikely to appear composed and likely to stand upright for long or slouch for long. On the other hand, if one is excited, he or she is likely to change posture and movements frequently than when one feels sad. At one point, you must have felt highly excited, you probably walked fast, jumped, sat, and stood up frequently than usual.

Additionally, gestures are the other form of nonverbal communication. Focusing on hand gestures, they are used to beckon, wave, point, or direct. In most cases, hand gestures happen without much intervention from the conscious mind. The meaning of most hand gestures varies across cultures. An innocent message created by a hand gesture in one country may be offensive in another country. One can read the emotional states of a person from their hand gestures even if they speak contrary. For example, when one is angry, he or she is likely to throw their hands in the air in an uncoordinated manner. In most cases, hand gestures contradict verbal communication, especially where one is feeling emotional and tries to hide it.

Relatedly, there is eye contact that is an important aspect of body language. The way one looks at another person when communicating reveals hostility, affection, interest, and confidence. Individuals that have difficulties initiating and sustaining eye contact are largely considered shy. When an individual feels embarrassed, he or she is likely not to make and sustain eye contact. Sustained eye contact at a particular person or group of people is a stare and indicates judgment. Think of how your instructor looked at you when you were talking while others were writing. Prolonged eye contact is associated with intimidation and judging.

For touch as a component of body language, it evokes significant meaning and, in some cases, touch influences the development of a person. In the formative years, children need touch, reassuring fondle for them to feel secure and loved. Psychologists can suspect bonding issues where one of the parents shows reluctance to touch and stroke their kid. For adults, touch is expressed commonly as a handshake and a hug. A firm handshake indicates confidence and familiarity, while a weak handshake suggests a lack of confidence and unfamiliarity. A hug serves the same role as a handshake, but hugs for individuals in love may be prolonged.

Equally important, there is space as part of nonverbal communication. Getting too close to the person you are having communication with will make them feel uncomfortable unless it is in exceptional situations. For lovers trying to connect more, moving closer to each other may sound romantic. In teaching, there is what they call the professional distance, which is the standard distance allowable between a teacher and the student when communicating. When someone gets too close, then the other person may feel suffocated, trapped, and intimidated. Getting too far is also counterproductive as it makes the other person strain to participate in the communication.

Correspondingly, voice is part of nonverbal communication. How loud we speak communicates an emphasis. The pace by which we speak captures our emotional status. If one speaks fast may indicate that one has panicked or one is feeling insecure and wants to get through with speaking as fast as they can. The tone and inflection of the voice tell more about the attitude of the speaker and the nature of the message. For instance, the message may sound standard and devoid of emotions, but the tone and pitch of the speaker may bring out excitement or temper. The tone of the speaker may indicate sarcasm or anger.

While nonverbal communication can be manipulated or rehearsed, it is difficult to manipulate all forms of nonverbal communication in one instance. It is difficult to rehearse tone, gestures, touch, distance, and facial expressions to align with verbal communication. For this reason, body language remains a reliable source of reading and ascertaining the emotional status of an individual. However, it is possible to learn and exert control over your body language to enhance particular outcomes. Just as if we learn to focus our emotions and subsequent reactions, we can exert more control over body language. There is also a possibility of receiving confusing nonverbal communication, which is unintentionally sent by the source. In most cases, a confusing nonverbal communication harms relationships. At one point, you might have smiled unintentionally only for your friend to think you are rejoicing that they are suffering.

For example, Collins holds the view that he gets along well with his colleagues at work, but if you question any of the colleagues, they think that Collins is intimidating and very intense. Most of the friends think that Collins's eye contact is a stare that seeks to devour others through the eyes. Collins's colleagues are of the view that if he takes your hand, he lunges to grab it and then squeeze so hard that it hurts. Collins is a caring lad who wishes that he attracted more friends, but his nonverbal language keeps people at a distance and constraints his ability to advance at work.

On the other hand, Joan is elegant, is outgoing, and has no qualms meeting eligible men, but she has a hard time maintaining a relationship for longer than a few months. Joan is social and interesting but exhibits tension even though she constantly smiles and laughs. Her voice is shrill; shoulders and eyebrows are noticeably raised, and the body is stiff. Most people around Joan feel anxious and uncomfortable, and it is discomfort from people that makes Joan feels uneasy with her life.

Relatedly, even though Dennis thought that he had found the perfect match when he met Sharon, Sharon was not so sure. Dennis is good looking, a smooth talker, and hardworking but seemed to care about his thoughts than those of Sharon. When Sharon had something to speak, Dennis was always read with judging eyes and a rebuttal before she could finish her thought. All these developments made Sharon feel ignored, and soon, she started showing interest in other men. The inability of Dennis to listen to others makes him unpopular with many of the individuals he most admires.

Against this backdrop, all these smart and well-intentioned people are struggling in their attempt to socialize with others. The unfortunate thing is that they are unaware of the body language they communicate. If one wants to communicate effectively, they should avoid misunderstandings and enjoy a trusting relationship, both professionally and socially. One should understand how to use and interpret body language and enhance their nonverbal communication.

One of the most challenging and most valuable aspects of nonverbal communication is that it is happening even when one is not initiating. For this reason, body language can be frustrating, especially where one is trying to hide something while the body language keeps on giving them away. At some point, you have been in a relationship and detected lies from your partner despite the best attempts by your partner to cover their trails. On the other hand, nonverbal communication gives the most dependable indicator of the status of an individual even when the person is attempting to mask their true status.

Relatedly, most people feel frustrated by nonverbal communication because they cannot always control it even with rehearsals. Think of trying to assure your partner that you are not offended, but the tone and pitch of your voice suggest that you are upset. The listener will feel that you are not being honest with yourself and to the listener. It is important to match verbal communication with nonverbal communication and not the other way around. The inability to manifest the desired body language can be a source of distress.

If reading body language, try to pay attention to inconsistencies exhibited by the communicator. Usually, nonverbal communication should support or amplify verbal communication. Where inconsistencies manifest, then the individual is trying to mask their true emotional status. It is important to analyze nonverbal communication signals as a group rather than a single nonverbal cue. For instance, analyze the tone of the voice, hand gestures, facial expressions, and eye contact a group of related components. It is important to remember that some people are born with conditions that make them appear to show inconsistencies when communicating nonverbally, but they are honest in their communication.

For instance, they are people born shy due to parental issues that make them shy off when interacting with people. A shy individual will have challenges in initiating and sustaining eye contact, and this has nothing to do with their emotional status and honesty of their verbal message. There are persons born with hyperhidrosis, which is a condition that makes them sweat excessively even when the weather is cold and with no strenuous movement. The hands and feet of such people sweat, and they will avoid handshakes or eye contact, which should not be interpreted as panicking, insecurity, and anxiety.

Chapter 5: Hand Gestures and Arm Signals

It is important to read gestures in the context of other aspects of body language, but in this chapter, we will explore ways of reading gestures. We all talk with our hands often. For some people, the gesturing matches their message well. Some people do not deploy hand gestures while others overuse hand gestures. Most hand gestures are universal. A person that does not use hand gestures may be seen as indifferent. For this reason, the audience may feel that one does not care about what the other is talking about. If your hands are hidden, then the audience will find it difficult to trust you. If one's hands are open and the palms wide enough, then the individual is communicating that he or she is being honest and open.

Furthermore, randomly throwing hands in the air while talking may suggest that one is anxious or panicking. Extreme anger will also make one throw their hands in an uncoordinated manner. For further understanding, take time and watch movie characters quarreling, and you will note that most people being accused of something will throw their hands in the air randomly. It is something that they have little control over because most of the body language happens at the subconscious level of the mind. Randomly throwing hands in the air indicates that one is overwhelmed with emotions or that one has given up defending their position in the argument and have left the argument to the individual that started it.

Additionally, one may point at an object or a person. Pointing as a gesture helps the focus of the speaker and the audience to the focused area. During your school days, you probably saw your teacher point in a particular direction without speaking until the students that were talking had to stop. As such, pointing at particular students drew the attention of the entire class to their direction, making them become the center of attention, and they had to do a quick self-evaluation and stop talking. All these illustrate that body language communicates tone and emotions just as verbal communication.

Furthermore, pointing while wafting the index finger indicates a warning. When one points the index finger at someone and wafts it up and down, then you are denoting a stern warning and judgment to the individual. It is the equivalent of saying, "this is the last warning." Probably your parent or teacher may have a point and waft gesture to signal a warning that what you are doing is wrong and that you should stop. In movie characters, you might have observed that the police or the lead actor uses the index finger to warn someone. The finger signal singles out the individual and reduces the focus to just that one aspect of behavior that the speaker wants the target person to understand.

Relatedly, if one spreads all the fingers and holding them together against those of the opposite hand indicates strong personal reflection such as when praying or remembering the departed soul. The same gesture can be used when one is focusing the mind during meditation or yoga. The holding of each of your fingers against their peers of the other hand may also indicate feeling humble and thankful of everything. For instance, followers of the Catholic faith frequently use this gesture when praying. The gesture shows humility and thankfulness.

Sometimes one may tap on the head once or continuously. When one taps on the head using a hand or a finger, it indicates the individual is thinking hard or trying hard to recall something. For instance, when speaking and you try to remember what another person said you might use this gesture. Children often tap their heads once or continuously using one finger or the entire palm to signal attempts to recall something. The gesture is the equivalent of saying, "Come on, what it was?" or "Come on what was the name again!" and it is a prop to recall hard.

Similarly, a fully raised palm with fingers spread may indicate that one should stop. When stopping the vehicle on the roadside, one raises one of their palms high up, and it is taken as a sign to stop. The same is true in the sporting environment were raising one palm high up commonly communicates that the playing should stop. When arguing with your partner, if he or she raises one of their palms, then it is signaling the other to stop arguing or stop whatever action he or she is doing.

If one claps, the palms together may indicate applauding the message or the speaker. When the speaker is done with speaking, the audience may clap their hands together to mark appreciation of the message or both the message and the speaker. However, when the hands are spontaneously and violently clapped, then it is a message that the audience should stop because what they are doing is unethical or irritating. At home, one of your parents probably clapped their hands suddenly and violently to make you stop as well as draw attention to their presence, especially where you were playing loudly around the house.

Relatedly, if one interlocks one hand against those of the other hands and folding them. The application of this gesture indicates that one is attentive but unease at the same time. During an interview, meeting, or a class session, the audience is likely to interlock their fingers and fold them. In a way, the interlocking of the fingers is supposed to offer some form of assurance to the affected person that he or she is safe. One is likely to also use this gesture when he or she is mentioned negatively. Think of how you reacted when you were mentioned among noisemakers or workers having challenges following the rules of the company. Most probably, you interlocked your fingers and folded them.

Additionally, if one is feeling shy or uncertain, the individual is also likely to interlock their fingers and raise the interlocked fingers when speaking. The gesture in this context appears to give some sort of prop for the affected individual enabling them to navigate the anxiety. The gesture in this context is not just about communicating the physiological status of the affected person but as a coping mechanism of sudden anxiety and discomfort of the individual.

Still on body language and focusing on gesture, if one raises both hands behind the head and interlocks the fingers, then it is to act as a cushion for the head. The gesture is used to indicate that one is feeling casual, tired, or simply not tasked by the current conversation. The gesture may also indicate that the individual is feeling tired by the conversation or the activity. Think of how you react when feeling exhausted when talking to a friend or after watching a movie. You probably raised both of your hands behind the head and interlocked the fingers to act as a headrest. In most cases, when one invokes this gesture, then the individual is likely to let the mind allow other thoughts to escape from the current conversation.

Correspondingly, there is the gesture where one lets one of their palms to brush down their faces. The gesture is used to signal deeper thinking, processing new contradictory information, or accepting humiliation in front of the audience. The gesture suggests surrender. It indicates yielding to inner thoughts or views from the audience that one may have initially opposed. At one point, the class or your friends cornered a speaker facing the speaker to pause and take a minute to admit that he or she may have overlooked some facts about the issue. Probably, the speaker used this gesture to indicate defeat.

On the other hand, to indicate rejection or strong disagreement, both hands with palms wide are waved in an alternating manner to create letter X. In class, you probably drew the letter X using both hands to indicate that you disagree or reject what is being proposed. For instance, as a kid or as a student, you probably drew letter X to signal rejection that you will not follow instructions when the teacher sarcastically indicated that you should not follow his instructions. The sign also indicates retreat to your inner world to avoid listening or watching what the speaker wants.

For emphasis, when hands are open with palms down, then one is communicating that he or she is certain about what they are speaking. If your palms are facing each other with the fingers together, then you are communicating that you possess the expertise about what you are talking about. Then, there is the approximation gesture is performed by holding the hand horizontally with palm down and with fingers forward and then tilting the hand to the right and the left. The approximation gesture indicates that a statement is to be taken a close estimate of the truth.

Equally important, the gesture with a gentle rocking from left to right is taken to mean that it is not so good or not so bad. The same gesture is used to indicate that an event is equally likely to end in one of the two ways suggesting that it can go either way. The gesture can be used to signal the other person when a match is going, and the friends are watching in the house, and they do not want to wake up the child through loud talking.

Similarly, there is the beckoning sign, which has the index finger sticking out of the clenched fist and palm facing the gesturer. Then the speaker's finger moves repeatedly towards the gesturer as to invite something nearer. The beckoning sign has the general meaning of commanding someone to where you are standing. The beckoning sign is often performed with the four fingers using the entire hand depending on how far the recipient of the sign is. Depending on the circumstance, when performed with the index finger, it can have a sexual connotation.

If one feels that the speaker is not making sense, he or she is likely to keep his or her fingers straight and together while holding them upwards with the thumb pointing downwards. Then the fingers and thumb snap together to indicate a talking mouth. The gesture is used to indicate contempt for a person talking for an excessive period about a topic that the gesturer feel is trivial. In

Asian cultures, the gesture is used as a reaction to a dry joke. The gesture may also indicate that one is blabbering.

Additionally, there is the check gesture that is understood by waiters around the world to signal that a dinner patron wishes to pay the bill and get out. The gesture is manifested by touching the index finger and thumb together and denoting a wavy line in the air akin to signing one's name. Drawing a checkmark in the air using the fingers communicates that the individual wants to pay the bill. Equally important is a clenched fist that is used across cultures to communicate defiance among several groups. The clenched fist is considered hostile and without any notionally offensive connotations. The clenched fist is associated with Communists and other nationalist revolutionary movements. Most of the pro-democracy movements in dictatorial regimes will use the clenched fist to show defiance and inspire others.

Concerning the finger snap gesture, it is used to express that one is cornered. The gesturer usually holds one hand out in the direction of the adversary and snaps his thumb and middle finger accompanied by a high-nosed facial expression and then by crossing the arms. In the United Kingdom, snapping your fingers are used to indicate remembering or failing to remember. Children may snap their fingers to indicate that they are eager to answer.

Regarding the hanging gesture that is manifested by holding a clenched fist at the side of the head and tilting the head away from one's fist and making a choking sound, it is used to affirm that I would rather be doing it. The hanging gesture may also be accompanied by hanging the tongue loosely out of one's mouth and rolling the eyes back into the head. The hanging gesture is used to signify what I would rather be doing, and it can also be used to indicate suicide. The hanging gesture is increasingly being replaced by actual mimicking of a gun being shot at one's temple with the same meaning.

For emphasis, there is the horn gesture whose meaning varies depending on the context. The horn gesture commonly denotes the horned god by neopagans. It is thought to ward off or to bestow the evil eye. In some places, the horn signs indicate a sexual insult or charging a man with being a victim of cuckoldry. It is also used as a salute by fans of heavy metal music, usually with a repeated forward bend of the wrist. When done in the context of music, it is known as the devil horns.

From their critical role in communication, gestures help animate a conversation and add to the memorability of a conversion experience. You probably remember your teacher, coach, and preacher's message largely because it was accompanied by well-articulated gestures. Children and lovers may find gestures, fun, and validation of verbal communication. In this manner, gestures are essential for healthy parenting and an improved relationship between lovers.

Chapter 6: Eye Signals and Facial Expression

As suggested, facial expressions should be interpreted among the entire set of body language, but in this chapter, we will explore facial expressions solely. Wrinkles convey the intensity of emotions and the degree of originality of the emotion. In most cases, wrinkles convey hardship and suffering as well as extreme anger. Wrinkles indicate that one is always smiling, senile, or nasty.

Firstly, facial expressions can create an emotional experience. Smiling tends to induce more pleasant moods while frowning induces negative moods. In this manner, facial expressions may cause emotion by creating physiological changes in the body. Through the self-perception process, people assume that they must be sad or happy because they are smiling or frowning, and these cause emotions. Emotions are triggered by other factors beyond facial expressions. For instance, emotions are largely a function of the human system of beliefs and stored information. In other terms, you feel upset when you score less than average marks because the current system equates that to not being smart enough and the stored information reminds you that you risk repeating the test or not securing a plum employment position.

These entire terms make you feel hopeless, upset, and stressed. There is a possibility that if the belief system did not deem less than average as a failure and the stored information shows a positive outlook for a score that you will feel happy or excited by the score.

Secondly, twitching your mouth randomly, way suggests either that one is deliberately not listening or degrading the importance of the message. The facial gesture is realized by closing the lips and randomly twitching the mouth to either the right or left akin to swirling the mouth with mouthwash. The facial expression is also to indicate outright disdain to the speaker or the message. The facial expression is considered a rude way of expressing disgust with the speaker or the message and should be avoided at all costs.

Thirdly, if one shuts their lips tightly, then it indicates the individual is feeling angry but does not wish to show the anger. Shutting the lips tightly may also suggest that the person is feeling unease but struggling to concentrate at all costs. The source of the discomfort could be the immediate neighbors or the message of the speaker. Through this gesture, the individual is indicating that he or she simply wants the speaker to conclude the speech because not all people are enjoying the message.

If one is angry or strongly disapproves of what the speaker is saying, then the person will grin. A grin suggests that the person is feeling disgusted by what is being said. In movies or during live interviews, you probably so the interviewee grin when an issue or a person that the person feels is disgusting is mentioned. Showing a grin indicates that one harbors a strong dislike for the message of the speaker. An individual that is feeling uncomfortable due to sitting on a hard chair, a poorly ventilated room, or sitting next to a hostile neighbor may also show a grin which is not necessarily related to the message.

Furthermore, if one is happy, then one is likely to have a less tense face and a smile. Positive news and positive emotions are manifested as a smile or a less tense facial look. On the other hand, if one is processing negative emotions, then the face of the person is likely to be tensed up due to exerting pressure on the body muscles. A genuine smile like when one is happy is wide by average curve and is temporary. A prolonged smile that is very wide suggests that the individual is smirking at the message of the speaker. A prolonged smile may also suggest the individual is faking the emotion.

Similarly, a frozen face may indicate intense fear. For instance, you have seen terrified faces when attending a health awareness forum on sexually transmitted diseases or some medical condition that terrified the audience. In this setting, the face of the audience will appear as if it has been paused. The eyes and the mouth may remain stationary as the speaker presents the scary aspects of the medical condition. It appears negative emotions may slow down the normal conscious and unconscious movement of the muscles of the face.

As such, human beings can recognize facial expressions of at least six emotions with significant accuracy, and these include fear, happiness, sadness, surprise, and disgust. However, the universality and accuracy of facial expressions hold where it is a still photograph of an expression. The accuracy of such judgments rises when people are allowed to make a judgment of the facial expression in action. Due to the universality of facial expressions of emotions, it can be concluded that they are innate rather than learned behaviors. It has been observed that individuals with congenital blindness produce similar facial expressions to people with sight.

In addition to the cultural similarities, differences in facial expression of emotion happen across cultures. One, people are likely to correctly interpret the facial expression of people from their culture compared to those of other cultures. Nevertheless, people are still accurate when judging members of other cultural groups. The appropriateness of facial expressions varies among subcultures of the same cultural group. Compared to the Japanese, Americans readily manifest anger, and this shows that individuals express emotion differentially across cultures.

For instance, if you are a teacher or trainer, then you get facial expressions from your students frequently. Assuming that you are a teacher, and then you have noticed facial expressions indicating shock, uneasiness, and disapproval when you announce tests or indicate that the scores are out. Form some facial expressions; you will concur that the students feel uncomfortable, uncertain, and worried. The students will show lines of wrinkles, look down, eyes wide open and mouths agape when sudden and uncomfortable news is announced. Even though the students may indicate that they are prepared for the test, their facial expressions suggest otherwise.

Akin to all forms of communication, effective reading of facial expressions will happen where the target person is unaware that you are reading even though they understand that their facial expressions are integral to the overall communication. In other terms, when one becomes aware that he or she is being studied than the individual will act expectedly or simply freeze expected reaction. As part of human behavior, we tend to act expectedly once we realize we are being studied.

The underlying emotion affects the facial expression that one shows. As indicated previously, the body language overrides verbal communication that helps reveal the true status of an individual. One possible argument of the body language triumphing over verbal communication could be because the body prioritizes its physiological needs over other needs. The physiological needs are critical to the survivability of an individual. Over the centuries, the human body could have been programmed to increase survivability rate by prioritizing physiological needs. Body language largely indicates the physiological state of an individual who is meant to help the individual and others respect the true physiological status of the person.

Think of what could happen where one is sickly, and it is worsening, but the person manages to manifest a convincing body language of happiness and enthusiasm. The outcome would be prioritizing the emotional needs of the individual over the physiological needs. Apart from laboratory tests and physical examination, it would be difficult for other people to realize that something is amiss and ask the individual to take rest. Without illness, when one feels anxious about the audience, then he or she manifests disharmony of the physiological status, and there is a necessity to make the person and the audience aware that the individual is suffering and that they should be understanding of the individual.

Chapter 7: Eye Contact

The purpose of reading eye contact is that it can help one establish the true status of the target person, even where verbal communication seeks to hide it. As indicated, body language should be processed as a group of nonverbal communication instead of focusing only on one aspect of it, such as eye contact. However, since the reader needs to understand each element of body language comprehensively, then it is necessary that we tackle each segment independently and deeply.

Notably, the pupil dilates when one is interested in the person that he or she is talking to or the object we are looking at. During the conversation, the pupils will contract when one is transiting from one issue to another. We have no control over the working of pupils. When one is speaking about a less interesting topic, the pupils will contract, and this will manifest even if the verbal communication wanted to mask it.

Establishing effective eye contact is useful when having a conversation with people. Eye contact suggests that one looks but does not stare. Persistent eye contact will make the target person feel intimidated or judged. In Western cultures, regular eye contact is desired, but it should not be overly persistent. If one offers constant eye contact, then it is seen as an attempt to intimidate or judge, which makes the recipient of the eye contact uncomfortable. Various studies suggest that most children fall victim to attacks by pet dogs if their eye contact is constantly regular, which causes them to feel threatened and defensive. Initiating an overly persistent eye contact is a sign of an individual's over-awareness of the messages they are emitting. Lying can be detected by the individual avoiding eye contact.

For instance, evasive eye contact indicates discomfort. We avoid looking at a person if we feel ashamed to be communicating at them. When we feel dishonest about trying to deceive people, we avoid looking at them. While it is okay to blink or drop eye contact temporarily, people that consistently shun making eye contact are likely to be feeling uneasy with the message or the person they are communicating with. For emphasis, staring at someone will make him or her drop eye contact due to feeling intimidated. Evasive eye contact happens where one deliberately avoids making eye contact.

Equally important is that people cry due to feeling uncontrollable pain or in an attempt to attract sympathy from others. For this reason, crying is considered as an intense emotion associated with grief or sadness though it can also denote extreme happiness known as tears of joy. When an individual forces tears to deceive others, then it is known as crocodile tears, which imply faking tears to deceive others. If one cries, then the individual is likely experiencing intense negative emotion.

In some instances, blinking is instinctive, and our emotions and feelings directed towards the person we are speaking to can make us to subconsciously alter our rate of blinking. If the average rate of blinking is six to 10 times per minute, then it is a strong indicator that an individual is drawn to the person they are speaking to, and it is indicative of flirting. In normal contexts, men and women blink at the same rate as each other.

Notably, the direction of the eyes tells us about how an individual is feeling. When someone is thinking, they tend to look to their left when they are recalling or reminiscing. An individual that is thinking tends to look to their right when eliciting creative thoughts and it can be interpreted as an indicative sign of someone trying to be deceitful in some situations such as creating a version of events. For left-handed people, the eye directions will be reversed.

Furthermore, when one is interested in what you are speaking, he or she will make eye contact often. Some studies found that when people are engaged in an interesting conversation, then their eyes remain focused on the face of their partner, about 80% of the time but not wholly on the eyes. Rather the eye contact on the eyes of the other person is for two to three minutes, then move down to the lips or nose then back up to the eyes. For a brief moment, the person initiating eye contact will look down then back up to the eyes. Looking up and to the right demonstrates dismissal and boredom. Dilation of the pupil may indicate that someone is interested or that the room is brighter.

As such, sustained eye contact may be a signal that you want to speak to the person or that you are interested in the person sexually. At one point, you may have noticed a hard stare from a man towards a particular woman. The stare is hard and long to the point that the woman notices and asks the man what is all that for. In this case, eye contact is not being used to intimidate but to single out the target person. You probably have seen a woman ask why that staff is staring at her then she proceeds to mind her business, but on looking at the direction of the man, the stare is still there. In this manner, eye contact is used to single out an individual and make them aware that one is having sexual feelings towards the person.

Nevertheless, people are aware of the influence of body language and will seek to portray the expected body language. For instance, an individual that is lying is likely to make deliberate eye contact frequently to sound believable. At one point, you knew you were lying but went ahead to make eye contact. You probably have watched movies where one of the spouses is lying but makes believable eye contact with others. The reason for this faked body language is that the person is aware of the link between making eye contact and speaking the truth.

Akin to verbal language, body language and in particular, eye contact can be contextual. For instance, an individual may wink to suggest that he or she agrees with the quality of the product being presented or that he or she agrees with the plan. Eye contact in these settings can be used as a coded language for a group of people. At one point, one of your classmates may have used a wink to indicate that the teacher is coming or indicating that the secret you have been guarding is now out.

Chapter 8: Nonverbal of Legs and Feet

Like the other limbs, legs, and feet are used to communicate as a form of body language. If one is seated and continuously taps one of the legs on the floor, then the individual is not focusing on the conversation. The tapping of feet on the floor is a way for an individual to channel his or her energy elsewhere, and this denies the person the focus to process the body language of the speaker as well as the emotions. Different reasons can make one tap their feet on the floor, and one of them is an attempt to escape from a hurtful message. For instance, if the speaker is touching on a sensitive issue and is insensitive, then the part of the audience may continuously tap on the floor as a means of avoiding processing the message. Individuals with low concentration levels may inadvertently tap on the floor because they want a distraction.

Additionally, if one is speaking and stands on one leg, then the individual is feeling tense. When speaking before a large audience, one is likely to feel scared for a while before regaining confidence. In most cases, one will stand on one leg with the other leg folded at the knee-level and checked on the straight one akin to a flamingo standing. The posture serves a coping mechanism for the individual as he or she tries to process the stage fright without appearing visibly scared. In most cases, the individual will relax the folded leg and stand on both before reverting to this position. For most people, this body language usually is brief as the person quickly gains confidence and assumes normal body posture.

Similarly, standing with crossed legs at the ankle-level indicates that one is feeling unease with the speaker or the message. You probably have noticed that some people cross their legs in an alternating manner when speaking. If one crosses the legs when speaking, then probably the individual is feeling unease with the message or the audience. The crossing of the legs suggests that one is feeling defensive and wants to shield the personal space even further. In a manner, the individual is trying to safely process unwanted message or unwanted emotions by crossing the legs. For some reason, most shy people may cross their legs when speaking, which is an indication of being highly protective of their personal space.

If one sits on the chair and stretches both legs forward, then the person is feeling relaxed and casual. At home and especially when from work, you are likely to sit with all of your legs stretched straight forward as a way of relaxing. For this reason, this posture should be avoided in all formal settings such as workplaces. Chances are, if you were to visit someone with a managerial position and the person rocks the chair with both feet full stretched forward, then you will conclude that he or she is treating you casually. In most cases, this posture is realized when one is sitting on a raised or reclining chair.

Additionally, if one scratches the other leg using one of the legs, then the person is trying to get interested in the conversation. In most contexts, one will scratch one leg against the other as a way of eliminating a distraction such as an itch or recalling some information that will interfere with listening. For emphasis, if one scratches the other leg-using one of the legs, it does not necessarily mean that the individual is not listening. It is most likely a way of avoiding attending to the distraction, such as an itch or struggling with safely processing negative emotions such as anger. Most public speakers are likely to scratch one of their legs using the other when asked a disturbing question because this body language can be used as a coping mechanism for processing negative feedback.

Relatedly, sitting with both legs wide open, indicates disinterest in the conversation. Recall how you sit watching boring news or TV program. Most likely, you relax your legs far wide apart and in a slumped position when watching or listening to a dull interview or movie. For this reason, this posture should be avoided as it communicates tiredness and disinterest in the message as well as the speaker. Perhaps you noticed that during your high school days, some of your colleagues would exhibit this posture.

Expectedly, men are likely to exhibit this posture due to cultural considerations that dissuade women from sitting in this posture.

If one sits upright with both knees nearly the same level and close enough, then the individual is highly alert and actively participating in the conversation. A person in this posture is fully occupying their personal space and feeling comfortable. Keeping the knees at the same level and close is a mechanism to enhance focus at the speaker or the message. During church sessions or a meeting of state officials, most members seated in a hall are likely to manifest this posture, and it is because they are deliberately trying to listen. Again, using the example of a school, chances are that during an address by the school principal, the students were neatly seated with their knees close to each other and the same level because they purposely wanted to remain alert.

Correspondingly, stretching both legs straight while seated upright indicates the casualness of the person regarding the message or the speaker. As earlier on mentioned, if one sits with all the legs straightened and stretched, then the individual wants to induce relaxation and feel casual. At the end of a class, there are chances that you or one of your classmates stretched their legs while in a seated position to indicate that they are inducing relaxation and feeling casual than they were. While this posture appears like just any other posture, it can be important for an individual that is feeling restless. Using this posture, a restless individual can be helped to induce the much-needed relaxation of the body and mind.

Additionally, standing at the same spot for more than five minutes when speaking may indicate that one is not natural with the speaking. Indeed, standing at the same spot for more than five minutes indicates that one is operating under a fixed schedule and a defined set of expectations such as giving a speech or dictating notes to a class. For instance, a preacher is operating under fewer time constraints and expectations and will speak at random but predictable physical spots compared to a minister reporting on a disease outbreak. For this reason, the unrestricted movement of feet through walking indicates freedom of thought, unlike speaking at the same physical spot.

If one taps their feet on an object, then the person is not actively participating in the conversation. One of the best indicators that one is not listening to an interview is when the individual taps on the floor, desk, or wall. The tapping of feet on an object is an attempt to ease the mind of processing what is being said because it is demanding or disturbing. For instance, at one point, you noticed that one of your classmates taps on the wall or floor when talking about an essay or project because the colleague does not feel as good as others do. This behavior is meant to help the individual process negative feedback safely because continued active listening will make the individual get overwhelmed by emotions.

Furthermore, if one knocks against their knees, then the individual is feeling embarrassed or disinterested in the conversation. Knocking the kneecaps or shaking the legs with knees almost touching indicates uneasiness, inadequacy, and embarrassment. In most instances, this posture is attained when one is seated. Knocking of knees or almost knocking the knees against each other is also a way of expressing extreme anger where one tries to process the negative emotion safely. Either you or your colleagues probably waved their knees to almost touching because you were feeling frightened, intimidated, or upset and wanted to process the emotion safely. Since this posture is mostly done when one is seated, most speakers commonly miss it, but a keen observation of the shoulders may indicate the individual is waving the knees against each other.

Relatedly, if one places one or both of their palms in between their two thighs clamped together, then the individual is feeling embarrassed. Children commonly exhibit this posture, and it is meant to indicate that he or she is feeling cornered or embarrassed. Adults also manifest this posture of clamping one or both palms of the hands between their thighs when feeling embarrassed or scared. Fortunately, this posture can be observed with ease, and the message read accordingly. In some extreme circumstances, this posture communicates that one is feeling erotic or sexual, especially when done by one of the lovers towards the other.

If one walks excitedly across the stage when speaking, then the individual is likely to be excited. As earlier on suggested, moving animatedly across the stage or physical area where the communication is happening may suggest that one is happy and at ease with the message and the audience. Think of how preachers utilize the stage by moving animatedly across the stage. Most storytellers also utilize random and firm movements across the stage to indicate that they are feeling confident and involved in the message and the audience. Most artistes tend to move randomly and excitedly across the stage to show eagerness, happiness, and active participation of what they are delivering to the audience.

On the other hand, if one walks slowly across the stage when speaking, then the person is focusing more on the message content over everything else. When the speaker wants to draw attention to the message over everything else, then he or she will move slowly across the stage to ensure that the audience recalls more the words rather than the body language. For this reason, slowing down during speaking may help the audience lend more criticality to the message rather than the speaker antics. It is the reason why most interviews are conducted while one is seated.

Even when given an entire stage, a politician is likely to move least because he or she wants the audience to remember the content of the message as opposed to other aspects of communication. In communication, any unwanted message is known as noise and if a speaker wants the audience to remember the presentation, and then, if the audience remembers the dressing or dancing of the speaker, then this can amount to noise. Noise in communication is thus contextual contrary to the broad assumption that noise in communication is always universal.

There is also the closed posture where one crosses the arms across the chest or crosses the legs away from someone or sits in a hunched forward position as well as showing the backs of the hands and clenching the fists are indicative of a closed posture. The closed posture gives the impression that one is bored, hostile, or detached. In this posture, one is acting cautious and appears ready to defend himself or herself against any accusation or threat. While we insist that certain postures should not be encouraged, it is important to realize that they should be expressed as they help communicate the true status of the individual.

For the confident posture, it helps communicate that one is not feeling anxious, nervous, or stressed. The confident posture is attained by pulling oneself to full height, holding the head high, and keeping the gaze at eye level. Then pull your shoulders back and keep the arms as well as the legs to relax by the sides. The posture is likely to be used by speakers in a formal context such as when making a presentation, during cross-examination, and project presentation. In this posture, one should stand straight and deliver the message.

Then there is the crossing of the legs from the thigh through the knee while seated on a chair, especially on a reclining chair. In this posture, one is communicating that he or she is feeling relaxed and less formal. In most cases, this posture is exhibited when one is at home watching a movie or in the office alone past working hours. If this posture is replicated in a formal context, then it suggests boredom or lack of concentration. If a speaker reads this body language, then he or she should realize that one of the members of the audience is feeling less interested in the message and should activate self-feedback. Self-feedback includes things such as am I speaking fast. Should I give them a break? Should I vary the tone?

For the posture where one crosses the legs from the ankle to the soles of the feet while seated, it communicates that one is trying to focus on an informal context such as at home. For instance, if a wife or a child asks the father about something that he has to think through, then the individual is likely to exhibit this posture. If this posture is replicated in a formal context, then it suggests boredom or lack of concentration. Akin to all aspects of communication, it is imperative that the audience generates feedback for the speaker to take into account and adjust accordingly. While some forms of body language indicate casualness, they are not entirely deliberate, and they are merely stating the true status of the affected individual. What is important is for the speaker to adjust the communication by simplifying it, introducing breaks, varying tone, and being sensitive about how the audience feels.

Chapter 9: Posture and Body Orientation

Even though posture is affected by our health status and sometimes the furniture, in standard environments, our posture is largely mediated by our emotional states, and for this reason, body posture can help communicate more about an individual character, personality, and emotion. One of the advantages of body language is that it is hardly influenced by the conscious mind, and this makes body language a highly reliable source of profiling a person. We require reading body language so that we can ascertain the truth-value of the claims of an individual. If a person says that they are feeling sorry for what they did before you can accept their apologies, you will need to ascertain the honesty of that claim, and this where reading body language comes in. As indicated, some professions such as medical, law enforcement, and conflict resolution require near accurate reading of an individual's body language.

As suggested, posture and body, orientation should be read in the context of the entire body language to develop the full meaning being communicated. Starting with an open posture, it is used to denote friendliness and positivity. In this open position, the feet are spread wide, and the palms of the hands are facing outward. Individuals with open posture are deemed more persuasive compared to those with other postures. To realize an open posture, one should stand up or sit straight with the head raised and keep the abdomen and chest exposed. When the open posture is combined with a relaxed facial expression and good eye contact, it makes one look approachable and composed. Maintain the body facing forward toward the other person during a conversation.

Regarding the closed posture, one crosses the arms across the chest, or crosses the legs away from someone or sits in a hunched forward position as well as showing the backs of the hands and clenching the fists are indicative of a closed posture. The closed posture gives the impression that one is bored, hostile, or detached. In this posture, an individual is acting cautious and appears ready to defend himself or herself against any accusation or threat. If this posture is exhibited in an audience, then the individual is feeling insecure by the message, the speaker, or due to the actions of another member in the audience.

Additionally, there is a confident posture that helps communicate that one is not feeling anxious, nervous, or stressed. The confident posture is attained by pulling oneself to full height, holding the head high, and keeping the gaze at eye level. Then pull your shoulders back and keep the arms as well as legs to relax by the sides. The posture is likely to be used by speakers in a formal context such as when making a presentation, during cross-examination and project presentation.

One should also take note of the postural echoing and is used as a flirting technique by attracting someone in the guardian. It is attained by observing and mimicking the style of the person and the pace of movement. When the individual leans against the wall, replicate the same. By adjusting your postures against the others to attain a match, you are communicating that you are trying to flirt with the individual. The postural echoing can also be used as a prank game to someone you are familiar with and often engage in casual talk.

Sustaining a straight posture communicates confidence and formality. Part of the confidence of, this posture is that it maximizes blood flow and exerts less pressure on the muscle and joints that enhances the composure of an individual. The straight posture helps evoke desirable mood and emotion that makes an individual feel energized and alert. A straight posture is highly preferred informal conversations such as during meetings, presentations, or when giving a speech.

Relatedly being in a slumped position and hunched back is a poor posture and makes one be seen as lazy, sad, or poor. A slumped position implies a strain to the body that makes the individual feel less alert and casual about the ongoing conversation. On the other hand, leaning forward and maintaining eye contact suggests that one is listening keenly. During a speech, if the audience leans forward in an upright position, then it indicates that they are eager and receptive to the message.

In this manner, if one slants one of the shoulders when participating in a conversation, then it suggests that the individual is tired or unwell. Leaning on one side acutely while standing or sitting indicates that you are feeling exhausted or fed up with the conversation and are eagerly waiting for the end or a break. Think of how you or others reacted when a class dragged on to almost break time. There is a high likelihood that the audience slanted one of their shoulders to the left or right direction. In this state, the mind of the individual deviates to things that one will do next. In the case of a tea break, the mind of the students will deviate to what one will do during or after the tea break.

As earlier on suggested, if one stands on one foot, then it indicates that one is feeling unease or tired. When one stands on one foot, then it suggests that the person is trying to cope with uncomforting. The source of uneasiness could be emotional or physiological. For instance, you probably juggled your body from one foot to help ease the need to go for a short call or pass wind. In most cases, one finds himself or herself standing on one foot when an uncomfortable issue is mentioned. It is a way to disrupt the sustained concentration that may enhance the disturbing feeling.

Furthermore, if one holds their arms akimbo while standing, then the individual is showing a negative attitude or disapproval of the message. The posture is created by holding the waist with both hands while standing up straight and facing the target person. The hands should simultaneously grip on the flanks, the part near the kidneys. In most cases, the arms-akimbo posture is accompanied by disapproval or sarcastic face to denote attitude, disdain, or disapproval.

Should one cup their head or face with their hands and rests the head on the thighs, then the individual is feeling ashamed or exhausted. When the speaker mentions something that makes you feel embarrassed, then one is likely to cup their face or head and rest the face on the thighs. It is a literal way of hiding from shame. Children are likely to manifest this posture though while standing. When standing this posture may make one look like he or she is praying.

If one stretches of their both shoulders, arms, and rests them on chairs on either side, then the individual is feeling tired and casual. The posture is akin to a static flap of wings where one stretches their shoulder and arms like wings and rests them on chairs on either side. It is one of the postures that loudly communicates that you are bored, feeling casual, and that you are not about the consequences of your action. The posture is also invasive of the privacy and space of other individuals and may disrupt their concentration.

Relatedly, if one bends when touching both of their knees, then the individual is feeling exhausted and less formal with the audience. The posture may also indicate extreme exhaustion and need to rest. For instance, most soccer players bend without kneeling while holding both of their knees, indicating exhaustion. Since in this posture, one is facing down, the posture may be highly inappropriate in formal contexts and may make one appear queer.

If one leans their head and supports it with an open palm on the cheeks, then it indicates that one is thinking deep and probably feeling sad, sorrowful, or depressed. The posture is also used when one is watching something with a high probability of negative outcomes such as a movie or a game. The posture helps one focus deep on the issue akin to meditating.

Similarly, crossing your arms to touch shoulders or touch the biceps indicates that one is deliberately trying to focus on the issue being discussed. Through this posture, an individual tries to avoid distractions and think deeper on what is being presented. If you watch European soccer, you will realize that coaches use this posture when trying to study the match, especially where their team is down. However, this posture should not be used in formal contexts as it suggests rudeness. The posture should be used among peers only.

Lastly, there is the crossing of the legs from the thigh through the knee while seated on a chair, especially on a reclining chair. In this posture, one is communicating that he or she is feeling relaxed and less formal. In most cases, this posture is exhibited when one is at home watching a movie or in the office alone past working hours. If this posture is replicated in a formal context, then it suggests boredom or lack of concentration.

Finally, for the posture where one crosses the legs from the ankle to the soles of the feet while seated, it communicates that one is trying to focus on an informal context such as at home. For instance, if a wife or a child asks the father about something that he has to think through, then the individual is likely to exhibit this posture. If this posture is replicated in a formal context, then it suggests boredom or lack of concentration.

Activity

a. Collins is attending a meeting on security, and the role that employees play in helping maintains the organization secure. During the first ten minutes of this meeting, Collins is seated upright with the head slightly leaning forward. Comment on what this implies.

b. Thirty minutes later, Collins slumps or slants in the chair while raising his head up and backward. Comment on what this means.

c. Forty-five minutes later, Collins has slanted his left shoulder and is supporting his head with the left hand while watching the speaker. Comment on what this implies.

d. After a twenty-minute break, Collins sits upright with his arms crossed and palms touching the biceps. Comment on what this means.

e. After fifteen minutes, Collins stretches both of his arms across the top edges of the adjacent chairs while listening. Comment on this posture.

f. After twenty minutes, Collins crosses his legs from the thighs through the knees while listening. Comment on what this implies.

Chapter 10: The Voice

As with any form of body language, the voice should be analyzed against the entire set of body language to make a reasonable conclusion. Individuals that work in customer care or call centers understand the value of voice. It is what the customer meets and forms an opinion of the service and the company. Concerning voice, what counts most is what one hears. As a fan of music, you probably have comprehensive exposure to the role of voice in communication.

For pitch, a high pitch communicates nervousness, and one should pitch inflection to convey energy and sound persuasive. Pitch concerns how loud a voice is when one is speaking. At one point, you might have felt unease having to shout on the phone due to the mouthpiece or network issues because it makes you sound nervous, and that is not how you want to be perceived. Listening to an individual that appears to be shouting suggests that the individual is irritated, tired, or unwell. A speaker that sounds like he or she is shouting comes across like someone that is offended or irked by an issue or the audience.

Then there is the speed of speaking. Speaking fast indicates panic and selfishness. Slowing down the speed of speaking allows the receiver to effectively process what is being spoken. Speaking fast also indicates that one is in a hurry and wants to move on to the next. If you have ever called a call center and got an agent that spoke faster than usual, then you felt the agent was not listening or that the agent was not valuing your concern, as it should be.

Furthermore, pitch concerns the lowness or highness of the voice and is highly critical in the English language. Through pitch, we express emotions and attitudes by changing intonation. From the pitch of the voice, we can determine if one is feeling stressed. Variation of pitch helps make the conversation sound natural, as emotions are not static. From the analysis of pitch variation, one can determine if one is a native or non-native speaker of a language. A monotone voice is not expressive and not interesting to hear.

Regarding tone, it is critical because it can mislead or enhance the outcome of the conversation. If one has an angry tone, then it does not matter the neutrality of the message, as the receiver will assume that the speaker is upset. A professional and understanding tone is preferred. A critical tone makes the person sound as if he or she is judging the audience. A professional tone makes one appear diplomatic and knowledgeable in what he or she is presenting to the audience. Organizations invest significantly to attain a professional tone.

Relatedly, the tone also includes verbal communication, especially the choice of words. The kind of words that one employs affects the intended tone despite the best intention of the individual. However, in this context, we are focusing on nonverbal communication. At one point, you tried making a joke, but no one laughed, or you had to offer apologies because the audience processed differently. Part of this mishap was due to the way you voiced the joke making it appear like shouting, taunting, or disdain. Even the best comedians lose the audience in some instances due to the way they expressed their jokes.

Equally important, having a consistent content tone of voice enables the audience to view you as consistent. At school or campus, you profiled and expected your teachers or dons to speak in a speaking manner. Part of this profiling is attributed to the consistency of their voice's tone. Take time and search the late and former United Nations secretary-general Koffi Annan to appreciate the pitch and voice of a speaker. There is a justification for insisting on tone during communication. Overall, tone is likely to be associated with your personality and profession, and it is the reason organizations invest time and resources to evoke the right tone that connects them with their clients.

Exhibiting a unique tone can help charm and convince your customers. It is not just about having a pleasant tone but also about creating an identity. If one exhibits a consistent and particular tone, then the public is likely to form an image of your values and personality, and this can make it easier to connect with customers. For instance, your favorite social media influencer has a particular tone that you associate the individual with and have learned to find it a unique way to approach issues.

Furthermore, tone replaces face-to-face communication, and this makes tone highly critical to avoid misconceptions and backlash. As earlier on indicated, as most services go online, most customers occasionally need assistance with applications and access to online services, and this requires a responsive call center. When customers contact the call center, the only thing they interact with is the tone of the speaker. The tone of the call agent can worsen the emotions of the client or thaw their emotions and make it easier to solve the issue facing the customer.

For emphasis, the role of tone in communication is to make one appear human. People prefer to deal with humans, and tone helps create a relatable personality that the customer can bond with. The rising and falling of tone help make the communication natural, and the recipient of the message views the communication as not rehearsed. Having the same tone will make one sound monotonous as well as appear rehearsed. If you sound monotonic, then it is suggesting that you cannot elicit the emotional aspects of the communication, and this makes you appear less human to the audience. Most probably, one of your favorite actors effectively uses tone to convey different emotions.

At the national level, your favorite political figure varies the tone making the message appear live and relatable.

As such, the tone helps establish authority. You most probably know someone that sounds commanding, authoritative, and uncertain courtesy of tone of the person. The preferred tone is a consistent and natural tone that communicates confidence in what one is speaking about, and this makes the person appear in charge. Try watching National Geographic wildlife documentaries or TED talks, and you will realize that the narrators and speakers have a consistent and natural varying tone to suggest confidence in what they are talking about. Most documentaries provide a learning opportunity for the role of tone in communication.

It is through a tone that one sustains the focus of the communication. Expectedly, tone helps keep the audience positioned in what the speaker intended. For instance, a professional tone helps maintain communication as formal. Again, using the call center example, most call agents politely try to keep the conversation formal even when the caller tries deviating the communication. The tone of the conversation makes the audience appreciate the formality level of the conversation. During interviews, the formality of the tone helps make the content delivered by the interviewee sound believable.

Lastly, tone helps one develop an identity. As indicated, you regard certain people as commanding, comical, or reserved based on their tone, among other factors. Again, try recalling which celebrity or politician sounds convincing, professional, commanding, or angry. The tone is connected to the way people feel the emotion you are trying to communicate. In some cases, the tone contradicts the intended emotion distorting the emotion.

Activity

Search YouTube for industrial strikes in the United Kingdom and the United States and listen to the pitch and tone of the leaders. Now search for industrial strikes in any African or Asian countries that speak English and listen to the pitch and tone of the leaders. Then comment on the tone variation or lack of tone variation in the selected leaders of the industrial leaders. Go further and comment on the pitch of the selected leaders of the industrial strikes. Then, listen to any speech by Barack Obama and a speech by Teresa May. Which of the two sounds convincing and natural to listen to?

Chapter 11: Distance in Communication

Focusing on the United States, there are four types of distances that people use to communicate on a face-to-face basis. These distances are **intimate, personal distance, social distance**, and **public distance**. Starting with intimate distance, it is used for highly confidential exchanges as zero to two feet of space between two individuals marks this zone. An example of intimate distance includes two people hugging, standing side-by-side, or holding hands. Individuals intimate distance share a unique level of comfort with one another. If one is not comfortable with someone approaching them in the intimate zone, he/she will experience a significant deal of social discomfort.

Firstly, personal distance is used for talking with family as well as close acquaintances. Even though it grants an individual a little more space compared to the intimate distance, it is still proximity to that of intimacy and may involve touching. The personal distance can range from two to four feet. Akin to intimate distance, if a stranger walks into the personal zone, the one is likely to feel uneasy being in such proximity with the stranger.

Secondly, there is the social distance that used in business exchanges or when meeting new people and interacting with groups of people. Compared to the other distances, social distance has a larger range in the range that it can incorporate. Its range is four to twelve feet, and it depends on the context. It is used among students, acquaintances, or co-workers. As expected, most participants in the social distance do not show physical contact with one another. Generally, people are likely to be very specific concerning the degree of social distance that is preferred, as some require more physical distance compared to others. In most cases, the individual will adjust backward or forward to get the appropriate social distance necessary for social interactions.

Thirdly, we have public distance, which is twelve or more feet between individuals. An example of public distance is where two people sit on a bench in a public park. In most cases, the two people on a bench in a public park will sit at the farthest ends of each other to preserve the public space. Each of the earlier types of proximity will significantly influence an individual's perception of what is the appropriate type of distance in specific contexts. One of the factors that contribute to individual perceptions of how proxemics should be used is culture. Individuals from different cultures show different viewpoints on what the appropriate persona; space should be.

Fourthly, there is the concept of territoriality where individuals tend to feel like they own and should control their personal areas. We are inclined to defend our personal space. When someone invades this personal space, then the individual will react negatively as it is an invasion of territory without express permission. At one point, you asked a stranger to keep some distance from you because you felt uncomfortable with the person standing close to you. Sometimes standing next to a person may also denote that you are creepy and may be intending to harm the person.

If one is talking to someone, the person violates your personal space, and you allow it, then it signals that you are okay to intimate ideas. Intimate ideas in this context include highly personal issues that one can talk with another person. For instance, if you walk and sit close and in contact with a woman watching television and she approves your behavior, then it is indicative that she is likely to allow you have a personal talk that may be intimate in nature. Such discussion may include your health challenges or mental health and not necessarily sexual issues. For this reason, one should carefully weigh the need to invade the personal distance.

Regarding children, violating personal distance will make them freeze due to feeling uncomfortable. If a teacher sits next to a student or stands next to a student, then the student is likely to feel uneasy and nervous. However, they are instances where the invasion of personal space is allowed and seen as necessary. For instance, during interviews or when being examined by a doctor, invasion of private space by the person with advantage is allowed.

The panel during an interview may move or ask you to move closer, which may violate your personal space. A doctor may also stand closer to you, invading your personal space, but this is necessary due to the professional demand of their service.

As such, when one avoids personal distance, and the individual is expected to be within this space, then the individual may be feeling less confident or feeling ashamed. For instance, if a child has done something embarrassing, he or she is likely to sit or stand far from the parent during a conversation. For this reason, it appears that one should feel confident, assured, and appreciated to approach and remain in personal space when needed.

Additionally, staying in personal space during intense emotions may portray one as resilient, understanding, and bold. Think of two lovers or sibling quarreling, but each remains in the established personal space. The message that is being communicated is that the individual is confident that he or she can handle the intense emotions from the other person. For most people, they only allow their lover to stay in their personal distance when feeling upset because they trust that the person can handle the known behavior of the affected person. Since being in personal space places a person within physical striking range, most people will only allow trusted and familiar individuals into their personal space.

Equally important is that invasion of personal space is justified because it is part of professional demands. Think of a new teacher that is trying to help a student solve a mathematical equation. In this aspect, the teacher is a stranger because he or she is new to the school. By sitting or standing close to, the student, the teacher is invading the personal space, but the established norms in this context allow the student not to feel unease. For emphasis, this case is not unique as it aligns with stated expectations that people will welcome known or unfamiliar people in their personal space only if they trust them and, in this case, the student feels safe with any teacher. For this reason, the operationalization of distance in communication is mediated and moderated by established culture.

In most cases, one can start with public distance before allowing the interaction to happen in personal or social space. For instance, as a student during tournaments, you could have initiated nonverbal communication with the student from the other college before suddenly feeling connected to the individual and allowing him or her to move into personal space as a potential girlfriend or boyfriend. At first, the target person saw you as a stranger but allowed you to make nonverbal communication within the public space. When the person felt the need to connect more with you and have given you the benefit of the doubt, the person allowed you to move through public distance and social distance to enter their personal space.

For instance, a lot can be learned from studying distance and space in communication. Being allowed into the social and personal distances implies that the person trusts that you will not harm them emotionally and physically. For the intimate distance, being allowed into this distance implies that the person trusts you so much and is confident that you can never harm them and that you share a lot. For instance, a mother holding her baby close enough to her signals that the baby is feeling assured of security and protection. When two lovers move, closer until their faces are almost touching suggests trust and confidence that the other person feels safe and protected.

Relatedly, if arguing with your child or lover and the individual moves farther from you physically, then it suggests that the person no longer feels safe with you being within their personal distance. Issues that can cause someone to expand the distance between you and them include the risk of violence from you and emotional issues. If you occasionally act violently, then chances are, your lover or children will expand the personal distance to social distance because this is where they feel safe due to your personality and character. It then appears that your prior behavior will also affect the distance during communication.

Nevertheless, they are other issues that cause individuals to extend the distance of interaction, and these include having a medical condition or having hygiene issues. For instance, if you are sweaty, then chances are that the other person may prefer to extend the distance of communication between you and them. Having oral hygiene issues may also make the other person move far away from you because the smell turns them off. For this reason, interpreting the distance between communicators should also include hygiene and health-related issues that impact this distance.

For instance, some medical conditions can make people maintain some distance from you or be closer to you physically. For instance, some conditions may attract uneasiness, and this includes epilepsy. People with epilepsy get seizures, and this can make people feel unease being closer to them because they inadvertently fall. On the other hand, having hearing issues or sore throat may make people move closer to you physically to facilitate effective communication. However, these are exceptions when analyzing space and distance as forms of nonverbal communication, but they should be taken into account where necessary.

In some cases, it is welcome to invade personal distance merely by circumstances. For instance, when attending a match in a full packed stadium or sitting to watch a movie in a movie theater, one will have his personal invaded due to the sitting arrangements. In this context, one may feel uneasy with this arrangement, but he or she has little control of the situation.

While we value and seek to protect personal spaces, some situations make us allowing invasion of this space because it is beyond control.

Activity

a. Mark is talking to his girlfriend, and their noses are almost touching. Comment on what this means. Do you feel that the actions of Mark are appropriate? Why or Why not?

b. The following day, Mark is talking to his girlfriend while standing nine feet away. Comment on what this means.

c. An elderly person asks Mark to assist him in how to shop online using the smartphone. Richard is standing right next to this elderly person. Comment on what this means.

d. On Saturday, Mark argued with his sister. He was visibly angry, but they continued exchanging words while seated on the same sofa set. Comment on this distance and space in communication. Comment on the importance of trust and assurance for people who share this space.

e. Mark met his girlfriend while attending a football match. It all started when Mark threw a hard stare at her at the farthest end of the stand. When the girl reciprocated the stare, Mark moved closer to her after the game and they walked holding hands. This is an example of allowing someone to transit from public distance to personal distance. Using analysis of distance and space in communication only, why do you think the girl allowed Mark to shorten the distance and welcome him into the personal space?

f. Nicole works as a nurse at the local clinic. When one of the patients asked for a nurse, Nicole moved close enough to the patient and touched his hand to examine it. What is the justification for this distance in this communication?

g. Nicole and her husband quarreled last night, and today they sat eight feet from each other while pretending nothing happened. Using the concept of space and distance only, suggest two reasons for this behavior?

h. As a new mother, Nicole holds her baby closer, making her nose and that of the baby touch while making sounds to the baby. Justify why this distance and space in communication is allowed?

i. Last month while seated on a bench in a public park, a stranger walked and sat right next to Nicole even though the bench had only Nicole. Nicole decided to stand up and walk away. Why do you think Nicole walked away? Use only the concept of distance and space to explain.

Chapter 12: Mirroring Body Language

One of the critical roles of mirroring the body language of the target person is that it alerts them that you are taking deliberate interest in the person and want to strike a rapport with the person. Mirroring helps create a connection between the participating parties in a conversation. Akin to any other aspect of communication, one needs to learn the right way of mirroring body language to realize the maximum benefits of the concept.

First, start by building your connection through fronting. In fronting, you want to lend the other person, complete attention. Go ahead and square your body so that you are directly facing the target person and try to make them the focus of your universe. Then establish eye contact, which may first appear invasive. Eye contact is critical in communicating your level of interest in the target person by communicating that you are giving undivided attention. Eye contact is also thought to elicit warm feelings that enhance a close connection. You should go ahead and initiate the triple nod, which does two functions. When one does the triple nod, then the target person is likely to speak three or four times longer, making them feel that they are being listened or what they are communicating is important. Additionally, if one nods, then it communicates that you are in tandem with what the person is saying, and this creates a receptive environment for sustained communication. One should elicit questions that will invite nodding. For instance, start by asking if the weather is warm. Then, pretend, followed by not pretending. In this instance, you are fronting the target person and initiating the right eye contact and applying the triple nod will help strike a rhythm with the individual. In this instance, you are likely feeling a strong connection, but to realize its full benefit try using the power of imagination by pretending the target person is the most interesting individual you have ever met. Try to imagine it and act accordingly followed by ceasing the pretense. In all this, significant levels of mirroring are likely to happen naturally on its account, but the following techniques can help enhance the mirroring of body language to attain intended goals.

Relatedly, exploit the pace and volume as many times people think of mirroring body language as mimicking the physical actions. However, mirroring body language includes all aspects of nonverbal communication, such as pace and volume. For instance, mirroring the pace and volume of the target person's speech will help initiate a connection and rhythm between the two. If the target person is, a fast talker and loud then enhance your volume and animation and if they are soft and slow, then relax and match them at their level instead. Compared to physical actions, mimicry, pace, and volume matching are easier. Recall how you felt when one of your friends adjusted their pace and volume of speaking to match yours at those instances you probably felt that they want to hold a conversation with you.

Additionally, identify the target person punctuator. Assuming that you have been carefully paying attention to the target person, you are mirroring all this time; then you will notice their favorite punctuator that he or she uses to emphasize a point. For instance, it could be an eyebrow flash such as quickly raising the eyebrows. The punctuator could also be a form of hand gesture, such as the one certain politicians use. For instance, it could be that each time the target person insists on an issue, he or she makes a certain finger gesture, then you can encourage the individual by nodding when he or she makes the particular sign. After his or her submission, you should mimic that gesture to suggest that you align with the submitted views. In all these interactions, you will not utter a single word but are connecting and communicating with the target person.

Equally important, you should test the connection with the target person in several ways. For instance, make an overt unrelated action to the conversation and observe if it is reflected. An example is where you are giving a keynote speech, and a member of the audience comes up to you, and you discuss the similarities that he and you had with your fathers that had both participated in the World War II. At that instance, while talking, you get an irritating itch on your nose that you quickly scratch but then you realize that he reached up and scratched up his nose all the while continuing with his story. Even though it seemed out of place, you go ahead to evaluate if the test was a fluke and a moment later, you scratch your head, and suddenly the target person does the exact thing. It appears odd, and you almost laughed aloud. It is important to avoid repeated testing as it will break the connection and make the entire exercise appear like a prank against the best of your intention. It is also necessary to only mirror positive body language and avoid mirroring negative nonverbal communication such as turning away, closing your eyes, locking with your arms folded, or looking away. Akin to any other aspect of communication, comprehensive practice is important for one to attain efficacy levels.

As indicated, mirroring helps create a rhythm with the target individual. The main intention of mirroring the nonverbal communication of the target person is to make them notice you and fall to your pace of communication—nonverbal communication. Recall your school days when in a sporting activity or a hall with a visiting school. One of the ways that you initiated a conversation was by looking directly at the eyes of the other student that you did not know, and he or she responded. You then slowed your breathing and blinking of eyes to mimic the target student until you felt as if you are talking to each other using words. All these actions constitute mirroring to create a pattern of communication nonverbally with the target person.

For instance, if you smile at a child, it is likely to smile back at you. A common example of mirroring is when you look at your baby or any baby directly in the eyes or smile at them. In most cases, the babies will replicate the same action that you paused at them. For instance, if you clap your hands, they will also clap their hands at you. Though for the case of babies, they may lack the conscious level to perceive what they are doing, it represents the efficiency of mirroring body language. Babies with difficulties reflecting your actions can suggest that something is amiss, enabling you to investigate their welfare deeper.

Compared to men, women are more likely to mirror each other with ease. It emerges that women are likely to mirror the actions of another woman enabling two strangers, women, to connect instantly. If you are a woman or have female friends, then you must have noticed that women appear to easily connect, and it is largely due to mirroring the body language of each other. For instance, if one of the women adjusts her hair, then the other is also likely to the same and all these increases the likelihood of striking a rapport and creating a rhythm.

It is important to take into consideration your relationship with the target person when mirroring. When mirroring the target person's actions remember that the power relationship between the two of you. For instance, mirroring your supervisor may not be a good idea. At the same time, mirroring a colleague of the opposite sex may be misinterpreted to mean that you are attempting to flirt with them even if they are responding to the mimicry. Similarly, mirroring in some contexts may appear unprofessionally and a violation of work ethics. For instance, a teacher mirroring a student or a doctor mirroring a patient may appear as a mockery even if that is not the intention. Overall, the power relationship with the target person should mediate and moderate the level of body language mirroring.

As such, mirroring body language is an efficient way of building trust and understanding fast. From all these what we learn is that mirroring body language helps initiate trust between two people, especially where the two have a passive history of interaction. As indicated earlier on, you might use mirroring body language during a random interaction such as a sporting event, a party, and any social function where you want to initiate communication and rhythm of communication to build a long-term relationship. In a way, mirroring body language acts as a technique of testing waters before one can verbalize their intentions. Chances are that if the mirroring of body language backfires then the person is likely to the walkway and make the target individual understand it was just a prank or casual moment, but if mirroring body language elicits positive responses then the two individuals are likely to go ahead and connect.

Lastly, like any other form of communication, the feelings of the target person should be taken into consideration. Even though mirroring of body language is a nonverbal and mostly passive form of nonverbal communication, a human being is an emotional creature, and it is necessary to listen and respond to the feelings of each other. For instance, if the body language of the target person indicates anger, then you should cease or adjust your actions to show consideration and care for the affected person. If the target person that you are mirroring body language is happy, then you should also exhibit positive emotions to increase the shared ground spectrum and encourage the person to exude emotions that are more positive.

Chapter 13: Touch

As human beings, we engage in touching routinely, and it includes patting someone on the back or granting someone a hug to indicate that we care. We commonly shake hands as greetings or assign to signal shared understanding. Touch, as a form of communication, is called haptic. For children, touch is a crucial aspect of their development. Children that do not get adequate touch have developmental issues. Touch helps babies cope with stress. In infancy, touch is the first sense that an infant responds to.

Notably the workplace, touch is among effective means of communication, but it is necessary to adhere to conventional rules of etiquette. For instance, a handshake is a form of touch that is used in the professional environment and can convey the relationship between two people. Pay attention to the nonverbal cues that you are sending next time you shake someone's hand. Overall, one should always convey confidence when shaking another person's hand, but you should avoid being overly confident. Praise and encouragement are communicated by a pat on the back of a hand on the shoulder. One should recall that not all people share the same comfort levels when using touch as nonverbal communication. For instance, an innocent touch can make another person feel uneasy, and for this reason, applying touch requires reading the body language and responding accordingly.

Most forms of communication require some kind of touch. A handshake is a primary touch in social touches. Handshakes vary from culture to culture. It is socially polite and allowed one to shake another person's hand during an introduction in the United States. In some countries, kissing on the cheek is the norm. In the same interactions, men will allow a male stranger to touch them on their shoulders and arms, whereas women feel comfortable being touched by a female stranger only on the arms. Men are likely to enjoy touch from a female stranger while women tend to feel uncomfortable with any touch by a male stranger. Equally important, men and women process touch differently, which can create confusing and awkward situations. In most contexts, it might help unnecessary physical contact in social contexts, especially those of the opposite sex. One should try to follow societal norms and to take cues from those around you. For instance, while you stand close to a stranger on an elevator, it is not acceptable to engage in any unnecessary physical contact with him or her.

Additionally, at the workplace, touch can become complicated when touch is between a boss and a subordinate. Standard practice is that those in power are not allowed to touch subordinates than the other way around. For this reason, you should examine your motives for even the most trivial of touches and resolve to enhance your communication techniques with your juniors. A standard measure is that it is better to fall but on the side of caution. Functional touch includes being physically examined by a doctor and being touch as a form of professional massage.

Notably, the types of touches allowed between friends vary depending on contexts. For instance, women are more receptive, touching female friends compared to their male counterparts. The touches between female friends are more affectionate often in the form of a hug, whereas men prefer to shake hands and pat each other on the back. Within family members, women touch each other compared to men. Additionally, same-sex family members are more likely to touch than family members of the opposite sex are. Displays of affection between friends are critical in expressing support and encouragement, even if you are not a touchy person. One should be willing to get out of their comfort zone and offer their friend a hug when he or she is going through a difficult time. Helping others enliven their moods is likely to uplift your moods as well.

Commonly, arousing touches are elicited intense feelings and are only suitable when mutually agreed upon. Arousal touches are meant to evoke happiness and pleasure and can involve kissing, hugging, and flirtatious touching that is intentional to suggest sex. One should be careful about their partner's needs. One can greatly improve their communication skills and relationships by paying attention to the nonverbal cues that you send to others via touching behavior.

Relatedly, in romantic relationships, touches that communicate love to play a critical role. For instance, the simplest of touches can convey a critical meaning such as holding hands or placing your arm around your partner, which communicates that you are together. Adults pay more attention to nonverbal cues compared to verbal cues during communication according to recent studies on communication. In the earlier stages of dating, men tend to initiate physical contact in line with societal norms, but in later stages, it is women that touch first. Women place more premiums on touch compared to men, and even the smallest of gestures can help calm women they were upset.

Correspondingly, our sense of touch is intended to communicate clearly and quickly. Touch can elicit subconscious communication. For instance, you instantly pull away from your hand when touching something hot even before you consciously process. In this manner, touch constitutes one of the quickest ways to communicate. Touch, as a form of nonverbal communication, is an instinctive form of communication. In detail, touch conveys information instantly and causes a guttural reaction. Completely withholding touch will communicate the wrong messages without your realization.

Try patting someone on the back when you grant him or her praise. If your colleague or friend has graduated, earned a promotion, or married, and then pat them on the back. Giving a pat suggests that you are happy with the person and are encouraging them. Touch has a therapeutic value that relaxes the mind and the body as well as helping an individual feel secure and appreciated. At school, you must have felt valued and loved if you were patted on the back.

Then initiate discussions with a touch to create cooperative relationships. Studies have established that touching a person increases their willingness to cooperate and work with others. They are establishing physical contact with an individual that you wish to initiate a conversation with can help. Sometimes the target person may not realize that you touched them but will register subconsciously and establish a bond.

Equally important—extend the handshakes. Shaking hands shows confidence and simplicity in interacting with others. Touch helps build trust between two people. Make your handshakes firm when shaking hands with people. It is also necessary to remember that some health conditions may make one shy away from shaking hands, and this includes hyperhidrosis, which makes the palms of the person sweat. With sweaty hands, the individual is likely to shun handshakes, and this has little to do with the context of the conversation.

For emphasis, touch is contextual. For instance, the Japanese do not favor shaking hands, and a person in this environment will avoid shaking hands at all costs. In the American context, shaking hands is encouraged. For this reason, one should adjust the touch-type depending on the contexts. It might be welcome to hold the hands of your partner continuously while the same is creepy when talking to a stranger or a colleague at the workplace.

The other form of touch is tickling, which is mostly reserved for lovers, parents versus children, and peers. For instance, a mother may tickle her baby, which is a therapeutic touch and is permissible. On the hand, children or students of the same age set may tickle each other, which are permissible. However, it is inappropriate to tickle an adult when you are not lovers or the relationship between you and them is formal.

However, there is a thin line between permissible touch and physical abuse. If not certain, one should avoid initiating touch unless fully certain of its meaning to the target person. Pushing someone or pinching someone is considered a form of physical abuse. Kicking or striking someone, as well as strangling, are forms of physical abuse.

There are some contexts where a touch is a form of the game, especially teasing. Touch as a form of the game should only happen where the participants are peers and are receptive to it. For instance, your friend or classmate may blindfold your eyes with the palms of their hands from behind. The participants in this tease may touch each other; for instance, the blinded person may try to feel your arms or head to try to guess the identity of the person teasing. In this form of touch, the scope of touching allowed is large and may be equivalent to that of lovers.

Chapter 14: Paralinguistic

Paralinguistic refers to a type of nonverbal communication that is premised on the qualities of voice and the manner one vocalizes. The accent, pitch, and tone of our voice communicate more about our personality and us. Our accent can tell where we come from or our teachers. The audience will, for instance, form stereotypes based on your accent. An individual that talks slow may sound tired, thoughtful, or perhaps not intelligent. An individual that talks fast may sound shady, anxious, or excited. Inflection, vocal volume and stammering do influence verbal messages and affect the processing of the intended meaning by the audience.

As such, paralinguistic entails the aspects of spoken communication that does not involve words. For this reason, paralinguistic emphasize or diminish the intended meaning of what people say. Other aspects of body language are part of paralinguistic. The paralinguistic features of the language are critical as they directly influence the message. Better conversation can be realized by being more aware of the subtle nuances of verbal communication by promoting deeper understanding and connection with others. Overall, the study of voice and how words are voiced is paralinguistic communication.

Correspondingly, speaking faster or rapid rates of speech are linked to composure and self-assurance. One should try to speak at a rate similar to the individual they are communicating within the conversation. In the TV series, "Young & Hungry," watch a single episode and focus on Gabi Diamond. In the TV series, Gabi Diamond speaks fast, and this makes her look like she is exhibiting composure and self-assurance. However, if you watch several episodes, you will realize that she speaks fast to hide her insecurities and disappointments with love largely due to her quick nature of approaching love issues. Against this backdrop, speaking rapidly may suggest composure and self-assurance, but it is not necessarily the true status of the individual.

Relatedly, think of a classmate or colleague that speaks fast. Chances are that the individual has composure and self-assurance or the person is masking their insecurities. People that naturally speak fast are the ones that may be exhibiting composure and self-confidence. However, individually that suddenly speaks fast than usual may be showing attempts to hide their weakness. In public speaking, an individual may speak fast, try to display all before the expiry of the indicated time. In overall, the assessment of the rate of speaking should largely be naturally fast speaker versus induced fast speaking. Speaking fast for an individual that does not speak at that rate may be indicative of attempts to trivialize the situation or create lies.

In most languages exhibit unique rhythms and rhythm is critical, especially for the English language. A person from Korea and one from Bulgaria will speak at a different speed and rhythm. In most cases, people will speak a second language at a rhythmical pace similar to their native language. The overall aim of acknowledging rhythm is that you should try to speak at the same rhythm with the individual, and the chosen rhythm should be the one that is slower than the other is. At one point, you tried having a conversation with a person that is not a native speaker of English, and you had to slow down the conversation to enhance understanding.

For instance, search YouTube for "Kids stories English India" and note the rhythm of Indian speakers of English. You will realize that the speakers try to speak close to the rhythm of their native language. Again, go to YouTube and search for "President's speech Uganda, Kenya, Nigeria, or Zambia." You will observe that the speaking rhythm is close to the native language rhythm of the speaker.

Correspondingly, the person with fast rhythm has to adjust to the slower rhythm. Search YouTube for "BBC interview with Uganda's president Museveni" or "CNN interview with Kenya's President Kenyatta." In many instances of these interviews, you will realize that the interview tries to slow their usual rhythm of speaking to match the relatively slow rhythm of these African countries' presidents. On the contrary, if you voice the person with the slow rhythm to match up to your fast pace, then the conversation will negatively be affected, as the individual will have to rush their thoughts and reactions.

Notably, speaking loud suggests that one is assertive, confident, and bold. Think of a politician or any leader that you recognize. Chances are that the individual speaks loud enough, which shows that the person is confident and assured of what he or she is saying. When addressing the entire school, your college principal spoke with loud volume, which indicated authority and certainty of what he or she was saying.

Additionally, speaking with low volume shows shyness and insecurity. For instance, in school, the groups that had not done adequate preparation during presentation probably spoke with low volume. The ones that had researched and fine-tuned their work spoke confidently. If you are a parent, you will notice that if your child has done something awkward, then he or she will reply in a low almost muffled voice.

Relatedly, speaking with a high-pitched voice makes one sound childlike. Lower pitches are primarily associated with higher credibility, authority, and maturity. Try listening to Bernadette Rostenkowski, the character wife to Howard Wolowitz in the TV series "The Big Bang Theory." She is featured from Season 6 onwards. Take note of Bernadette Rostenkowski's pitch in the TV series. The most important thing is that the pitch you choose should be your most powerful vocal range. You should not force a lower-pitched voice even if it is considered more credible as you risk losing the vocal power.

As indicated earlier on, speaking in low-pitched voice indicates that you have owned the space and are confident in what you are expressing. Most people find people with deep voices as appealing to listen to and hold a conversation with. Men have an advantage when it comes to low-pitch voices, and this easily makes them come across as composed and in charge. The low pitch voice is a critical element of talk therapy as it gives reassurance and calming effect to the target person.

Against this backdrop, vocal variety or inflection concerns the variations in the pitch of the voice. Some contexts demand variations in pitch such as when narrating a story to children while other contexts demand less variation in pitch, such as in the corporate world. A few singing exercises when showering can help improve tone variation of the voice. The other great way to practice is to record and listen to oneself to analyze the quality of your inflection.

If listening to someone, pay attention to inflection. A person that shows expected tonal variation of the voice is speaking naturally and probably is truthful. People that speak a monotone are likely disinterested or not being truthful. However, some instances may justify speaking with no tonal variation in casual contexts. For instance, people that are not native speakers of English are likely to speak with a flat tone and this because they lack the native perception of the choice of the words used. Additionally, for most people, when reading a text are likely to use a flat tone as opposed to speaking their minds literally.

In some cultures and languages, favor variation of tone. For instance, American English and Lingala language are widely spoken in the Democratic Republic of Congo naturally demands tonal variation of the voice. The phonetics of these languages give the speakers the quality of varying tone compared to say the Swahili language widely spoken in East Africa. In this manner, the cultural context of the language may enhance or lower the degree of inflection when one is speaking. Lastly, a tonal variation of the voice does not imply shouting as one can speak softly but vary the tone.

Notably, the attribute of voice that enables you to distinguish one voice from another is known as the quality of the voice. For instance, identifying a voice as feminine or aloof constitutes the quality of the voice. The quality of a voice is a function of pitch, rate, and volume of voice. Even though the quality of voice can be learned, in most cases, it is innate. Some people are born with a commanding voice or a feminine voice. The quality of voice is largely monetized when one decides to work as a musician, narrator, or news anchor. Despite having different voice qualities, some contexts seek and use different voice qualities, especially in animation movies and general movies where the different quality of voices are critical to eliciting laughter and relatable aspects of the production.

One of the best illustrations of different voice qualities is the TV animation series, "Family Guy." Search for an episode of "Family Guy" and notice the different voice qualities. Before you search, kindly appreciate that some of the content may sound offensive to people with disabilities, and ethnic minorities. However, most of the content is standard with a touch of humor. Listen to the quality of voice of the character Louis and that of the character Peter Griffin. Again, listen to the quality of voice of Joe and that of Stewie, all characters. You can also look for any animation, and I suggest "The Storks" and "Penguins of Madagascar" to appreciate the quality of voice. Most animation movies present different voice qualities within a short period enabling you to register and analyze them.

Concerning tone, it is the intensity of the voice. The tone of a voice reveals more about the emotions behind the words being spoken. If the listener is assertive, then he or she will quickly connect and create a rapport with someone on the telephone by utilizing aspects of paralinguistic communication. Creating a rapport can be enhanced through matching and mirroring vocal attributes devoid of mockery. All these lead to greater understanding and more effective paralinguistic communication. Realizing awareness of your paralinguistic vocal strengths will enable one to subtly influence the speaking and listening so that one comes across as a powerful communicator.

Additionally, the loudness of a voice varies across cultures. For instance, men in Saudi Arabia may sound aggressive when compared against the loudness of voice in the United States. Among Arabs, a soft tone implies weakness. Personal social class also influences the loudness of voice with people in lower classes using lower volumes when speaking. The tone of the voice is what makes one feel that one is upset. Without taking into the environment of an individual in consideration, a loud voice should be avoided during the conversation.

For instance, for non-Americans outside America, they may struggle to notice the sarcasm in the laughter of some Americans. Americans tend to apply sarcasm in speech and laughter that non-Americans may miss unless they understand tone. When speaking or interacting with a non-American, one should understand that the person may not get the sarcasm, and this may impede effective conversation. Overall, when using tonal variation to elicit sarcasm, one should be careful concerning the ethnic and nationality composition of the audience.

Chapter 15: Mind Control and How to Defend Yourself

First, having gone through in what constitutes body language, the role of body language and how to read body language then it is important that one learns on ways of benefitting from reading the body language of people. In this context, the benefit realized from reading the body language of people is not to torment or use people but rather to enhance your interests that are acceptable such as increasing business deals.

Secondly, mind control refers to a context where one is taken advantage of and appears not to have the mental willpower to understand or control what is happening to him or others. Even though mind control may involve hypnotizing, it mostly occurs without using hypnosis. As earlier on discussed, one of the ways of controlling the mind of another person is to mirror their body language and create a communication rhythm making the person feel connected to you. People that employ mind control are seeking short-term or instant gains, especially by controlling your emotions and how you react to their emotions.

From an ethical viewpoint, mind control largely qualifies as unethical. The moral question arises because one is tapping into the weaknesses of the target person to accomplish your interests. For instance, one can mind control you to make sell an insurance package that you do not need, but the seller needs to be paid. A partner may mind control to enhance loyalty levels in the relationship, which may not be what you are genuinely feeling. As such, with mind control, the question of ethicality dominates the application of mind control.

Fortunately, through understanding body language, one can detect an attempt for controlling their minds and activate defensive measures. First, take note of attempted body language reading to win over a difficult customer or person. At one point, you have encountered a difficult person to understand and get along with despite the best of your efforts. Armed with body language reading competencies, you can correctly analyze their tone, posture, touch, eye contact, and facial expressions to connect with the individual correctly. Similarly, a person trying to control your mind will try to read all these body language cues. For instance, they will employ paralinguistic skills; try to strike a rapport with the person. Some customers are defensive, but if you are armed with, body language reading skills, then you will easily manage to manipulate them to your advantage. Similarly, the manipulating individual will try to apply these tactics on you. For instance, the manipulating person will try to read if you speak in high-pitched voice, then probably the customer is angry or frustrated by workload or other life issues. Using this knowledge, you can predict how the manipulating person will react to your voice pitch.

Secondly, most manipulators target negative feedback and negative emotions because this is where most people show weakness and create room for mind control. A manipulator will exploit body language to create perceptions of care, love, and sympathy as well as empathy that most people fall for during their challenging moments. By realizing that you are most vulnerable to manipulation when processing negative news and negative emotions, you will be able to manifest high mental awareness levels.

Expectedly, most manipulators that want mind control will seek to precipitate conflict and take advantage of the festering differences. However, by learning and applying effective conflict resolution can be realized by reading the body language of the target person. Assuming that you are an arbiter in a conflict, you should read the body language of the feuding parties to discover any shared ground and the emotive issues. Individuals will show panic, uneasiness, and stiffness when emotive issues are raised such as grinning, crossing arms, breathing fast, and showing cold stare. Individuals will nod if something they agree to is mentioned. They may also stamp their feet, clap hands, and shake hands to show a willingness to talk or strike a compromise. An arbiter will use reading body language to identify hardliners and use body language to thaw the hard stance of such people. The participants themselves can also read the body language of the other party and appreciate their stance and attempt to initiate meaningful conversation. All these combined efforts will give one an edge in solving conflicts.

Furthermore, watch out for attempts to make conversations interesting. We also would like to enliven conversations, but it is not always the case, and manipulators understand this. One effective way that manipulators use is to improve how other people perceive them is to understand their status and adjust your words and body language. For instance, if a manipulator reads the body language of the other person and realizes that, he or she is feeling disinterested or exhausted; he or she can suggest a break or crack a joke. Through eye contact, you can make the other person feel recognized and wanted to join in the conversation. If the entire group or audience feels disinterested in the conversation by yawning, slouching on their chairs, crossing their legs, and losing eye contact, then the speaker should conduct a quick self-feedback and adjust the communication. It is important to watch out for deliberate attempts to make you attached to the conversation.

Relatedly, taking advantage of reading body language can help one to recognize any dishonesty and pretense in a conversation and help you notice the lack of honesty from the manipulator. Focusing on verbal communication alone is not enough to accurately determine if one is pretending. For instance, your child may say that he is comfortable going out to play while his body language suggests otherwise. For instance, the child could be replying in a high-pitched voice and laugh sarcastically that he or she is comfortable going out to play. The parent will use this body language to address the true feeling of the child. In an intimate relationship, determining the true emotional status of your partner is critical for peaceful and constructive interaction. For instance, if your partner states that she believes you, but her voice is high-pitched, and she is throwing gestures randomly, then chances are that she does not, and, in fact, she is angry with you.

Relatedly exploiting body language reading can make one make a good first impression, and you should critically analyze the first impression. A good first impression is critical when selling, during an interview, and when seeking a life partner. Armed with reading body language one can deliberately enhance positive body language such as nodding to a speech, using gestures when necessary and speaking in a low-pitched voice to sound professional. When one feels tired and wants to shuffle feet or lower eye contact, one can compensate for that by interrupting the speaker to ask a question or take notes. Expectedly, one will offer a firm handshake and accompany it with a smile. Making a good first impression can improve and open opportunities for you in the case of negotiation, interviews, making sales, and seeking a marriage partner.

Furthermore, taking advantage of the body language can help one to correctly identify issues in a relationship by analyzing body language. Apart from just reading the body language and improving social and intimate relationships, one can also use reading body language to determine the presence of issues in relationships, which includes identifying attempts of mind control. For instance, you might notice that when you talk on certain issues with your partner, his or her body language suggests defensiveness and anger. For this reason, reading the body language can help get to the underlying issue even in cases where the partner is determined not to open up. Using body language to identify issues can also help a parent to determine what is bothering a child in cases where the child retreats to its world. The parent can try talking over general issues as well as specific issues and watch the body language of the child to guess the issues or challenges that the child is facing.

Equally important, effectively teaching or sharing ideas can be enhanced by reading the body language of the target audience. A manipulator will seek to adjust the experience to prioritize their needs rather than mutual needs. For instance, a teacher can improve understanding of the students by taking note of signs of lack of concentration such as yawning or staring at the ceiling. However, if the teacher wants to attain mind control, then he or she will manipulate the body language to prioritize only his or her needs over the others. Just like verbal communication, body language can also contain noise where the nonverbal cues of communication distort the intended message. Outside the teaching context, one can improve on sharing ideas by reading the body language of the audience and evoking the desired emotion and reaction. For instance, one should ensure that the target audience is relaxed and alert by evaluating the sitting posture, eye contact, and facial expressions before starting a presentation. Sharing ideas effectively depends on accurate timing and actors, orators, and politicians understand this well.

Finally, taking advantage of reading body language will lead to improved emotional intelligence and social skills to make one more appealing and understanding. Emotional intelligence involves being aware of how you feel and acknowledging how others feel to enhance mutual understanding. For this reason, body language is a critical avenue to read the emotional status of the other person. Emotional intelligence requires correctly reading the emotional status of an individual to enable you to empathize with how they feel. Against this backdrop, reading the body language of a target audience gives an added advantage to an individual to evoke and apply social skills as well as understand self-deeper. Think of speaking to a colleague and manifesting nonverbal cues that you are offended, but the person is not registering what you are feeling. In this context, effective communication will not only be hampered, but the social relationship will also be affected negatively.

Activity

a. Watch the movie "The Wolfstreet" and observe how manipulation works

b. Watch the movie "Get Hard" with lead actor Kevin Hart and assess if the hand gestures align with verbal communication. If possible, watch the entire movie and note the gestures and facial expressions exhibited when one is angry.

Chapter 16: Manipulation and Dealing with Manipulators

Manipulators simply exploit effective body language reading and effective nonverbal communication to attain their self-serving interests. The choice of body language is because, at some point, we become completely unaware that they are leading us on and fall for their schemes. Perhaps some of the common instances of manipulation happen in relationships and during sales. For this reason, defending oneself against manipulation requires improving your awareness of body language reading skills that will enable you to detect and activate defense mechanisms.

First, improve body language reading skills by observing people in your daily life. Like any form of reading, one has to engage in reading other people frequently. The best starting point is the people close to you as you get to test the accuracy of your body language reading skills. For instance, observe your roommate's body language and try to guess his or her emotional status. Even though it might appear as spying on the person, you can go ahead, label the person as Specimen Y, and maintain a journal of their body language and what you concluded. Try to determine if they are behaving in a particular manner to manipulate you.

Secondly, manipulators understand the behavior of people in a group and may help initiate actions that will make the entire group mimic while they intend to get a single person out of the group with the others being akin to collateral damage. People in groups such as in a class, a stadium or workplace tend to mimic each other. If one person takes a selfie, the chances are that the others will also take selfies. If one person starts taking a walk, chances are that the rest will also join inadvertently. It appears that when an individual is placed in a group setting, then he or she is likely to let others dictate how they act and react. In most cases, people will deliberately suppress undesired emotions and actions to accommodate others or simply fit in. For this reason, create a room for self-doubt when participating in informal group activities.

For emphasis, you should exhibit awareness. You should pay attention to everything that the person is doing and when the person is doing it. While this appears trivial, each small and subtle detail about the target person is necessary for one to profile the person accurately. Manipulators have to communicate also, and a keen examination of their body language may reveal they are the true intention. For instance, if the target person adjusts earing, you should not assume that this is a mundane aspect and does not constitute body language. Being awake to every aspect of behavior, actions, and movements of the target person are critical to effectively reading the body language of the individual. Awareness requires that you also understand yourself first, and this can be realized through emotional intelligence competencies.

Another means to enhance your awareness of manipulators is to study politicians as most are, study people you admire. Another way of attaining this is to find any recordings or videos of the people, mute the voice, and study only the body language. With social media, people are sharing videos and audio recordings that one can learn from. You can also get a movie, especially the one that you are to watch, mute the volume, and analyze the body language. Then get a paper and profile each of the characters observed on their personality and emotion. Once you have completed the profiling, activate the volume, and compare the perceived character against the body language reading that you did.

At this point, you can attempt to read the body language of the suspected manipulator to determine the truthfulness of their emotions and personality. Try to mirror the target person by mimicking their body positions, matching their tone, and carrying the same pace of the conversation. When mimicking the individual, ensure that it is done subtly. Through mirroring, one creates a synergy and connection that enables you gets into the mind of the target person. Mimicking another person's body language should be carefully done to avoid making it appear as if you are trying to flirt or that you are creepy.

Then scout for additional cues when you encounter that the target person is crossing their arms and legs. Crossing the arms and legs denotes that one is defensive, but most people cross their arms and legs when feeling comfortable or if they want to concentrate more on what is being spoken. If someone holds a drink on the table using the opposite hand, then the person is showing a lack of confidence. Overall, body language cues should be read, as an entire set as focusing on one can be misleading. Where necessary, consider the cultural or learned behavior that may elicit a different meaning from what the body language is suggesting. For instance, people that stammer may throw gestures randomly or stomp their feet, and this does not imply that they are lacking confidence or are scared.

As indicated, most manipulators seek to exploit any gaps in communication, especially weak eye contact from the target person. Try to have more eye contact with the individual. You can initiate eye contact with the target person and observe their eye contact behavior. Eye contact, just like touch, communicates much more about the person and their emotional status. Staring at the ceiling or on the floor may indicate that the individual is bored and not interested in what is being said. However, an individual may look on the floor or stare at the ceiling if the news being given is negative and painful such as the loss of a friend or loss of a job. In this context, avoiding eye contact does not imply that the individual is not listening, but instead, the person is thinking deeper about how to navigate the negative emotions. There are also extreme situations where eye contact can mislead, such as people that shy who will avoid eye contact.

Relatedly, observe the shoulder position of the target person to read their body language. If the person holds their shoulders by their ears, then it is a sign of tension and can make the speaker become unease as well. Relaxed shoulders indicate that one is feeling calm and alert. If the person tries to retract the shoulders closer to the trunk of the body as if an umbrella closing, then the person is feeling embarrassed or unease with the environment or the message being passed. Fortunately, the posture of the shoulders can be read from a distant position.

It is also necessary to examine the sitting posture of the individual. Slouching on the seat suggests casualness or tiredness of the target person. If the person spreads their legs wide while seated, then it indicates that the individual is not participating in the conversation. Crossing the legs may indicate that the person is feeling unease or relaxed when participating in the conversation. It is important that you take note of the sitting posture of the target person as it communicates about the attitude and emotional status of the individual. It might be necessary to walk near the audience and take note of their sitting posture.

As with any other form of reading, recognize, and address personal bias and stereotypes. Each one of us has ingrained biases and stereotypes, which is largely a function of our parenting and environment. For instance, if you grew up in a strict Christian family, then you may show disdain to an atheist, and the contrary is true. There are visible attributes of a person that can trigger biases that will distract making an objective conclusion about the target individual. For instance, the skin color or gender of the target person can distort the objective reading of the target individual. If you are a man and you, notice that the target person, a woman is staring at the neighbor who is a man also then your biases may make you think they are in love because that is how you view women. It is important to recognize and work on personal biases to help you objectively profile the target person.

Expectedly, a manipulative individual will still engage in all forms of communication, including the touch aspect of communication. If there, is an opportunity, study, and analyze the handshake or hug offered by the target person. When analyzing the handshake, try to assess it in combination with the facial expression exhibited. For instance, if you shake the hand of the other person and the person shakes your hand firmly but looks down then the person could be naturally shy, and this may imply that the person is confident as the one that shakes the hand firmly and maintains eye contact. On the other hand, if you shake the hand of the person and the individual firmly shakes your hand but frowns, then the person could be feeling unease and irked by your previous behavior or comments.

Finally, like any other form of reading competencies, it is necessary to prepare for reading body language by going through resources that discuss and analyze body language. For instance, get a book, presentation, or documentaries on body language and study them. You can only analyze what you know at first. For instance, there several aspects of touch that people do not and will not consider them when reading touch. The same is true for posture and facial expressions. The more theoretical knowledge you have on body language, the more effective you will be at reading the body language of people.

Exercise

Search for TV series "Gary Unmarried" and pick one episode then focus the lead character Gary and the ex-wife Allison. With time, you will notice that Allison the ex-wife quickly discerns any attempts by Gary to manipulate her. From just the episode you have selected, why do you think this is possible?

Chapter 17: Detecting Lying and Deception

Notably, each one of us would like to easily determine deception at any level such as personal, social, and organizational levels but it is not that easy. Some professions that rely wholly on determining the truth in personal and social contexts such as law agencies, health agencies, and media agencies invest heavily in determining the truth value of their productions, but they fairly fail despite having immense resources. However, if we go back to chapter one of this book, we will realize that human behavior is dynamic and this implies that what proves a lie in one context may also prove the truth in another context.

There is only one reliable way to determine lying and deception, and that is establishing a baseline for the target individual and comparing against this baseline as well as doing the adequate prior investigation before confronting the person. Unfortunately, creating a baseline for each and conducting relevant background study is not always assured due to the time factor and resource constraints and this implies that a speedy analysis of body language and verbal communication can help determine a likelihood of a truth or a lie.

Verbal Hints of a Liar

Liars Tend to Respond to Questions That Were Not Asked

If a person is lying, then he or she wants to cover as much ground as possible, and this includes answering questions that were not posed. By answering questions that were not asked, the individual is prompting the speaker to a particular direction and does not want to be caught off guard. Answering questions that are not asked may also give the individual lying an opportunity to deny the speaker adequate time to analyze the answers given by continuously bombarding the interrogator with new information and ideas. Lastly, answering questions that were not asked also helps the layperson to appear well prepared and knowledgeable in what is being asked.

Liars Tend to Answer a Question with a Question

Expectedly, most liars will respond to a question with another question to shift the burden of thinking and responding to the interrogator. Most politicians employ this tactic when being interviewed, and it is meant to buy them enough time to recall information to the main question. For most liars, not responding is akin to affirming that they lack memory of what is being asked or what happened. The other purpose of responding to a question with another question is to irritate the interrogator and derail his or her composure. Responding to a question with a question is a defensive tactic indicating attempts to hide something.

Most Liars Tend to Make Self-corrections to Avoid Sounding Uncertain

As indicated, most liars want to ensure that each area is covered to eliminate any doubts because allowing room for doubt may expose them. For this reason, most liars tend to self-correct to ensure the information given is irrefutable. In most cases, liars will repeat the correction to ensure that the interrogator and the audience also capture the self-correction. As expected, the liar will blame the need to self-correct on a slip of the tongue or the fast nature of the interview. Another reason for self-correction by a liar is that the individual has a premeditated script and outcome and keeps forcing everything to align with the premeditated picture.

Liars Tend to Feign Memory Loss

As expected, most liars need a safe escape button when cornered and feigning memory loss is a favorite excuse for most liars. When a liar is cornered, then he or she will cite memory loss and later institute self-correction to attain the preformed script. Try watching interviews with politicians to appreciate how they feign memory loss to escape explaining something and pretend to have recalled the information when there is an opportunity to sound believable.

Most Liars Tend to Report What They Did Not Do as Opposed to What They Did

People that lie will give an account of what they did not do to avoid being held accountable. If a liar dwelled on what he or she did, then the individual can be held accountable, and this is not something that a liar wants. However, if a liar dwells on what they should have done, \ he or she has a large degree of freedom to give any answer and avoid scrutiny. Again, try watching a recorded or filed interview with any politician to appreciate how this technique is employed.

Liars Tend to Justify Their Actions Even When not Necessary

Expectedly, most liars are insecure and are uncertain that they sound convincing. For this reason, they over-justify everything because they feel that no one believes them even when people have fallen for the lies. When examining a potential liar, look for signs of unnecessary justification, and again, politicians will provide a good case study of over-justification.

Most Liars Avoid Mentioning Emotional Feelings in Their Version of Events

Since a liar is faking everything, he or she will avoid mentioning feelings that were associated with what is being reported. Mentioning emotions may force one to show them. For instance, if you were talking about an exciting event that you witnessed, then your facial expressions and voice should manifest positive emotions, and this is not something a liar wants because he or she is not assured of the consistency of verbal communication and body language.

Most Liars Are Careful, and Will Insist on a Question to Be Repeated

Finally, liars focus more on what is being asked because they only want to accept a question that they are certain of responding to. Liars dwell more on what the question is and what the interrogator wants to help them generate convincing information. The other role of wanting questions repeated is to help the liar elicit a response by making up one because there is none.

Nonverbal Hints of a Liar

Liars Randomly Throw Gestures

The hand gestures are among the best indicator of positive and negative emotions and are difficult to fake in a consistent manner. If one is angry but is pretending to be calm, he or she will throw gestures randomly. Most liars get irritated when taken to the task of what they just said and are likely to throw random gestures in the air even as they try to sound calm.

Against the Norm, Liars Speak Faster than Usual

People that normally do not speak fast will suddenly speak fast when they are lying. Speaking fast helps, the person denies the audience adequate time to listen and analyze the information. Speaking fast also allows the liar to exhaust all of the rehearsed information, as any interjection will throw the liar off balance. Speaking fast also indicates that the person is uncomfortable with the audience or the message and wants to finish fast and end the experience.

Liars Sweat More Than Usual

People sweat, and it is normal. However, more than normal levels of sweating even when the weather is fine may indicate that one is panicking and feeling cornered. All these may indicate a sign of a liar.

Liars Avoid Eye Contact

Most liars shun eye contact or give a sustained stare to intimidate the target person. Shunning eye contact indicates that the person feels awkward or embarrassed about what he or she is presenting to the audience.

Pacing Up and Down

If one paces up and down more than necessary, then the individual is likely lying. All these indicate feeling uncomfortable with the message and the audience.

Conclusion

Overall, the reader is carefully introduced to aspects of behavioral psychology to understand why human behavior is complex as well what motivates human behavior. For instance, under the investment model, one seeks to maximize returns by committing certain actions. While the book invokes reputable psychological theories and concepts to make the content quality and applicable, the author ensures that the book is easy to read for any reader. Throughout the book, the author employs simple and easy to understand the English language with the understanding the audience of the book is likely to be of native and non-native speakers of the English language.

Additionally, the author systematically presented content and concepts allowing the reader to build familiarity and complexity towards the end. The author presented the book as a manual, guide, and informative piece of ways of reading human body language. All these were possible through extensive reading of related topics on the issue from reputable scientific journals and presenting it in a readable, relatable, and simple language. Against this backdrop, this book managed to introduce human behavior psychology, discuss the role of analyzing people, ways of becoming an analyst of people, and presented different forms of nonverbal communication. Towards the end, the book discussed ways of mirroring body language, mind control, manipulation, and ways of detecting lying and deception. As such, you should find this book an easy and informative guide to reading body language.

Dark Psychology Secrets

Introductory Guide to Discover How to Stop Being Manipulated, Avoid Mind Control, Covert Persuasion, Deception and Learn the Art of Reading People.

Diana Brain

Introduction

In this book, we analyze the dark sides of personalities also known as the dark cores. We all may portray one or more of these dark personalities.

A research that was done indicated that if you have one of these traits, then chances are you also have several others that you are not aware of.

This book also takes a keen look at the minds of people who love controlling other people, of the different subtypes of narcissists i.e. the introverted narcissists and the narcissist and the impersonal and difficult people in relationships.

We will look at these types of people including those who hurl subtle insults at other people, portray sullen behavior, stubborn in nature and those who have tendencies of not completing tasks and projects.

We also give you a deep and in-depth explanation of mind control and how it's used in real life.

We will compare brainwashing and mind control.

The book will also help you to clearly identify the individual who is holding a gun to the head, why they do it and what they hope to gain from their acts in the long run.

In this book, we will clearly define and break down susceptibility in dark psychology. We will also disintegrate cult psychology including paranoia, brainwashing, public humiliation and self-incrimination.

The book takes you through the mind of individuals who practice dark psychology.

We will also analyze the psychology of manipulation.

We will give you an insight into global vs ordinary manipulation.

The book shows how each of these manipulations are applied to our day to day lives.

The book also explains why not all forms of manipulations are immoral including examples.

The book will also clearly explain the characteristics and traits of people who are manipulative in nature.

In the final chapters of the book, you will get to learn more about the human rights that you may be violating when practicing manipulation.

While it is evident in our society that there are individuals who have no respect for the right of other people, we will show exactly how to avoid such people including techniques such as keeping your distance, avoiding personalization and self-blame, focusing on asking probing questions and many others.

The book also looks at deception tactics including how to gain manipulation tactics, how to use and various manipulation techniques.

The book also looks at persuasion techniques and deception tactics.

In this book, we will take a deep look at what it takes to analyze some of these characters, including how to decipher the truth from lies.

You also learn what it takes to have a clear comprehension of the characters and traits that affect humanity in the world of psychology.

Instead of trying to understand these people by yourself, the book addresses some of the deep issues that have affected the course of humanity including cults, leadership, introversion and the possibilities of being lied to by relatives and friends or the people closest to you.

You should be able to grasp a few basics regarding why manipulators are good at what they do and why they delve into such traits, yet they can still get what they need in life without deceiving others.

In the long run, you will also learn more about what to take into consideration when dealing with such individuals.

This book is also one of the first steps you're taking towards understanding what you need to do in order to evade manipulative people who will ruin your life.

Since the world is continuously developing into a chaotic place filled with various issues affecting the world, the information provided in the chapters will help you to handle some of the crucial issues affecting you as an individual who is dealing with other issues of life.

With the knowledge passed through this book, you'll be in a position to understand the possibilities of being abused by some of the closest people you have in life.

You'll also be in a position to analyze the impending nature of humans and their focus on the use of dark psychology to harm humanity.

You'll learn more about how to deal with people who tend to manipulate others in their course of life.

You'll also learn to manipulate your way out of their traps and study human nature and its application in real life.

In the long run, these chapters will disseminate critical information about how to analyze the possibilities of being useful in other people's lives when it comes to protecting them from people who mistreat them.

Some of the principles that have been highlighted in this book will help you to comprehend the nature of human beings, including how to handle different characters.

With the persuasive techniques outlined in these chapters, you'll be in a position to successfully manipulate others and convince them to join you on your way of handling issues.

You will also be able to read minds through learning more about people's thoughts, including how they approach matters that affect them in life. You will be well-positioned to convince other people by learning various mental tactics that can be applied in real-life scenarios.

Chapter 1: Defining Psychology

Psychology refers to the scientific study of the brain as well as the mind's behavior. This is often regarded as a multifaceted subject that includes various subtitles and fields, including the study of areas of sports, health, clinical as well as social behavior and cognitive processes.

With that said, psychology is also a new discipline in science that advances as time goes by.

It has been a subject in the field of science for more than 150 years. But, its origin can be traced to ancient Greece between 400-500 years before Christ. The main emphasis, in this case, was a philosophical one where great thinkers, including Socrates, influenced Plato who would later pass the same effect to Aristotle.

As such, philosophers would take over different discussions to highlight the pleas of the people in their communities using psychology.

In the initial days of psychology, there were two main dominant theoretical perspectives.

There was an American practicing psychologist known as William James who created different policies and developed an approach known as functionalism.

The professional argued that the brain and the mind are two significant elements that are taking different changes in the face of the world. It's, therefore, pointless to look for various constructive blocks of experience.

Rather than that, people should focus on how an organism takes a specific action.

It was also suggested that professional psychologists need to look for the main underlying issues that cause changes in behavior.

This emphasis was on the causes and consequences that have influenced contemporary psychology.

Structuralism is the name that was given to the approach that Wilhelm Wundt came up with.

The word hailed from Edward Titchener, who was a psychologist hailing from America and trained by Wundt.

The subject of structuralism highly relied on the trained introspection as well as research on the subjects.

This was based on the disciplines related to what was happening in their minds when performing a particular task.

Over the course of the years, it turned out to be pretty unreliable as a method that could be used in assessing the wellbeing of patients. Structuralism also relied on various trained introspection.

This was a research method in which subjects related to the ongoing actions of their minds as they performed various tasks.

The method was not reliable since there were several individual variations in their experiences as well as reports regarding the research subjects.

While Wundt failed in the aspect of introspection, he figured out the history of psychology since he opened a laboratory that was devoted to the study of the human mind. That marked the outset of modern psychology. Wundt became vital since he separated the study of psychology from the philosophy of analyzing the existing workings of the mind by utilizing more objective as well as standard procedures.

Since psychology is a science, it tries to investigate the varying causes of the systematic character of the mind including procedures of observation, analysis, backed up by any existing theoretical interpretations, explanations, predictions, as well as generalizations. Psychologists are well known for defining and examining the character and behavior from different perspectives.

Each one of the elements is underpinned using a shared set of various assumptions regarding what people are and what is vital in the study of psychology.

Some specialize in the study of the mind and brain, as others major on how people process information. Some also specialize in the impact of evolution on society as well as the environment.

The classic perspectives in psychology in adoption various scientific strategies and policies were majorly behaviorists who were also renowned for their existing reliance on laboratory experiments as well as the rejection of unseen subconscious forces that affected human behaviors. As such, cognitive psychology took over a rigorous and lab-based approach too.

Using memory and cognitive development, psychologists focused on understanding human brain development as well as all the existing actions that surrounded their characters.

Chapter 2: The Dark Side of Your Personality (secrets of psychology)

Dark psychology is human consciousness as well as constructive study regarding the human condition since it relates to the nature of psychology where people prey on others.

The character is often motivated by the psychopathic and psychopathological criminal drives that usually lack purpose as well as general assumptions of instincts and drive. It is also driven by evolutionary biology as well as social sciences theory.

All humanity has the capability to victimize humans as well as other living creatures successfully.

Although many will restrain from this character, some will take action on their impulses.

Dark psychology is also defined as the art of manipulation as well as mind control. Although psychology is known as the study of the human character and it's central to human thought, interactions, as well as actions, the word Dark Psychology is a great phenomenon where people use various tactics in motivating and persuading others in order to get what they want.

Dark psychology is also an overview of the existing psychological persuasion that humans have over other people. In the current world, dark psychology is a powerful force that's used in several sectors.

Great influencers across the world also utilize it. Those who aren't aware of the risks of this dark force may have it used against them in different scenarios. To be safe from such harmful elements in society, you need to familiarize yourself with the effects of dark psychology in the community, including families as well as different individuals.

While some people restrain this character, some will take action upon their feelings, thereby delving into certain characters.

Dark psychology also seeks to comprehend the different thoughts and feelings as well as perceptions that may lead to existing human predatory behavior.

It assumes that the production is natural and purposive and carries some rational and goal-oriented elements at that time.

The remaining percentages under the umbrella of dark psychology refer to the brutalization of the victims without any purposeful intent coupled with a reasonably defined science as well as religious dogma.

In the next century, there will be predators as well as their acts of different actions of theft, violence, coupled with abuse.

It'll become a major global as well as an international epidemic that will affect society. There will also be cyberbullies and sexual predators that will harm different people.

Just as portrayed in the study of dark psychology, abuse is going to become an international phenomenon that will affect every part of the earth.

There will also be a review of all existing deviant behavior on the continuum of depth and purposive intent.

As such, the theory of predators takes up the same framework. However, it revolves around the abuse as well as the assault of different people using information and communications technology.

With that said, egoism, psychopathy, sadism, as well as spitefulness are some of the traits that have been standing in for dark psychology.

Results from a project show that was spearheaded by various scientific researchers also indicated that these traits stand for the dark sides of the human personality.

They are defined as the dark core.

Therefore, if you have one or more of these traits, you are likely to possess others as well. In the world of history, life is full of perfect examples that people are using to exude their characters while acting mercilessly towards others.

Most of these individuals are not only selfish but self-centered.

They are barely supporting their friends and relatives in handling their projects. For that reason, there are different names for such traits.

Some are known as psychopaths, while others are better defined as narcissists.

While at first glance these traits appear to be well defined such that the differences can be seen, and they seem more acceptable at first glance, they also appear to be a bit confusing for learners who are seeking to understand the effects of dark psychology in the community.

As such, most dark traits have been misunderstood by people seeking to learn more about psychology and understand their friends as well as relatives.

New research on the same indicates that other traits that can be categorized in this discipline are such as sadism and spitefulness.

Many dark traits can be comprehended as a major flavored manifestation of the common underlying issue that directs researchers to disposition.

With that said, the dark core of a person's personality is what is defined as the dark psychology.

It implies that if a person is known for having the tendency of exuding these dark traits, they are also likely to have a strong, viable additional trait that has not been discussed yet.

According to research, the common denominator, in this case, is the D- factor which can also be defined as the general main tendency of a person's ability to maximize their utility by disregarding and accepting the disutility of other individuals.

This is usually accompanied by the belief that serves as a justification. In other words, it implies that dark traits can easily be traced back to the tendency of putting one's own objective as well as interests over other people's preferences.

This act is usually to the extent of rejoicing when another person encounters any misfortune in life.

The main intention is to hurt others while pleasing oneself.

The research based on this study indicated that dark traits come along with certain justifications that can generally be understood as different instances of the common core.

While these aspects may be different in different ways, they all sum up to one major trait that is known as the dark psychology.

The justifications point to narcissism since there's an aspect of provocative characters. A psychology professor known as Ingo Zettler has demonstrated how the common denominator applies in the study of dark psychology.

Here are a few factors he pointed out towards egoism, moral disengagement, self-interest, spitefulness, psychopathy, Machiavellianism, and psychological entitlement. These are some of the important elements he realized that needed the input of trained professionals in deciphering the truth behind their effects on humanity.

In a different series of over 2,000 individuals, moderators realized that most people who were asked to what extent they agreed to disagree with sentiments such as it's challenging to delve into projects without being manipulative here and there, and, it's worth the struggle of trying to find out what the project really entails exuded tendencies of aggression as well as impulsivity.

These are the main measures of selfishness as well as unethical characters and behavior.

The researchers also mapped out the main D–factor, which ended up being published in the academic journal of psychological reviews.

The subject can largely be compared to the works of Charles Spearman which were published more than 100 years ago when he stated that people who often score highly in a certain type of intelligence test would most likely score highly in a different test. This is because there is a general aspect of both cases.

In that same way, it was established that the dark elements of the human brain and personality have a certain common denominator which implies that one can easily say that they are in the expression of the dispositional tendency.

For instance, in a person, the dark factor is usually manifested as narcissism and psychopathy.

It may also be any other form of a dark trait such as a combination of the two. However, with the correct mapping of the common denominator, one may easily ascertain that a person has the dark factor in their brain.

This is because the element indicates how likely an individual is to engage in different behaviors linked to one or more of the dark traits.

An individual who exudes some of these traits is likely to carry some elements of malevolent behavior, too.

They are likely to humiliate other people by cheating, lying, as well as stealing. The updated nine dark traits aren't the same.

They may also result in various kinds of characters. Nonetheless, at the core of these traits, every trait can majorly result in certain kinds of behaviors that end up setting them apart from the rest.

The dark traits in a person are not the same for everyone.

Every element in those traits differs in different persons.

At the core of the characters, the dark traits have common elements that may end up setting them apart.

Knowledge regarding this dark core can also play an important role in the life of researchers as well as therapists who often work with specified people in assessing the existing dark personalities in individuals.

As it may be, the dark trait and factor that affects various types of reckless as well as malicious person's behaviors in addition to actions have often been reported on media. For instance, it has been seen in extreme cases, that many of these cases involve people who lie and manipulate others, thereby ending up killing them.

It has also been established that some of these people with the D-factor of characters have ended up deceiving officials in the public sector.

Here, vast and extensive knowledge regarding a person's D-factor can be a useful tool in assessing a person's traits in the long run.

Also, it's going to be used against them in order to prevent them from taking more actions against humanity.

A Major Fact Box of Dark Psychology

Dark psychology is a powerful force that works in the real world today. It's one of those factors that majorly control the world in many ways.

It's used by the world's most powerful influencers to control most of the actions taking place in different scenes, including politics, the health sector, and the entire economy generally. It is also one of the main forces behind different industries across the world.

Dark psychology has been applied by professionals who are aware of its implications in the world and its economy.

You should not be at risk of receiving the actions of those people who understand this game better.

As such, many people are encouraged to find the real meaning of this subject before associating with other people in different matters.

Every chapter of this book seeks to identify the traits involved in dark psychology while addressing some of the impending issues that need to be dealt with.

In the long run, these chapters also address some of the main applications of dark psychology not only as a subject but a trait in many people who would like to manipulate others.

In the subject of dark psychology, ideas are usually illuminated using various examples in order to make the duty of comprehending the actual factors slightly easier.

Besides, the chapters of discussion also have case studies as well as useful profiles on the existing types of people who have utilized black magic in order to get through life every other day.

As a learner, you're likely to come across different studies that analyze the application of dark psychology in matters of real life.

Once you have lifted one curtain up, there will be no going back as you'll be left studying the remaining chapters of the book while seeking the real truth of the subject matter.

You will also have a clear understanding of the issues affecting the center of humanity, especially when it comes to seeking the truth about how people treat each other.

People with dark market traits are often considered to be callous, cold, dishonest, as well as impulsive in every action they take.

At their workplaces, these individuals can easily endanger the eventual success of their teams while seeking to become the best versions of themselves in order to be identified as winners in the long run. Also, one other popular conception is that they may risk the lives of their team members without their knowledge.

This implies that such individuals should be separated from society. They are not only psychopaths but harmful individuals who can easily harm their families, too. Some people with such traits can also be slightly different.

Research indicates that such individuals may also tend to be slightly normal in different cases.

As such, they may end up having two personalities that come together to form psychopaths. While they can occur together, they really don't have to.

Regarding this matter, some people have argued that psychology is a matter of common sense.

Others have stated that it's a matter of answering one question with another. As it may turn out, many psychologists understand more than they answer. They also seek to address underlying issues that people affected by the subject may not be in a position to address of look at in any way.

Psychologists barely rely on the evasive tactics, especially when someone asks a direct question that seeks a direct answer.

They have a tremendously well-established knowledge reservoir where they can draw important knowledge based on the needs of their people.

Psychology is also a fascinating element in science. Understanding the existing reasons as to why some people have certain behaviors as well as their mysteries and personalities is a subject that needs to be addressed at length.

Secrets of Psychology

Secret 1

Therapy is a viable treatment method that has worked for many individuals seeking to receive treatment in the psychological department.

It does not have to last indefinitely. The existing misconceptions regarding therapy are very rampant in the media fraternity.

Nonetheless, the most vital factor, in the long run, is that these misconceptions are hardly advertised.

Also, at the same time, the misconceptions regarding therapy majorly portray it as the base of the ongoing process that may go on for decades.

In order for therapy to be defined as being effective in the industry, some elements need to be present.

This discipline is also known as the therapeutic alliance. Short, focused therapeutic interventions last 8 to 10 weeks.

They are also used successfully in treating various symptoms such as mood disorders as well as anxiety.

Secret 2

The second secret covers the six degrees separation, which was a concept of the past that was invented by a professional psychologist.

The secret is psychological trivia. In some movie, the play seeks to address a common study conducted by Stanley Milgram, who was a psychologist known for his research regarding obedience to authority.

His studies identified the Small World Experiment that used some chain letter method in establishing the average length of chains found between random people in the United States of America.

Secret 3

A professional serving in the psychological sector doesn't need a lie detector to tell if someone is not telling the truth.

If one needs to know if their friend is making up some lie to cover up a canceled date or if the co-worker has been talking about someone behind their back, there is no need to get a polygraph machine. According to psychologists, there is a viable system to tell if someone is telling lies.

This is appended to their breathing rate and blood pressure.

Their sweating hands can also determine this. The face and the palpation of the eyes can also tell a lot regarding the truth or lie.

The micro-expressions of a person's eyes are the most impossible ones to disguise. If you understand where you should look, therefore, you'll be in a position to spot any forms of deception.

This is especially specific if the individual does not make the professional use of a psychologist's input in telling the lies.

You may also use psychology in sniffing an online liar. This is going to be successful with the application of the input of a professional psychologist.

Secret 4

If you don't manage to encode successfully, you may not be in a position to retrieve it. Many people go through various memory failures that are not appended to the fact that they forget what they knew in the past. These issues are largely linked to the fact that they didn't know the information. This is a fact that's easily demonstrated and highlighted using the penny experiment. You can try to remember all the existing details of a penny. You can recall the date and what's on its back.

What can you see or what have you seen in the past? Supposing you're a coin collector, then you'll be stumped. The main issue is that people don't really pay attention to the problems affecting society. If you attempt to recall where you placed something that you may have lost, perhaps the best strategy, in this case, is to think of what you were up to when you were putting the item away. One second is enough to help you in encoding your attention and making sure that it pays off instantly. This is while trying to dredge the information from long-term memory.

Secret 5

Many of life crises can be overrated to some extent. For instance, adolescents encounter painful as well as destructive life seasons. The existing mid-life crises often stress middle-aged adults and burdened by the fact of being in the sandwich generation. Right? Babies end up spending most of their lives missing their mothers as well as fathers. They may also be unable to cope with such separation. These are life crises that can happen to anyone in the world. However, the fact is that they don't. Prominent psychology's mentality will often over-emphasize the extent to which such issues affect humanity.

Others will also highlight how these issues have impacted other people's lives to the extent of hurting them in one way or the other. As such, it has become vital for people to focus on the research of psychological issues and how they are attached to the human character. Therefore, these individuals are often in a position to withstand separation. On the other hand, adolescents can explore other life's alternatives. Middle-aged individuals don't really feel sandwiched in the long run.

Secret 6

Psychological studies hardly involve deception. Like you read in Secret 2, Stanley Milgram was known for his extensive psychological studies that focused on obedience to authoritative elements. Participants held to the fact that they were shocking a different human being.

They also didn't find out until their experiment was completed. The research study has since been the most prominent psychological investigation that involved deception. It's factual that a number of different psychological studies in the current world could not be conducted unless there was some element of deception involved.

Nonetheless, the majority of existing psychological, social experiments are completely transparent in their objective. The American Psychological Association is known for having a code that spells out various conditions that psychologists need to abide by, especially when they carry out experiments on animals as well as humans. It was discussed that one of the main conditions with humans entails informed consent where risks, as well as benefits and other additional conditions, are discussed and explain prior to the extensive study of humans as well as animals.

One of the main conditions involves informed consent where risks, as well as benefits and other additional conditions, are vastly explained before the outset of the study. In a different debriefing, which demands that researchers have to reveal their reason for conducting the study after extensive research, it was highlighted that hospitals and other sponsored institutions that carried out research could specifically have ethical conditions that can protect their participants.

Secret 7

In this chapter of analysis, it has been discussed that the saltier the soup, the more challenging it will be for one to taste the main difference when more salt is added. In a report issued by the psychological department of the American studies, it was stated that the Weber's Law tells the difference in threshold between two major existing principles of two levels of stimulus where one is harder to detect the stronger version against the value of the stimulus.

There's often a mathematical function that will describe the existing relationship between stimulus intensity as well as the main difference in the threshold. This indicates that when people become deceptive, it becomes easy to tell the difference in the stimulus. This is often the reason why when you have a salty bowl of soup, you need to add more salt in order to sense some taste. The same is usually true when it comes to lighting a room. A match in the dark room is often easy to see.

But a match in an already lit space isn't easy to see. As such, even when it comes to sound, if the music is pretty loud, you will need to increase the volume in order to hear the existing difference.

According to Weber's law, which majorly reinforces what the world of psychology understands regarding sensation as well as perception, our senses do not record the nature of the stimulus on the face value and actual basis. Instead, the brain largely interacts with the eyes, nose, as well as ears and other sensory organs in order to have a major influence in the way perception is done.

Secret 8

In Chapter 8, the researchers indicate that it is essential to use or lose it. The phrase is originally coined by the sex researchers known as Masters and Johnson at a point when they were discussing various issues regarding aging as well as sexuality.

Of course, this applies to various areas of life, such as outside the bedroom.

Researchers who often study and analyze the aging process have also repeatedly demonstrated the possibilities of hanging onto your cognitive abilities through exercising the brain.

The types of mental gymnastics can be presented in several various forms such as board games, chess, bridge, in addition to teasers.

In cases where you'd like to benefit the body physically, you can take advantage of the strategies such as workouts and dance.

If these two seem slightly strenuous, a short walking workout can also provide you with the required dose. In other words, psychologists have a secret to help in keeping the brain in its topmost functioning position and state.

This can assist you in staying on top of your game. This is regardless of your age.

Secret 9

People aren't as logical as they are. This is demonstrated by the illogic nature of the mind of the human being as presented by psychologists. In social psychology, personality psychology, as well as behavioral economics, it has been discussed that there are several examples of the existent errors in the thought of waves. For instance, everyone understands that to some extent, horoscopes can't really help in the prediction of the future happenings.

They also can't predict the possibilities of something happening in life. Yet, via the Barnum Effect, it has been established that genetic predictions are made from the horoscopes.

Therefore, the feedback from the magazine quizzes coupled with the mind-reading portfolios plays a role in contributing to the experiments spearheaded by stage magicians.

The logical abilities are often challenges beyond their recognition by slightly simple tests that need people to use their cognitive skills in seeking the right answers to life's most challenging questions.

When it comes to the issue of decision making in life, people are often fooled by the obvious cues, including the size of the plate as well as the color. In the long run, we need to know better. However, we don't.

Secret 10
There is a correlation that can easily equal causation, mainly if the required techniques are applied.

This is a well-identified fact in the scientific method since it can only be used in various experimental studies that can demonstrate causation.

The question, what's really up with the secret? While looking at it, correlational statistics went through a significant retooling a few years back.

It is, therefore, possible to utilize the sophisticated modeling techniques in performing various miracles such as controlling for confounding variables and drawing arrows that indicate directionality of the effects as well as charting complicated relationships over some period of time.

It's factual that correlational studies are always going to be flawed. As such, a correlation of hostility with a person's blood pressure can easily be conducted by any existing number of intervening variables such as smoking, strained personal relationships, in addition to genetics.

Also, when a person throws in such variables into some modern statistical program, they may be in a position to overcome the existing correlational studies limitations. It's also clear that people will never be in a position to manipulate another person's hostility levels in a social experiment.

However, it's possible to successfully improve on the impending issues affecting society by plotting the problem against the other elements that raise personality issues in people.

Also, it's vital to note that the next time a person decides to learn the actual results of a correlational study; they may find themselves regarding the findings with some aspect of respect.

This is as long as the research study has properly been conducted. With that said, it's also important to note that some people actually enjoy such facts of psychology.

Therefore, if you've enjoyed this chapter, feel free to explore other related postings that cite the elements of psychology and their impact on humanity. It's also vital to look at all the factors of psychology that could be having a direct relationship with dark psychology in the long run.

These facts can apply to your daily life since they have been studied and proven to have a direct impact on different people's lives, including how they face different life's challenges.

It's also factual that such issues have a direct impact on people's ability to make decisions regardless of their life's situations.

Therefore, everyone needs to be keen on the issues that affect their daily lives in order to find the underlying factors.

Chapter 3: The Dark Side of Your Personality

Dark psychology is also the analysis of the human condition, including its relation to the psychological nature of human beings who like to prey upon others. All human nature has the ability to victimize other humans and animals successfully.

As such, although many restrain the tendency or character, some will take action upon their feelings and impulses.

Dark psychology is a discipline that seeks to study the tendencies as well as the production of some rational and goal-oriented motivation based on the time.

The 1 percent that remains under the dark psychology refers to the brutal victimization of other people without having a reasonably defined evolution of science as well as religious dogma. It's evident that dark psychology is also related to various subjects and terminologies such as the arsonist who is an individual who is obsessed with fire setting.

Such people will have developmental histories that have sexual as well as physical abuse.

Common to these traits are individuals who also have been linked to serial killing and loners. Some of these people have few peers.

They are also fascinated by fire as well as their methodologies of setting these fires. Also largely preoccupied with fire setting, fire setters often fantasize as well as fixating over how they can plan their schemes which are largely related to fire setting.

They will set their targets on fire and experience some sexual arousal while proceeding with episodes of masturbation in order to please themselves and feel satisfied with their encounters with the fires.

As such, these individuals also seek to have some pleasure in the long run. They will watch as they take turns while pleasuring themselves.

This occurs in instances where there are groups of obsessed individuals. Over the years, it has been noted that such people have also been in a position to explore their psychological and pathological patterns, which include ritualistic patterns that serial arsonists have been involved in. As such, they feel proud of their actions. Thanatophilia, Necrologies, in addition to Necrophilia, are just some of the definitions that are appended to dark psychology in the segment of obsessed arsonists. These people exist.

They have a major sexual attraction to dead bodies. The main point of diagnostic as well as a statistical manual of the mental illness founded and published by the American Research Psychiatric Association puts this type of character and personality as a preoccupation that has objects, situations, as well as individuals that are mainly not part of the normative stimulation.

These people can easily cause distress as well as pressing issues that may end up affecting the people they are closely related with. It's also clear that these people can cause distress to their societies.

Therefore, a Necrophiles is a person who is sexually aroused by using an object, which in this case is a deceased person. Experts who have successfully compiled various profiles of Necrophiles have indicated that they have tremendous challenges when it comes to experiencing a certain capacity of intimacy with other people. For such individuals, sexual intimacy with dead bodies feels safer as well as more secure because they don't have an emotional attachment with other people.

As such, they have divulged their feelings to the dead in order to have some control over the universe. In the company of a deceased person, these people feel like they have a sense of control over something. Therefore, they end up taking some action in order to delight themselves. With that said also, these people lack the basis of self-control when interacting with real human beings. Necrophiles are also known for divulging during interviews since they have some feeling of control when it comes to connecting with actual humans. This, to them, often translates into an excellent feeling of control. As such, some sense of connection also becomes a secondary element to the initial need for control.

The iPredator

The iPredator is always known as a child. It could also be a group of adults who engage in various psychological as well as physical victimization and theft as well as disparagement. They are always motivated by malice, spite, and peer pressure, in addition to criminal and deviant intent by the application of technological and telecommunication objects. iPredators are also known to be driven by deviant sexual fantasies and aggressive desire for control and retribution, religious fanaticism, in addition to political as well as psychological distortions.

Personal, as well as monetary gains, also motivate them. These individuals can also be of any age as well as sex. Regardless of the persons they are, neither bound by the social-economic status or by their racial-national heritage, they can be from any society. With that said, such people are exposed to terrible societal character and they are also driven by the need to become overly obsessive in a way that can be harmful to others in the same society.

In the next century, it's going to be clear that such individuals, together with their characters of violence as well as theft and abuse will be international in terms of influencing the world of dark psychology. Therefore, they are likely to take over the world and impose their actions on other people in the long run. Just as suggested by dark psychology, these people are going to be a squashing epidemic of different societies. Other than that, they are also going to take over the remaining parts of the world as the main controllers who seek to interfere with any on-going projects that are being presented in different sectors of the world.

They will also be at warfare with the remaining world. As the dark psychology chapter suggests, it's going to be important and reasonable for such people to take over the world and control the main dockets that have an impact on the health care sector and other businesses. All criminals herein have deviant characters that need to be contained by the use of psychologist professionals. The offender may be a cyberstalker or a cyber harasser. It could also be a cybercriminal or an online sexual predator or terrorist who is looking for a prey. The person could also be a consumer or a distributor engaged in the online retail business. They fall within the category of an iPredator who will harm someone in the society.

There are three main criteria of defining a person who is in this category, and they include a person with some element of self-awareness that forces them to cause harm to others. This could be directly as well as indirectly. It could also be a person that uses information technology in gaining viable information about someone and using the information to harm others in the long run. The person could also be an individual who seeks to have a general understanding of the cyber stealth and then to use it to stalk as well as engage a target in the form of a friend.

The character can use the garnered information to delve into different activities that profile others while identifying them and locating a target. Unlike most human predators, before the information age, these iPredators highly rely on the use of multitude benefits and advantages provided by information technology to gain a platform where they can exchange information that seemingly defines their success in gaining access to viable data. As such, these individuals also seek to use the existing data to exchange current information that can guide them into accessing what they prefer to use in gaining information in the long run.

Habitually, these individuals use their technological ability to reach to destroy the peace that humanity has sought to create in the world. They also use ICT in different abstracts to manipulate others online while taking notes about their whereabouts, including how to destroy their families. iPredators will attempt to create as well as sustain complete anonymity as they involve themselves in different ICT activities while planning their assault meeting.

The team will hold a meeting to discuss and investigate the innovative surveillance technologies as well as researching the social profiles of their victims. Also concurrent with the known concept of Cyber Stealth, iPredator victims use their aptitude to target minors and adults. They can do so online and offline using their psychological weaknesses and technological surveillance and capabilities. This helps in increasing their chances of success, including criminal ramifications, and cyber-attack.

The Necrophilia

Necrophilia is also known as the necrophilism or necrolagnia. This is a sexual attraction involving dead bodies. It's often classified as a prominent paraphilia by the American Psychiatric Association. In a research report by Rosman and Resnick, it was established that there were 34 cases of people who were obsessed with having sex with the deceased. These people reported the habitual desire to have sex with dead bodies in order to feel as if they were taking charge of something or someone. They resisted actual partners, reunions, or a romantic relationship with their significant other.

They also sought self-esteem by indulging in such characters. In the long run, they were found to enjoy being with a homicide victim. This was a pretty sad state of affairs that led professionals to seek the help of well-established psychologists who can support the well being of different people in society who were at risk of associating with such individuals. While at it, these people liked to express their power over homicide victims. They were perceived as loners who have deep-seated forces that control their decision-making capabilities. As highlighted earlier in these chapters, the arsonist is well known for finding pleasure in being a serial killer. They found gratification from the fire setting processes.

While these episodes of setting the fire seemed erroneously precarious, they also delved into the project to seek some enjoyment at that moment. It was later discussed that such people can definitely cause harm to other people. This implies that their objective is finding joy in harming others. For one serial arsonist, perhaps the big payoff is finding pride in the distorted perception of inflicting pain as well as bodily harm in others. As such, it has become important to address such issues in society.

The character of the arsonist is highly reprehensible and precarious. However, typically, it does not involve any form of premeditated murder. These people often live within some comfort of internal obsession. Even though the train is not focused on causing a lot of pain to another person as well as victimizing them, the actions of these people are bizarre. They are also absent for some significant period of time when there's no element of logic. The need for perceived control is also seen as insidious to the extent of developing a sexual connection with a corpse. The character of the arsonist is not only reprehensible but precarious in every way.

It also does not entail premeditated murder. These people are just obsessed with killing. Therefore, they focus on subjecting others to pain. The serial killer, on the other hand, is referred to as an individual who murders more than three people over 30 days. During interviews with such individuals, it has been discovered that most of them tend to cool off after killing. The killer's period of cooling off is directly appended to the fact that there's a consistent refractory period in which they are certainly satiated with their demand and feelings to cause some pain to other people.

In the process of killing, these people are usually in pursuit of achieving some gratification, which can only be found brutally in their world. After murdering, these people feel some sense of relaxation and release from a bondage that needed them to kill. They also feel some sense of gratification since they have now become wanton of the feeling as well as experience of releasing extra gratification. The term serial killings refer to a number of killings that have been committed in the US having common traits that may suggest there is a reasonable possibility that these crimes were committed by the same individual. Sexual assault, as well as rape, humiliation, and torture, are some of the issues involved during the course of these reported murders.

As such, experts have admitted that other motivations besides anger, attention-seeking, and monetary gain, in addition to rage are some of the traits that accompany these killings. Eventually, serial killers will exhibit similar characteristics and patterns while seeking to cause harm to victims. These patterns can be used in assessing and evaluating their characters and progress in the long run.

Chapter 4: Inside the Minds of Controlling People

Perhaps you have been wondering what makes people who are overly controlling tick? Well, these individuals seem to spend their time bossing others around. The character in bossing might range from direct as well as explicit imperatives. These individuals may say things such as I want that book dropped on my desk immediately. Others may utter words such as put more salt on the steak since it'll taste great. Others may also command their friends as well as relatives to take up some classes in the belief that these individuals can become successful in their quest for a better life.

In the long run, such individuals will be asked to delve into tasking projects that may end up helping them to be better persons. Sometimes if the other person objects, it may seem like they are unreasonable to some extent. With that said, what really separates such a person from that best friend from the bully? What's the difference? As it turns out, the bullies, as well as besties, are slightly alike. They both want things to be done as they please. However, this is an ongoing process that helps in ensuring that the world perfectly matches internal ideas for everyone.

With how people are going about their business, some may apply identical methods to attack issues. The businesses may also be approached in the same manner. However, when it comes to controlling and manipulating people, this is usually a psychological issue that is appended to the dark psychology and its secrets. Usually, the agenda for bullies is to involve other people in their actions. They majorly focus on other's characters, especially when it comes to making them feel miserable about themselves.

They also have a certain view regarding how things need to occur or unfold in the long run. As such, these people do what they like. They are also determined to pursue their demands and the need to satiate their need to successfully frustrate people by their character and ability to delve into decision making. Friends, as well as other people whom you may not think of as controlling, also have certain views regarding the ways in which some things should be done. The main difference is that people have different views regarding how others should behave.

There's also a major difference in opinion. Therefore, as an individual, it becomes important to weigh such issues and come up with a viable idea that can be passed across respectfully. However, this is not usual for control freaks that are committed to frustrating people. Such individuals are usually focused on making others feel bad about themselves, and this is usually through controlling them. Also, friends, as well as other people who may not be regarded as controlling individuals, have certain views regarding the manner in which things need to be done. Their views are standard and reflect the need to be positive about many things in society, including how to approach matters. They may also have views regarding how to conduct themselves in different situations.

Over and above, maybe that is the main difference between real friends and control freaks who seek to manipulate and control others. The bully is known to have defined and well-fixed ideas regarding how the result should be acquired in the long run. On the other hand, besties seek to highlight key areas where an individual needs help in order to improve in either life or career in general. The ultimate outcome is based on assisting one person to become a better version of themselves. Also, such people recognize that there are different ways to gain access to positive vibes in the overall chase for a better life.

And maybe this is the main difference between toxic people and good-hearted individuals. So, therefore, what's really inside the mind of a controlling person? A lot of objectives is the right answer to this question. We might also think of their ideas outcomes, wants, demands, expectations, standards, coupled with should in the long run. The objectives of bullies and dictators, as well as manipulative people, tend to be based on making the right way for themselves in such a way that people should think or dress just as they do. Such differences may be illuminated and illustrated using an example of classrooms as well as teachers.

As such, a teacher, as well as most scholars, would think of as an individual who is controlling is the one who aspires to see students take certain actions in school. They enjoy seeing students sitting in a certain way as they look into a particular direction while producing a certain amount of work. These individuals may think that there is the right way of doing things in school. They may also think that there is a specific hairstyle that every student needs to have. Teachers who do not seem to be this controlling are often more relaxed when it comes to addressing the posture of students while they are writing as well as the particular attire that they need to wear.

These tutors are more interested in the academic performance of their students and not how they eat or dress. In the last research analysis, individuals who have been bossing other students around and those who probably care about how students will score excellent grades are totally different. The main difference in these people is that one group is more focused on how students will make it in the future while the other team is more focused on how they dress or run or even present themselves while not in school.

This is a perfect social experiment for different people. Such teachers are also more interested in their student's educational outcomes more than how they fair on as individuals seeking to create friends in the institution. In the last chapter of research and analysis, it was discussed that those who are interested in bossing others around as well as those who are looking forward to keeping friends have different traits and personalities. They are probably seeking the same aim in the long run. Therefore, the main difference is that autocrats are known for making their jobs slightly harder. By pedantically making various specifications of how other people need to behave, these individuals are building upon their traits and tearing down other people's ability to focus on their lives.

Therefore, they are likely to irritate each other in the long run. They two sets of individuals also don't get along because one is always obsessed with following the other and finding out how they lived in order to irk them. It all boiled down to getting to understand what would annoy the other person in the long run. As such, even the individuals who we often think of as people who are not as controlling are pretty much controlling to the extent of ruining other's lives in many ways. They aspire to realize what the outcome of their actions would be when it comes to issuing controlling elements in other people's lives.

In regards to wanting to find out what a certain outcome would entail, but always leaning on a more relaxed version of oneself, these manipulative individuals seem to appreciate the fact that if they highlighted issues about the final destination and then delved into certain discussions, there would be the need to specify all the impending actions needed for an individual to get there. With all that has been said and highlighted in regard to how manipulative some individuals may be, the need to be controlling on others may not make some sense right now; especially not to you.

If you are a person who enjoys life and loves others, including friends and family, you would not want to control anyone. Even if you are in the behavior of being perfect, you will remain in your own space and not someone else's. Therefore, controllers are in the world to ruin life for everyone. They would like to micromanage other people, including what someone says, how they act, what they think, in addition to what they would like to eat or have in an event. Such individuals ruin the chances of someone making new friends.

They also want to impose their beliefs on you. You cannot be yourself around such people. They often insist on becoming your top priority. Also, they want to influence your life in all ways they could even if it would be in a negative way. Such people might also push all your buttons in order to get an emotional reaction out of your peaceful self. This is simply because they would like to exploit you at your weakest points. They also have no respect for your boundaries.

There are different theories that highlight reasons as to why someone would want to have major control over you. One highlights the fact that people who cannot control themselves often become suspects of controlling others. This occurs on an emotional level where people seek to take control of others who seem weaker in character in their opinion. When a person is insecure to the extent of seeking comfort in other people's misfortunes, it becomes obvious for them to seek some sense of positivity from others since they have low self-esteem. Therefore, such individuals can also hide their despair in other people since they will be looking for somewhere to dispose of their disappointment. As such, maybe control freaks are scared of being abandoned for their miserable character and desperation.

They do not really feel secure in any type of relationship. Therefore, to seek comfort in life, they tend to lean towards becoming control freaks in other people's lives. Perhaps the main paradox is that these people's character creates what they may fear the most. Controlling people are also known as narcissists. They aspire to control the environment they live in by any means possible. That would imply that other people are treated as pawns. The main issue with this perspective is that these controlling bullies will make others wonder why they have been selected as pawns. If it is nothing personal, why do such people feel like the main target of the issue being highlighted?

The main reason is the person is not just good but admirable. There is really nothing wrong with them. As such, they don't really have a target on their back, and they don't deserve to be disrespected in any way. Simply analyzed, there is nothing wrong with these individuals. They are only a target for people who have issues with themselves. The controller is the party that seeks to control everyone and everything around them. Eventually, then, we have some element of being control freaks to some extent. The main difference is that there are some of these control freaks who we would rather avoid. Then, there are others who would rather get to understand and be friends with. It turns out that the main issue is not control but the need to display some sense of control in public for the person to be seen. Others just want to form strong fragment social bonds.

Subtypes of Narcissists

It's not easy to be in a superior position to everyone. Someone once said so. As such, narcissism has already been defined as a person's tendency to consider themselves as superior as well as entitled with the ability to marginalize and demean other people in order for them to feel good about themselves. In the "I" centered status-conscious as well as the materialistic society; such people have become toxic to society, thereby leading to highly destructive environments. Narcissists aren't really the same. Some are known to be chronic, while others have a manipulative tendency. Therefore, there are subtypes of narcissists arranged in different unique orders that many people should familiarize themselves with in order to get hold of certain traits that could be destructive to others. It's also vital for people to be aware of how such individuals can affect their lives in order to avoid being disappointed in the long run. These are the different types of narcissists:

Over Narcissist

An over narcissist is an individual who possesses several of the most common traits appended to narcissism. They include grandiosity, attention-seeking, exaggeration, excessive self-importance, charm, one-upmanship, negative put-downs, in addition to blatant entitlement and aggressive manipulation. Generally, such individuals often exude some element of a strident lack of empathy towards people. Specifically, only what they think is of value and importance. That is what matters to them most of the time. They also expect everything to be done according to their wishes since they think that the world revolves around them.

You could be sick, but their question would be what if you could drive them to the mall? Such people have a buried personality that they fail to express in the actual sense. They also fail to express themselves in truth as a response to early injuries. They have replaced such elements with highly developed compensatory falsehood. This alternate personality to the actual self is grandiose. Such people are self-absorbed. The over narcissist is also raging with anger within. They have passive aggression towards other people.

The Introverted Narcissist

The introvert is also known as the convert. This individual will often use statements such as they cry since other people are stupid. That often makes them sad. With that said, not all narcissists are really grandiose or offensive. Some are pretty calculative when it comes to pinpointing other people's issues and using their problems to attack others. Also important to note is the fact that many authors have successfully identified this type of person. Their traits include but aren't limited to self-absorption, the lack of empathy, smugness as well as quietness, and the need to judge other people harshly.

Although the introverted narcissist is usually misunderstood most of the time, these individuals take pride in their shy and quiet nature. They are overly obtrusive when it comes to demonstrating their false superiority complex. They will successfully subtly manifest their hidden conceit. Most of the time, it will be something like not really not saying it but demonstrating their actual actions using their smirk as well as body language. It's vital to note that not all introverts are really manipulative in any way. This is just a subtype of narcissism and can be categorized under people who would rather use their personality to hurt others.

The individuals who may have influence over others around them can make them feel slightly unaccepted in the society. What introvert and extrovert manipulative persons share in common when it comes to character is the fact that they hide their real character in order to gain access to their next target. They also seek to plot calculative moves on their friends and relatives with the need to satiate their hunger in the long run. In many ways, these individuals seek to use their personality against others while trying to harm their friends as well as relatives. Therefore, they end up harming others. They always think that they are better than others too. The extroverted one is always so quick to point it out, but the introverted one will silently display these feelings while looking down upon the others. That is the main other difference between an introverted as well as an extroverted manipulative individual in this category. Here are additional traits of introverts with the main reference to psychology and manipulation.

- Quiet Smugness/Superiority

Many of extroverted narcissists are easy to spot. They have an extra grandiose of mannerism coupled with attention-seeking traits that match machinations. On the other hand, introverted narcissists are pretty more challenging to pinpoint when it comes to analyzing and understanding their true characters and origin. This is at least at the outset of everything when someone is still seeking to understand them. In the long run, these individuals are keen on silently manipulating others and taking advantage of them by making sure that they are taken advantage of. While they may not express their negative minds outright, you'll be in a position to successfully analyze their characters based on their ability to control or manipulate you.

Such individuals also have the tendency to yawn as well as a groan or sigh in the presence of other people. When they take any form of action, including speaking, their comments begin to critically take some certain sense of direction while focusing on their concerted views. This is a seemingly impenetrable smugness that is a front covering a sense of vulnerability in these individuals. Therefore, it's vital for victims to be aware of such personalities before they become part and parcel of their lives, especially in this current century. Part of these people's insecurity is usually the inability to relate to other people meaningfully as other human beings successfully.

- Self-absorption

Don't be fooled by covert narcissism. These individuals are as dangerous as any other subtype of narcissists. Some may highly emphasize one personality more than the other. A person with an outgoing personality can easily show-off. They may also need to be at the center of everything since they are pretty much attention-seeking. A person with an outgoing personality may be very narcissistic when it comes to bullying and victimizing others. They may also become stubborn when it comes to initiating successful projects either at work or school because such people are driven by the fact that they can easily destroy others in a blink of an eye.

At the same time, these individuals want to work with people who have no control over their lives. They want to be the center of attention when it comes to initiating peaceful projects. They are majorly attracted to self-centeredness since they wish to take over every project but in the wrong way. Such individuals are not pushed by the need to address issues in a positive manner in the society. Instead, they are focused on how they can change their lives by harming others in every way that they can. Some of these people are self-absorbed individuals who are not easily identified. Some of them are also focused on challenging individuals in different ways that may seem manipulative.

On the surface, it can be challenging to identify these people. They can appear to be pretty shy and anxious. They can also look humble. You should not be confused by these characters because they are just on the surface. The actual person lies in the self-absorption nature of the individual who seeks to manipulate everything to suit their gains. Their gratification can also be pretty indirect through their emotional investment in a different person. With that said, it becomes challenging to decipher the traits of a person, especially when they have been hiding their true traits. They take things personally, in many cases.

They feel distrustful and mistreated as well as unappreciated. An individual with an outgoing trait may always show off because they need to be the center of attention in different ways. As such, it may be impossible to seek help from these people because they are likely to judge you. Such individuals may also come across as bullies. They may be entitled playboys or authoritative people who may be over-excited with becoming over-controlling over other people's lives. On the surface, it can be challenging to identify these people.

They can appear to be pretty shy and anxious. They can also look humble. You should not be confused by these characters because they are just on the surface. The actual person lies in the self-absorption nature of the individual who seeks to manipulate everything to suit their gains. Their gratification can also be pretty indirect through their emotional investment in a different person. With that said, it becomes challenging to decipher the traits of a person, especially when they have been hiding their true traits. They take things personally, in many cases. They feel distrustful and mistreated as well as unappreciated.

They often dream of greatness even though they understand that they cannot accomplish such success in real life. Some public figures and celebrities exude traits of extroverted narcissists. These are people who completely crave attention. According to radio host Dr. Wendy Walsh, this is not accepted in the industry of entertainment. It's actually a requirement since it provides the people with a higher rating. Either way, these people still make it to the list of individuals with a narcissistic personality disorder.

This is particularly when wanting admiration and lacking empathy as well as feeling entitled in matters that don't concern the. They are still self-centered since they expect special treatment from everyone they interact with.

They also often feel that others don't fully appreciate their specialness. As such, they may tell their friends as well as relatives that feel unappreciated and misunderstood. They may also say things such as people have not fully recognized and respected their unique nature when it comes to matters of handling business or any other project. Either way, these people still make it to the list of individuals with a narcissistic personality disorder.

This is particularly when wanting admiration and lacking empathy as well as feeling entitled in matters that don't concern the. They are still self-centered since they expect special treatment from everyone they interact with.

Many introverts are known to be quiet. They are good listeners too. However, these are not narcissists since they don't have a manipulative personality that can drive someone away.

With the latter, they will make a reticent as well as a poor listener. They will also make a very quick assessment of a person and tend to be slow to help others. Others may block you out of their lives because they are known to be selfish. In this case, they can be identified as individuals who hide their real and true characters in order to be in a position to harm others with their silent treatment.

While many mature adults are good at recognizing such tendencies, these introverts can be too manipulative for someone to recognize their true colors and decipher their personality.

As such, others find it interesting to tell and define the character of these individuals in order to evade encountering issues that can affect their relationships.

Introverted manipulative people will make a quick assessment of someone and end up becoming disinterested in helping them to become better versions of themselves. Such people will agree to things and then up not following through.

They will, later on, pretend to have forgotten or pretended that there was no agreement. With that said, it's important to note that all people with narcissistic nature and character are manipulative in many ways.

Covert or introverted narcissists are known to add some element of self-pity into their lives in order for them to get away with some character or behavior. Instead of directly putting others down, they may express envy.

This is also another way of controlling others in their lives. Because of their introversion, these individuals will brag silently about their life's accomplishments. They will act aloof as well as disinterested in making dismissive as well as discounting gestures such as sighing, yawning, and acting bored.

Although all people with such traits react poorly when it comes to criticism, the introverted narcissist will be a bit more sensitive.

They will also have the thinnest skin when it comes to addressing some issues affecting family or friends. This implies that they are not only dismissive but extra exploitative by nature. Instead of aggressive manipulation, they will delve into hypersensitivity coupled with anxiety in order to persecute the victims.

Usually, the danger in dealing with such people is failing to see through their façade since they are slightly overly passive.

They can also be destructive in nature to the point of running relationships. The emotional abuse that these people carry can be more silent.

However, it will always wear the other person down because they will feel demoralized. Their needs and demands for attention will also be discounted as well as ignored in the long run. Their victims can get sucked into attempting to console themselves or trying to help the manipulative person.

And even when attempting to assist these people, there is no way you can successfully fill their emptiness or create a different perspective in their mentality. Also, the self-esteem of the victim will gradually depreciate as they associate with such individuals. This type of person lacks empathy for other people. They will do anything possible to maintain some power over you.

Their pain, as well as demands, will always take precedence. Therefore, you'll be left fleeing alone if not neglected.

Extrovert narcissists, on the other hand, will act covertly if only to pout and get the better of their part of their victims in order to manipulate them in the long run. Do not get caught up in the different definitions of the psychological issues of manipulation. If your feelings are discounted, or if you feel manipulated, you can see a therapist in order to learn how to deal with the behavior.

- Lack of Empathy

While both the introverted and extroverted narcissists share this common trait, it's more inclined towards the introverted individual.

These people are usually oblivious to, and dismissive of other's thoughts as well as feelings. When you tell and try to discuss their attitude with them, their responses will be centered on themselves. That's where self-absorption comes in as a trait.

- Passive-Aggressiveness

Some of these introverted manipulative people deal with people who don't agree with them on some issues. Therefore, they exude the passive-aggressive nature. When they receive a reasonable request from you, they may end up saying things such as yes and of course. Others use a defense mechanism in order to fail to commit the cause. When you ask if they are in or out of a deal, they tend to give a passive answer that does not really confirm their actual side of the story or situation. When you try to find out why they didn't follow through an arrangement, these individuals may shrug a little with an excuse. They may also say that their way is always better than other people's. Now that you know what it takes to decipher the character of an introverted narcissist, how will you deal with these individuals? Most of us know how to spot such people.

While it does not feel good to be insulted, criticized, or belittled, at least, it's vital to know that you are hurting in some way. Nonetheless, at times, the people who are around us, such as friends and relatives, make us feel bad about ourselves. We may not be in a position to point out why. For instance, a colleague may fail to say hello to you when you meet. This can be utterly out of their own will or done knowingly. You may think that it could just be a slip even if you feel like something is amiss.

If this often occurs with one or more individuals in your life, then you might need to break down such characters and understand that you are actually dealing with a manipulative person known as a narcissist.

This behavior is usually harder to detect in most instances since these people have perfected the art of hiding their real and true characters.

Over and above, you may also find it important to take a look at a viable analysis of various characters that might manipulate you in one way or the other.

Passive aggression is a word that indicates that there is a major tendency to engage in the passive or indirect expression of unkindness and hostility towards others through various acts such as sullen behavior, deliberate failure, and subtle insults.

This is usually done in a quest to fail to accomplish certain tasks. To assist you in identifying these instances, here are a few strategies and elements to look at:

- The Silent Treatment

In the most basic form, the silent treatment comprises of ignoring someone and refusing to answer any question they ask regardless of the urgency of the matter.

It also includes refusing to share vital information regarding an important subject in that matter.

This type of treatment is not usually passive-aggressive exactly, but it's pretty explicit. There are also more subtle ways through which the person can subject you to their character of the silent treatment.

For instance, the individual may accidentally fail to identify the fact that you have been working hard at delivering in some projects. The same person may refuse to award you in case you have won in some case at work. During meetings, the individual may adamantly refuse to interact with you in any way. As such, it becomes an issue that needs to be addressed on a personal level during which other interpretations can be used to decipher this trait in the long run. Your colleague may also intentionally ignore your messages as well as comments just to hurt you.

- The Highly Sensitive Individual

The highly sensitive introverted narcissist is known for parading emotions when hurt. When confronted because of their mistakes, they tend to act like the victims of other people's actions. They will become defensive, therefore, throwing back the ball at the individual who has been asking questions about projects that have not been handled appropriately.

According to Glen Gabbard who is a professional psychiatrist, it's vital to note that some introverted manipulative people cannot take negative feedback and act on their actions especially when it comes to becoming a better person in life.

These people will also defend themselves for their bad actions. Others will fight or become dismissive in many ways. Typically, they won't let anyone on regarding how much negativity bothers them. At the end of it all, they will act as the victims who have been hurt by those who are questioning their negative actions. Apart from that, these people will even withdraw. In dark psychology, this person is often termed as a special individual who is often misunderstood. The self-perceptions of some of these people are such as they are special and one of a kind.

They could also refer to themselves as the most unique creatures in their classes. These are the common narcissistic tendencies that can be drawn from such individuals. These people tend to create a reassuring role that does not exist in the actual sense.

They end up submerging the actual true self, which is usually the vulnerable personality in this case.

The Impersonal and Difficult Individual in Relationships

As earlier mentioned, part of the society of introverted narcissists includes insecurity as well as the inability to connect with various individuals genuinely.

To that end, the aloofness in them is a defense mechanism they use to put people away.

They don't really want to have the narcissism exposed in any way since these are personal inadequacies.

Some of these individuals may also be narrowly focused on some self-absorbing tasks that can prevent others from realizing who they actually are in the real sense.

Some introverted narcissists delve into social networking, technology, as well as games and cliques.

This is usually a project geared towards helping them to remain antisocial when it comes to human interaction. These activities will also assist them in hiding their personalities.

Subtle Insults

The subtle insult is often recognized when people are overly insulted. However, subtle insults can majorly be harder to recognize for precisely what they are. Perhaps a colleague may pretend to compliment you on the work you have just completed. When you sit somewhere and try to think of it, you'll realize that it's some insult in disguise. This is for instance; you can turn a report to your boss. He then reads it and says it is almost as excellent as someone else's. A subtle insult can also comprise of a hidden as well as a semi-hidden reference to a person's weakest points.

This is for instance; the colleague in question may have earned a degree from a high-end institution. Maybe you received yours from a local college if the individual makes irrelevant references to your institution and then goes ahead to imply that it's not an excellent institution. That's an insult.

Sullen Behavior

When it comes to sullen character and behavior, it becomes uncomfortable being around people who are grumpy as well as sulky. It's also unhealthy to hang out with people who are grouchy or moody. It's almost as terrible as being near people who act explicitly. For instance, if an individual feels like they are answering you, they may choose to provide their answers using innocent comments such as remarks and questions in a slightly negative manner. As such, a sullen person will not smile. They will not flinch even when a colleague makes a small joke. Individuals who exhibit such characters and behaviors complain about everything they come across.

Stubbornness

Being stubborn is beneficial to some extent. It's a beneficial personality trait in some people. This is especially true when it comes to taking a stand as well as holding onto a certain position. However, at times, the trait becomes merely a way to punish others. The stubborn individual will defend their position or viewpoint religiously and have excellent arguments so that you can't simply have the time and energy to object what they are saying and advocating for.

This may also be a way through which these individuals can stay clear of the natural forces that may force them to have natural good and healthy arguments. Therefore, you cannot really dismiss what they have in mind at any given time. Besides, the stubborn character is going to defend themselves by applying various points that will help in protecting their character in the long run. Also, it's evident that these people will defend their position only because they understand that it won't annoy the other party.

Failure to Finish Projects and Tasks

Most people are quite familiar with stubborn kids who refuse to complete their tasks or projects. When the children reach a particular age, they succumb to peer pressure where they utterly refuse to become part of any other existing projects in the class or any other impending societal projects that they need to be part of. When they grow up, they also refuse to do what they are told. Kids are kids you'll often hear. However, in this case, the same kids are defying the orders of their parents or teachers since it's become a norm. It's often less easy to understand why they behave in a certain manner. You may have this colleague who will always find a way to avoid handling a task that needs to be completed on time. They will leave the full responsibility of handling these duties to someone else, yet they are the ones who were tasked with the duty of delivering the project.

If this is caused by a result of work-related health issues such as stress or stress at home, then it comes easy to procrastinate. This is known as a procrastinating personality that will end up interfering with the entire project in the long run. As such, people need to be taught how to handle their duties and roles from a tender age since that is the only way through which tasks can be accomplished later when they become adults. This is a frequent character and behavior in people who were raised to trust others to handle their duties. Therefore, they end up piling such roles on their friends as well as relatives in search of comfort eventually.

Chapter 5: Mind Control

Mind control is often known as the science of manipulation, brainwashing, mental power, as well as coercive control and malignant application of group dynamics in order to confuse others and distort them in the long run. This is a strategy that's often used by political and corporate societies in order to achieve what they would wish. Usually, mind control comes from the umbrella of persuasion by individuals who want to achieve something in their lives or businesses. It also centers around the need to make others believe in something that they would otherwise not consider to be a factor that holds water.

Mind control is a form of brainwashing activity that is used by people who want to deceive others into delving into their beliefs and ways of doing things. It indicates some form of deception that is created to allow the naïve individuals to take action in something they may not believe in. It is often used by people for their own good and benefit. Some people are known to argue that everything is about manipulation. This is not true since, in manipulation, distinctions are often lost. Therefore, it's much more useful for someone to think in the lines of influence as a major continuum. In the long run, on one end, there is a respectful influence while on the other hand, there are utterly destructive influences that will have a negative impact on the society and its people.

All in all, it also covers a person's ability to think. Mind control is a large discipline that covers the subject of cults as well as sects. These are small groups that use deception to control minds while applying tactics to take advantage of the vulnerability of others. These groups also apply several modern and proven to work tactics that may end up exposing others to danger. The cult leaders apply the same tactics in seeking the attention of the followers. It's also a movement geared towards assisting others in the cult to follow the cause while achieving their dreams. This is usually the term used by these people.

With that said, a one-on-one cult is often defined as an intimate relationship in which an individual abuses their power in order to manipulate others. It could be a teacher, preacher, or government official. It could also be a therapist who seeks to extort a client. In a different case, it could also be about a wife as well as a husband who is in the process of getting a divorce. The cultic relationship remains to be a version of the significant groups that may be destructive in the long run. This is because time, as well as attention, is directed towards one individual. With that said, therefore, what really is mind control?

Defining Mind Control and Its Uses in Real Life

You can think of mind control as an extensive system of various influences that disrupt a person. At its core, mind control is also defined as an element that has a system of forces that interfere with a person's system of beliefs, preferences, behaviors, character, while creating a new pseudo-identity. Like earlier discussed, mind control can be used in beneficial ways to help a group of leaders in achieving their life's goals and objectives. In this book, we are highlighting issues that can affect the growth and well-being of an individual because of the application of mind control.

According to Philip Zimbardo who is a professional psychologist, mind control is a viable process through which collective freedom of choice is often compromised by various agents who seek to modify or interfere with the system or process of the behavioral outcome. Mind control can also interfere with the manner in which things should be done in society. To some extent, mind control has a way of bringing people into some form of chaotic discourse that will end up interfering with other people's lives. The professional suggests that we are all susceptible to manipulation using mind control.

This is not some ancient issue that will only select a few people but a combination of group pressures could with words that have been packed in a single container in order to mislead others. Mind control is a discipline that highlights the vulnerability of other people who have the independence to decide what they like in life.

As such, the individual being controlled isn't usually aware of what's going on when it comes to being influenced. They also don't recognize the impending changes that are affecting their lives. There are some vital points that need to be made clear. For starters, mind control is defined as a subtle, insidious process in the world of psychology.

This implies that an individual is usually unaware of the extent of influence being imposed on them by their controller. These people often believe that they are making decisions based on their preferences and benefits. Instead, these decisions are made for them with the intention of doing them harm. Apart from that, it's important to note that it doesn't take place instantly. Rather, it takes time depending on the factors that will impact the benefitting team and the progress of the entire project. In the long run, the controlling party aspires to win in several ways, including using certain methods and skills to cause a harmful impact on the community.

There is a certain force also involved in castigating members of society while interfering with their lives in ways that can have a negative impact on their families. A controlling mind will issue threats of innocent people using specific skills that can be applied in a few hours. There is also a force and pressure involved in the entire process of controlling the minds of the vulnerable.

A Look at Mind Control vs. Brainwashing

Steve Hassan is an expert in this field. He is convinced that there's a clear distinction between mental control as well as brainwashing. He adds that in brainwashing, the victim understands the fact that there's an aggressor who is also the enemy. For instance, a prisoner of war comprehends the fact that there is an enemy who does the torture by seeking to understand that other people's lives depend on changing the system of belief. Other than that, it also becomes significant and apparent to the oppressor that the vulnerable member of society is exposed to such precarious actions caused by the oppressor.

They are also coerced using physical force into becoming involved in issues that should not become part of their lives. Over the years, psychologists have analyzed these people to the extent of disintegrating their characters and teaching the fragile members of society how to protect themselves from such people. Mind control is slightly subtle and sophisticated in that the individual spearheading the manipulation is considered a close relative or person such as a teacher or a friend. Usually, the victim isn't attempting to defend themselves. They could be willing to participate in the actions they have been asked to become part of.

In the process, they always believe that the manipulator is looking after their interest, such as health and well-being or any other prosperous objective that you can weigh. Usually, such people offer some information willingly which can be used against them in advancing the mind control games. This makes the game a precarious activity that can send someone into depression. It is more than the typical physical coercion. This implies that it may be more effective than torture or drug abuse.

Usually, in mind control, there is no physical coercion as well as violence in any form. It may be more effective when it comes to controlling an individual. This is because coercion can significantly change a person's behavior. To admit that someone who has been trusted by the vulnerable individuals has deceived them is pretty challenging. That's why it's not easy for various people to identify or recognize mind control when they are going through the phase. Even in cases where the victim is utterly free of manipulation, they still act and believe that they are still subjects of such manipulation. Their attitudes, beliefs, and decisions—or at least, so they think— are still under the influence of the manipulative individuals.

Who Is Holding a Gun to the Head?

Most manipulators are used to saying that nobody is holding a gun to the head of the vulnerable. This is an honest and powerful statement in several ways. To the person who is observing these actions, that is, the outsider, mind control is a dark vice that needs to be highlighted and discussed in many ways. It's difficult for such people to comprehend this subject. For the person who has been manipulated or who is being manipulated, they understand that it's factual that dark vices and individuals can easily control people. No one really holds a gun to these people's heads. Therefore, it reinforces the main idea that they have decided to delve into the practice by themselves. Decisions are therefore made personally. These decisions are powerful. The effects last slightly longer thereby propelling the manipulated individual deeper into the existing reality founded by the controller.

Who Uses The Gun?

The big question is who would use the techniques in manipulating others for their selfish gains. Another question is who would simply want to take control over other people in order to satiate their personal quest? The correct answer is psychopaths and narcissists since they seek to control everything around their environment. They do these things because they do not have a conscience. Since people do not understand the science of what it takes to become a psychopath, the manipulator is usually referred to as something else including abusive wife, controlling husband, or an emotionally abusive man. A look at a professional examination will reveal that such people have a destructive personality disorder.

Defining and Understanding Susceptibility in Dark Psychology

We are all susceptible. It's often a myth that some people are known to be weak and vulnerable and therefore susceptible. Such people also hold to the belief that maybe such things cannot happen to them. The attitude makes them vulnerable in many ways. They become exposed to mind control. This is because they are not on the lookout for the manipulative characters. The perfect way through which you can protect yourself from the people who want to recruit you into the cult and becoming subjected to mind control is by having a clear and detailed understanding regarding the tactics that these people use in attracting as well as keeping members.

Disintegrating the Cult Psychology

The psychology of cults seeks to disintegrate the main actions taking place at the cult and the surrounding society. Both fascinating, as well as terrifying, cults, tend to capture many people's attention to the extent of wanting to comprehend the invaluable lessons that they might garner from these secret societies. Cults are known for capturing people's attention based on the services and products they claim to offer in the long run.

The main question is usually, where does the management come from? What are some of the psychological elements of the cult? Who would live for that? In an effort to successfully answer these questions, people have joined cults blindly. With that said, we live in a world filled with challenges where people have abstract issues that need to be solved urgently. As such, these individuals may end up trying to find various solutions from cults. The same people may look for solutions in the wrong places. In the world dark psychology, people are seeing clarity based on the issues affecting them.

According to one Dr. Adrian Furham, who describes the issue in Psychology Today, humans are known to crave clarity in all forms possible. Therefore, it has become apparent for such people to address the impending and underlying issues that humans are facing from different world parts in order to help them in leading better lives. These people are blinded by those who would like to take advantage of them in several ways. They are also focused on improving their lives in every way they can.

People with low self-esteem are always more focused on learning what cults are about. For the better part of it, the average person is intrigued by the whole idea of a cult and its impact on people's lives. Many people have also successfully recruited others into their cults in order to maintain the life of the family tree. Generally, these individuals in the cults don't look to recruit individuals with health issues such as handicaps or the depressed. People with low self-esteem are recruited since they cannot properly defend themselves in any of life's most challenging scenarios.

And, where possible, these cults tend to take advantage of other people who are in dire need of community support when it comes to matters of physical and mental well-being. Most of the time, such individuals are compromised in one way or the other. The people also come from various backgrounds, including tax brackets as well as zip codes. Eventually, the idea is to recruit several people and grow the number of people following the cult in order to extend its life and relevance.

Cults generally don't get motivation from recruiting the best of the world's brains since it may be challenging to control such people. However, the cults will select a few people who seem confused about life and all it has to offer. These individuals can be controlled since they don't have a clue what the manipulative people can do in order to have control over their lives. In the long run, they end up submitting to such individuals. Once people have been admitted to the cults, they are usually bombarded with love and care. This is an odd trait and strategy that's commonly used in describing someone with low self-esteem since they are often flattered and complimented or seduced in order to help in training their brain to get used to the issues associated with the cult love as well as acceptance.

In the current world today, there are more abstract issues that most people seek to identify themselves with. Such are the problems that need to be addressed by the professional psychologists who understand how cults are. Cult leaders are known to promote messages that simply make sense at that moment in time. Past the scenario or in real life, such messages do not make sense. They do not contain any great content that can be substantiated. With that said, in certain research by the department of psychologists, it was disclosed that women would make up to about 65 percent of cult members across the world. Why, you may ask? This is because women, according to psychologists, are more vulnerable are always in a position to join cults in order to gain various advantages that have been promised including gaining access to education as well as funds to take care of their kids. Psychologists have also conclusively issued different ideas regarding why women are more susceptible to joining cults.

According to Dr. David of the prestigious Virginia Commonwealth University, women are simply intrigued by the fact that they can easily change their lifestyles just by joining a cult. Therefore, this makes them more statistically likely to become part and parcel of cults that will victimize them in the long run. Others have also suggested that it has to be linked to the fact that in history, women have always been oppressed. Therefore, they are better inclined towards finding solutions in such like arrangements.

Young women are especially exposed to such types of groups since they don't have the relevant experience when it comes to dealing with humans as well as becoming independent. To such women, it's all about seizing the opportunity and creating a better life for themselves. According to the opinion of many prominent psychologists such as Dr. Stanley H. Cath, many of these cult members need treatment after undergoing that phase in life. From his first-hand experience, it's clear that this is an interesting trend affecting masses of people in different parts of the world. Many individuals joining the cults have vastly experienced religion in their lives. They have also rejected it.

Maybe this is pretty surprising to some extent since cults are known to be religious. At least that is what they claim to be. In the opinion of Cathy, it's clear that this is a trend and a major sign of an actual deeper thing that needs to be addressed in society. Many of the individuals who end up joining cults are not only intelligent but hail from sheltered environments where people need the mental support of professionals who can offer them better diagnosis and treatment for their condition. Other than that, most people who have joined these cults are known for being exposed to emotional and physical abuse at some point in their lives. The idea has been to expose them to dark vices that will paralyze their ability to think positively or appropriately.

With that said, cults and secret societies are powerful since they are in a position to isolate the members from their initial lives that were not cult-related. One of the main ways through which this can be achieved is to make sure that the cult members are convinced that they are not just superior but can focus on falsely improving their lives in all possible ways. This is usually a "we" versus "them" mentality that highly destroys other people's self-esteem, thereby misleading them in their lives. They end up replacing all their relationships with the new ones with the hope of rekindling new lost lives that only exist in their heads. They also replace their relationships with the new ones. As such, leaders of a cult will tend to convince their victims to successfully separate themselves from a society in which they grew up. In order to successfully achieve this, the cult leader has to master the tactics of mind control and how to apply them to their personal gain. Some of these methods are such as

Public Humiliation
A new cult member will be love bombed immediately after their arrival into the cult society. However, when they have spent some time in the cult, they will have mastered all the existing emotional

blackmail strategies that may affect people's lives in a negative way. They will use these tactics to attract new members and make them conform to certain ways of belief. By using these methods to humiliate members of the cult too, leaders shall have conquered and won over the brains of other masses of people in the cult society. One such main method and strategy entails someone sitting in the arena of the cult society when they surrounded by various members who need to admit to their recent failures in life.

Self-incrimination

This is one of the most favorite tactics that the cult members should provide their masters with various written statements that detail their fears as well as mistakes. As such, the leaders can easily and successfully use the statements in shaming the individual members in public.

Brainwashing

When it comes to brainwashing, cult leaders are prominently known for repeating various lies as well as distortions until when a member finds it challenging to tell the difference between the actual cult life as well as the reality.

Paranoia

When it comes to paranoia, most of the time, there is the need to maintain as well as uphold some false sense of belonging and hope. Others may also think that the authority is out to seek them.

That usually offers false safety. Immediately, a cult member concludes that their families cannot provide a secure environment for them to live in, they start to worship as well as putting their faith in the hands of their leader. One person who is well-known for successfully achieving this is Jim Jones, who was skilled in playing mind control games. He would highly encourage members of his cult to tell on each other.

He also spoke through loudspeakers at different hours of the cult sessions and gatherings. All too often, he would implore the cult members to delve into different societal gatherings which he would control. Many cult members do not actually realize that they have become members of a broken system that deceives them. According to Dr. Margaret Thaler, who has spent most of her life attempting to understand the operating nature of the cults, most people join a cult with the hope of gaining some significant amount of power. She insists on the fact that some people are willing to highlight the perceived benefits of these cults in their lives more than they are able to see the dangers. She additionally mentions the fact that many individuals assume that cults are just religious even though they can also be political associations, including lifestyle groups and business groups.

Victims of cults will spend years trying to overcome the existing emotional damage that has been caused in their lives throughout the time they spent in the cults. All too often, psychologists who treat people who have been to cults will admit that they have been affected by the long term impacts of the cults. Their bodies and minds are not the same. Some of the symptoms they exude are such as lobe epilepsy which results from the cult conversions and increased irritability.

Chapter 6: Deception Tactics

When it comes to manipulation, the manipulator will always focus on getting what they want. They may use various forms of trickery so that they may get what they want from the other parties. Many people believe that manipulation is immoral. Since the psychological manipulators use various deception techniques, we will look into each of these tactics and offer a suitable solution on how people can defend themselves in case of any eventuality.

Method 1 – Gaining Manipulation Skills

Taking an acting class

When it comes to manipulation, it is good to learn more about how to master emotions while making sure that other people can become receptive whenever you tend to become emotional. To learn more about the various emotional techniques, it is good to enroll in an acting class. While in an acting class, it will be possible to gain some powers of persuasion. The most important point to note is that you should never inform other people that you have ever undertaken an acting class. Always focus on the main goal, which involves manipulating people. If you informed them about the period when you enrolled in an acting class, they might become suspicious, and many people will not believe you.

Enroll for a Public Speaking Class

The acting classes are meant to make sure that you can master your emotions. It will also be possible to convince other people, and you will always have your way as a manipulator. The main reason why enrolling for a debate class is advisable is because you will be able to learn more about convincing other people. You will learn more about how to organize your thoughts in a better manner. Additionally, a public speaking class will also enlighten you more about how to sound convincing.

Come Up With Similarities

Manipulators always make sure that they have learned more about the body language of their target victims. They also look into the intonation patterns of their victims before they can proceed with the manipulation process. Eventually, the manipulators will come up with persuasive methods, and they will also appear calm.

Being Charismatic

The charismatic individuals always have a way of getting what they want. When manipulating people, you will have to ensure that you have worked on your charisma. You should also be able to smile, and your body language should also showcase that you are approachable, and that means that people can easily approach you and talk to you. You must also be able to initiate a conversation with any individual regardless of various factors such as age. Some of the techniques that you can utilize to become charismatic include:

▪Ensuring that people feel special

The best way to achieve this is through maintaining eye contact while also conversing with a person. Make sure that you have also initiated a discussion about how they feel and the interests that they have. Always show them that you care and you want to learn more about them although you do not care at all.

▪Always maintain high levels of confidence

Charismatic people are always passionate about everything that they do. It is also advisable to have confidence in yourself. When you give in to your needs, people can easily trust you.

Learn from the Masters

If you have a friend who happens to be a psychological manipulator, you should approach them and also take notes. Always carry out a case study and ensure that the manipulators are the main point of focus. It will be possible to learn a lot from them. Pay attention to how these individuals get what they want. They can also share some insight into how they manipulate people. The main issue is that you may end up being tricked, but you will gain some insight into how to manipulate people effectively.

Learn More about How to Read People

Each individual has a psychological and emotional makeup, and it always varies from one individual to another. When you learn about the psychological and emotional makeup of a person, it will be possible to manipulate them. For starters, make sure that you have learned more about the individual that you are going to manipulate. Make sure that you have understood them fully. By understanding your target, you can formulate an approach that will come about as suitable when it comes to manipulating them. Some of the things that you may notice as you try to understand people include:

- Most of the people are vulnerable, and it is possible to reach out to them by evoking their emotional responses. For instance, some people may cry when watching a movie, and they may showcase some high levels of sympathy and empathy. To manipulate such individuals, make sure that you have joked around with their emotions while also pretending that you feel sorry and they will eventually give you what you want.

- Other people usually have a strong sense of guilt. Most of the individuals who have a guilt reflex grew up in a household that was restrictive, and they may have been punished for every wrong deed that they may have committed. As for such people, always make sure that they feel guilty about various acts and they will give in to your demands at the end of it all.

•Some people usually respond to approaches that are rational. For example, if you have a close friend who is always logical and they always keep up with the news, that means that they are always after information that is verifiable. In such an instance, always make sure that you have utilized your persuasive powers accordingly when manipulating them.

Method 2 – Using Different Manipulation Techniques

Impose an Unreasonable Request then Present a Reasonable One

This is a technique that has proven to be very effective, and many manipulators often use it. It is also simple to use. Whenever you want to manipulate anyone, always come up with a request that is not reasonable. They will reject the unreasonable request, and in that instance, you should come up with a request that is reasonable. The request that you come up with should be appealing to the individual who is being targeted. The best example to use in such a case is when an employee may not accept an offer to arrive early at work, but they will voluntarily accept a request whereby they are supposed to come to work early to handle various urgent duties. The employee will prefer engaging in a short-term request since it is less cumbersome as compared to the long term request.

Inspire Fear then Ensure That the Victim Has a Sense of Relief

As a manipulator, the main fact is that you have a target, and you have also chosen our victims wisely. In this case, you should make sure that a victim's worst fears have come to life. In the process, you will focus on ensuring that they have been relived and they will be happy enough to ensure that you have received what you were looking for. Such tricks might be mean, but they will ensure that you have gotten what you were looking for.

The best example to use in this case is—assume that your friend has a car. Try to shock them by telling them that the car was producing some funny noises. You may go ahead and tell them that the engine might be dead. At that juncture, the individual will be in fear. After that, go ahead and inform them that you realized that the strange noise was being produced by the radio. They will be relieved. You should make sure that the intervals through which you provide this information vary. Since the individual may be relived, you may go ahead and ask for another favor such as you may borrow the car once again.

Ensure That a Person Feels Guilty

As a manipulator, another way of getting what you want is through ensuring that you have invoked guilt in a person. For starters, carry out an evaluation and learn more about how you may invoke some guilt in the victim. Ensure that the person feels bad for a variety of reasons.

If you are targeting your parents, make sure that you have showcased that their parenting skills were wanting and that is why you are the way you are at the moment.

If you need to invoke some form of guilt among one of your friends, make sure that you have enlightened them about the number of times that they have let you down.

Bribe a person

When you are after something, you may issue a bribe. In such an instance, you do not have to use tactics such as blackmail so that you may get what you are after. You can always issue a reward to someone but in the form of a bribe. Make sure that the bribe is enticing. First, make sure that you have learned more about the needs of the person. Also, do not disclose various forms of information, including the act that you are issuing a bribe.

Pretend That You Are the Victim

When you pretend that you are a victim, you will attract some sympathy. Also, make sure that you have not overdone the act and you will get what you are looking for at the end of it all. Victims always appear helpless, and that means that the target will appear vulnerable as they offer to help you. Always ensure that you are well-composed. Pretend to be dumb although you know what you are doing. Also, pretend to be pathetic and helpless.

Use Logic

Logic is important in some of the day-to-day activities that you engage in. Always ensure that you have come up with a list of reasons as to why you would benefit from the things that you are asking. Always present your case in a calm and rational manner. As you present your issues, make sure that you have displayed some emotions and you will always get what you want at the end of it all. Make sure that each of your requests is logical.

Maintain the Character

Depending on the method that you have used, make sure that you have displayed some emotions that could relate to your current scenario. You may appear worried or even upset, depending on the matter at hand. Once you admit that you have been using manipulative tactics, you will realize that as per my point of reasoning, I have not deviated far from the truth.

Chapter 7: Dark Psychology – Persuasion Techniques

When it comes to manipulation, people will always make decisions depending on how manipulative people have persuaded them. We will focus more on the common persuasion techniques that have been used over the years, and they include;

- **Ultimate Terms**

There are some words that always seem persuasive as compared to others. The best example to use in this case is the words that people usually use during an argument. Most of these terms may seem charismatic. For example, people use the term God to showcase some form of attractiveness and positivity. The term devil will always showcase some negativity. As for the charismatic terms, they may include words such as "freedom." Some of these words are used to sway people who have come together to accomplish a certain goal. It is also evident that some of these ultimate terms are quote appealing, although some may be unreliable.

- **Talking Quickly**

The manner in which you deliver your words matters a lot. You may easily influence people by the way you talk. When you speak quickly, you may be persuasive to some extent. Also, when a person speaks quickly, it means that people have to be attentive so that they will not miss any details. Also, people cannot easily interrupt a person who speaks quickly during an argument. Although some problems may be present, the people will focus more on listening to what you have to say as they process every bit of information quickly. The audience that has gathered to listen to you deem you are knowledgeable and confident, which means that they regard you as a highly influential individual. It is easy to manipulate such people, and they may fail to realize what you are imposing upon them.

- **Using the Right Body Language**

Although you may be appealing with word of mouth, you should also ensure that your body language is desirable. As you speak, people will also pay more attention to your body language. Always make sure that you are standing straight and you should be relaxed. Ensure that you have not showcased nay form of uneasiness.

Additionally, it is advisable to make eye contact with your audience. Always make sure that you have exuded high levels of confidence and keep in mind that people will be observing your non-verbal cues. At the end of the address, you will leave an impression, and people will offer you their support depending on how you composed yourself.

Ensuring There Is Repetition

There are some instances whereby you might listen to a song, but you will not necessarily like it; however, after listening to the song over and over again, you will start to like it. As for the target audience, they may not be interested in what you have to say; however, if you ensure that there is repetition, they will express some interest in what you have to say.

Psychological manipulation is also known as the practice of undue influence via mental distortion as well as emotional exploitation with the sole intention of seizing power and control, benefits, as well as privileges at the expense of victims. In this analysis, it's vital to tell the main difference between healthy psychological influence as well as manipulation with the focus on understanding the subject in order to make use of the elements. Healthy social influence occurs in society among many individuals.

It is also part of the constructive relationships that encourage the give as well as take practice. On the other hand, in psychological manipulation, one person is often used for the benefit of the other person. The person who manipulates the team is known to deliberately create a major imbalance in power while exploiting the vulnerable in order to serve their agenda.

It's vital to comprehend the tricks that manipulative individuals use in coercing others into doing what they need to be done. While this list is not exhaustive, there are important points that you should master in order to benefit in the long run. With that said, a manipulative individual can easily insist that you have a meeting and interact in a certain area where they can exercise control in order for you to be their subject.

This may be the person's office, car, or home. In these areas, the people feel dominant while you feel the need to run for a cover or security. In a different scenario, some people, such as the sales representatives can allow you to speak first in order for them to prospect you and analyze your prospective response prior to probing questions. The person will then delve into the creation of a baseline to think about your character and evaluate your strengths as well as weaknesses. The type of questioning in this scene is based on establishing if you have understood all the relevant questions and answers during the interaction.

The panel may also want to know if you are a viable candidate for the position. You can rest assured that the person questioning you is well equipped with the right questions and answers to help you in understanding the scope of the business. As such, you should focus on exuding confidence.

How to Manipulate Anyone in Your Life

As a manipulator, you may develop different tendencies, including manipulating other people who are close to you in real life.

Manipulate Your Friends

When it comes to manipulating your friends, you might realize that it is a tricky situation. For starters, you will have to know your friends well enough before you put your manipulation skills to the test. You should not worry that much. It is still possible to make sure that your friends have submitted to your manipulation tactics. For starters, make sure that you have buttered your friend in case you need a favor within a few days. Always make sure that you have been nice while also doing some small favors. Ensure that you have told your friend about how good they are. The main point here is to make sure that you have done all it takes to become a "friend" without raising any suspicion.

- **Utilize Your Emotions**

  Your friends should be caring individuals; as a result, they will not want to see you upset. If you have any acting skills, make sure that you have used them accordingly to ensure that you will appear to be a very upset individual.

- **Constantly Remind Your Friend about How Good They Are**

Always ensure that you remember the periods when you have always done some good things for the sake of your friend.

- **Guilt-Trip Your Friends**

  You do not have to utilize the "bad friend" card. Always mention someone casually and remind them about how they have let you down. Always make it sound like your friend is uncaring without going overboard.

Manipulating Your Significant Other

When it comes to manipulating your partner, such a task should not be so hard. The best way to manipulate your partner is by turning them on and asking them for favors eventually; that means that your partner cannot get what they want unless they have heeded to your demands. If you don't want to use such a tactic, ensure that you have come up with different ways to manipulate your partner depending on what you know about them. The approach that you use should be effective. In most cases, make sure that you have made your request after lightening up the mood. You will always get that favor after reminding your partner about how good they are. The impression you use determines whether your manipulation techniques will subdue the target. Always make sure that you are deceptive and also swift. What matters most is ensuring that your image is still intact.

- **Utilize Your Emotions**

  Look into what your significant other would do when they realize that you are wallowing in sorrow. In most cases, your partner will ensure that they have reignited the happiness within you. If you are determined to solicit favor from your partner, make sure that you have utilized the waterworks approach in a public place. The best example to showcase the effectiveness of such an approach is— when a child tries to solicit favor from their parents in public, the parent will always give in to the demands of the child. When using this technique, use it sparingly.

- **Issue Small Bribes**

  If you want a man to do you a favor such as taking you out on a dinner date or any other event, always issue a small bribe.

- **Manipulating Your Boss**

  Use the approaches that are logical and rational when dealing with your boss. When you have some personal problems, do not discuss them in front of your boss. Also, do not appear at your boss's desk crying because of some personal issues. There is a high chance that you will be fired. When dealing with your boss, make sure that you are logical. Also, make sure that you have provided some good reasons regarding why you need some assistance from your boss. Make sure that you are a model worker. Such a technique will always work when you need to make a request. Also, make sure that you are working a bit late. Additionally, make sure that you are always happy and smiling whenever you are around your boss. You can also issue them some gifts in the morning.

When soliciting a favor from your boss, make sure that you have done so in an offhand manner. Always make the request in a manner that is causal. For instance, approach your boss in the office and tell them that there is an important matter that you wanted to discuss with them. When your boss hears that, they will issue you their undivided attention, and they will enact on your favor at the end of the day.

Try to ask for a favor at the end of the day. Do not engage your boss early in the morning. First, make sure that you have observed their mood. If they showcase that they are stressed, you could opt for another moment. If you want to approach your boss during a break, you can do so as they go to look for lunch. They will always grant all your requests, and they will not also argue with you.

Manipulating the Teacher

If you want to manipulate your teacher, you must do so professionally. Also, make sure that you have incorporated some emotions. During the specific day that you want to make a request, you should make sure that you have appeared before the teacher as a model student. Also, make sure that you have arrived in class early. Try to ensure that the teacher can notice that you have been reading a lot. In short, the teacher should note that you are taking your studies seriously. While in the classroom, make sure that you are active and you should be focused.

Always enlighten the teacher about how great they are, and you should do so casually. Tell them about how they inspire you. In some instances, also ensure that you have enlightened them about how much you love the subjects that they are teaching.

Mention some stuff about what is happening at home. Although the situation might appear to be awkward, the teacher will be able to sympathize with you since they will feel sorry and they might want to learn more about your situation.

As you discuss your personal life, ensure that you have done so in a strategic manner and your teacher will become uncomfortable eventually. If you had delayed when it comes to issuing your assignment, the teacher might have some pity on you because of your situation, and they will offer you an extension, which means you can submit your assignment later. If the teacher refuses to grant you an extension, always enlighten them that you understand that they do not extend the period when the students should hand in their assignments. Your voice should appear to be frail since you want the teacher to sympathize with you. There is a high chance that the teacher will give in to your demands.

If such a technique does not work, you can choose to cry since you must demonstrate that you are indeed emotional. You will start crying, and the teacher will become uncomfortable, and that means that they will have to heed to your commands.

Manipulating Your Parents

It is evident that your parents should always love you unconditionally. As a result, they may be more susceptible to your manipulation techniques. The main fact here is that your parents love you, and they will always support you in every way possible. You have to ensure that you are a model offspring for some time before you can make a request involving certain favors. Always make sure that you have not missed your curfew. Also, make sure that you have spent most of your time studying and assisting in handling some house chores. Afterward, you can go ahead and request a favor.

Ensure that your request is reasonable. For instance, you may want to attend a concert and the following day you should be attending school. When making such a request, make sure that you have done so casually. Always make sure that your parents can see the possibility in the situation, and they will not reject the proposal in the long run.

You can also pose a question to your parents while you are folding laundry. When handling such tasks, your parents will remember that they have a great son or a daughter, and they will always comply with your wishes.

Talk more about how you will engage in some of these activities together with your friends. When your parents hear that you will be engaging in a specific activity together with your friends, they will issue you the go-ahead to proceed.

Ensure that your parents feel guilty. For instance, you may have wanted to go to a concert. If your parents deny you the opportunity to take part in such an event, you will just tell them that it's okay. Always make sure that your parents will feel guilty since you may be missing out on an opportunity to take part in a major event.

Chapter 8: Analyzing the Psychology of Manipulation

When discussing the psychology of manipulation, it is good to note that it entails having some influence over a person without forcing them or persuading them rationally. People may be wondering whether having some influence over an individual without coercing them is manipulation. For starters, manipulation does not occupy the whole logical space, and the element of morality often distinguish it.

When a person manipulates another, their behavior is always criticized because of the acts that they have partaken.

The question now arises, is manipulation usually immoral? If yes, why is manipulation immoral? In some instances, manipulation might not be immoral, but, what matters most, in this case, is, what deems manipulation immoral.

An Insight into Ordinary vs. Global Manipulation

There are different forms of manipulation. Ordinary and global manipulation is differentiated by free will. Manipulation involves reprogramming a person's beliefs or their mental state. Global manipulation happens in an extra-ordinary method. For instance, global manipulation may be in the form of supernatural intervention or any other form of psychological conditioning. Global manipulation entails ensuring that the target victims do not have any form of free will.

Although there is a huge difference between ordinary manipulation and various forms of manipulation when it comes to denying other people of their free will, it is still good to learn more about the relationship between these forms of manipulation.

If the victim is denied their free will by global manipulation, are other forms of manipulation similar.

The Applications of the Theory of Ordinary Manipulation

Manipulation has existed for a long period of time. Recently, people began to view manipulation from a psychological view. In most instances, manipulation usually undermines the validity of consent. For instance, when it comes to medical ethics, the consent of a certain condition is not supposed to be manipulated. During the early discussions about manipulation from a psychological perspective, most of the medical ethicists usually undermine the validity of consent. Nevertheless, there is no agreement concerning how people can determine whether various forms of influence are manipulative. It is also good to note that manipulation also affects a person's decision-making process.

Learning More about Manipulation

When discussing manipulation, people are mainly interested in the identification question. The main focus is on the forms of influence that are manipulative and the ones that are not. The most satisfactory answer to this question may involve looking into the definition of manipulation. By looking into the definition of manipulation, it will be possible to also learn about the various forms of manipulative influence and what they may have in common.

When learning more about manipulation, it is also good to look into the evaluation. For instance, how should people evaluate manipulation? The answer to this question will allow us to determine whether manipulation is moral or immoral. If manipulation is immoral, we will also learn about why it is deemed immoral. Although the answer to the questions involving identification and evaluation are distinct, the answers are not independent.

When analyzing why analysis is immoral and the instances when it is immoral, it is also good to define manipulation. When you come up with an answer to the identification question, it is also possible to answer the question about evaluation.

The Relation between Manipulation and Identification

When looking into manipulation, you will realize that it has three main characteristics. For starters, manipulation bypasses deliberation. The second characteristic is that it induces some pressure. Third, manipulation is treated as a form of trickery.

Manipulation Bypassing Reason

Manipulation usually undermines a person's reasoning. In most instances, manipulation is meant to bypass an individual's deliberation. For starters, manipulation varies greatly from rational persuasion. It always influences a person's behavior by not targeting their rational capacities. The best example to use in this case is when a company is advertising one of their products. The advertisement may be highly influential, and it does not affect your rational deliberation; however, you will start using the products that have been advertised without considering different factors.

Some of these advertisements are meant to influence a person's behavioral conditioning since it is the most effective way to influence an individual. When defining manipulation as a way of bypassing rational deliberation, some of the examples that will be used would be exaggerated. Manipulation can be characterized in terms of bypassing deliberation altogether. When it comes to bypassing rational deliberation, you will have to introduce non-rational influences. Also, manipulation is also different from coercion, and it does not interfere with an individual's options. It usually influences the manner in which a person makes decisions while also trying to adapt to different goals.

Although psychology is beneficial to some extent, it can also prove to be detrimental. It is also good to look into how psychology relates to human behavior so that people can choose their actions wisely. Since we are discussing the psychology of manipulation, it is good to learn that there are some people who use manipulation to control the actions of others. For example, some people believe that every individual has a stable self that is usually consistent, and it is also predicted how a person will behave in the future.

The only issue is that people cannot be sure about how they can act when they are under extreme pressure. Most of the individuals would like to believe that they can act calmly while they are under pressure. Depending on the current scenario, people believe that they can act heroically while also maintaining their beliefs, such as being nonviolent. In some cases, people always act rationally. The best example to use in this case is, what if there is a zombie apocalypse? Would it be possible to maintain your moral code? Would you be able to take care of yourself, or would you resist any orders issued by the authorities?

The main point to consider is that it is not possible to predict the manner in which you can act while you are under intense pressure. The inability to determine the manner in which you will behave is mainly because of the unpredictability that is present in such cases. When people are under intense pressure, they can experience a fight reaction that will always evolve to ensure that a person has survived a potentially dangerous encounter. When such a move is activated, the higher functioning will be activated. For example, when you are in danger, your brain activity will be higher. The main issue is that your body will also consume high amounts of blood sugar, and that is why the body conserves the flight reaction mode.

Since manipulation may come about in different forms, the flight reaction system can ensure that you gave survived any attack. Furthermore, the body requires a person to function optimally when there is a scenario that induces some stress. Also, it should be easy to access the sugar. In short, when a person is subjected to high levels of stress, they do not act in an expected manner.

There are some people who also have an overview of psychology. Various experiments have also been conducted over the years to learn more about psychology. The researchers also focused on areas such as the psychology of manipulation. When looking into manipulation, it is advisable to reference the Stanford Prison Experiment. Phillip Zimbardo conducted it. After concluding the experiment, it was evident that people usually behave in scary ways whenever they are manipulated. A group of students volunteered, and they took part in a prison simulation. There was a basement that has been modified into a prison, and it was meant to be as real as possible. Some of the individuals were assigned different roles, and they acted as guards and prisoners. The experiment was to be conducted in two weeks, but it was eventually shut down since the behavior depicted by the "prison guards" was somewhat inhumane. At the onset of the experiment, the "prison guards" were not behaving in an inhumane manner. They would treat the prisoners accordingly. Before the experiment commenced, the prisoners thought that the "prison guards" would treat them well by acting morally. However, as the experiment progressed, they began to act in an inhumane manner. The "prison guards" were also highly unpredictable, and they would act in a manner that was unpleasant during the short period that the experiment lasted.

Social psychology came about as a result of this experiment. In most cases, people have been assuming that people within a group will always agree although they may be right or wrong. The main idea behind such a form of reasoning is that the group that has the majority will always win any argument. Such a character can be termed as deindividuation. In this instance, the party that has a majority was able to manipulate the minority. The minority individuals had to change their opinion since they had to support the majority. Some of the suggested conditions include safety, authority, and comfort.

The scary part about the research that was carried out about the psychology of manipulation is that it showcased some rapid forms of change. Also, there was some rationalism that was present. Some individuals will always rationalize their behavior while also trying to convince themselves that they had actually chosen the action without being influenced in any manner. It is rare to find a person who acknowledges that they had been manipulated.

People have perceptual limitations, and it is evident that we make some of these decisions in an unconscious manner and in most instances out, attention is always diverted to other areas. When referring to some suitable experiments that would help people to learn more about the psychology of manipulation, it is good to reference a group of people who have come together to watch a certain sport whereby each person is supporting a specific team. During some of these games, mascots are present. Since most of the viewers will be fixated on the progress of the game, they may fail to notice that the mascot has appeared on the screen.

Most of the individuals will have been focusing on the instructions while also counting the scores. By looking into the manner in which the people were not observant, it would be possible to note that the mascot may not have appeared on the screen.

When conducting another experiment, the person in charge of the experiment may be asking people for directions to a certain place. During the exchange, the other individuals carrying out the experiment may have walked past each other carrying a door. The experimenters would be swapped, and the people issuing the directions may fail to notice. In this case, it is evident that a lot of manipulation has taken place. It is also possible to note that there were some inattention and rationalization that also modified the behaviors of the people who had taken part in the experiment. To influence a person's behavior, you may use different phenomenon such as priming.

Such a phenomenon is meant to change the behavior of a person without their consent. For example, when reading a sentence, you may read it fast, whereas the other individual may read it slowly. Researchers have been claiming that people can be easily manipulated without their prior knowledge using different priming effects. However, the most common factor would be that every person would dismiss the fact that they were influenced and manipulated. Instead, they will start talking about how they had arrived at that specific decision on their own.

Many people may be shocked that some of these principles may have been applied many times throughout history. Some people may tend to assume that there were conspiracy theories present. The main point to note is that the psychology of manipulation represents the fact that human beings have the desire to be manipulated and dominated. As per the experiments that have been mentioned above, there is no individual that was forced into doing anything.

All the people that took part in these experiments did so on their own free will. What matters most is that everyone wants to achieve their own desires at the end of it all. For example, when you watch a certain advertisement, you will realize that you will have the desire to purchase the product that is being advertised. It means that you can be easily manipulated using some of these principles.

When purchasing these products, you should be sure that you have been manipulated using the principles that relate to the psychology of manipulation. When people act in a violent manner, the act of violence will be as a result of their beliefs. Also, it might be possible that these individuals may have been manipulated using social conditioning.

When discussing the psychology of manipulation, things might get scarier with time. Since technology has advanced greatly, it is good to note that there are various forms of technology that can be used to alter the brain functioning of an individual using a brain scan. It is also possible to see brain activity through a screen as well as the thoughts of an individual. The current forms of technology are also set to improve. Eventually, it will be possible to implant thoughts to people using various forms of technology. Using such forms of technology, people can also induce an abnormal mental state in others using TMS (transcranial magnetic stimulation) or ultrasounds. The mentioned forms of technology may prove to be effective, and they might also be widespread eventually.

To some extent, people may assume that all hope is lost and the psychology of manipulation will prove to be detrimental over time. It is not possible to identify how people can act in different situations unless they can seize a chance to act it out on their own. Most of the people may not know what to experience when they are subjected to different forms of stress. Some of the scenarios involving manipulation usually take place in a manner that the victim is somewhat unconscious.

People usually pretend that their actions were as a result of their choices. It is advisable to ensure that you have learned more about your behaviors. Also, you should be disciplined and conscious about all your actions so that you may test who is in control. If you notice that you are tempted to act in a different manner, you should try and look into the matter in an in-depth manner. Try and ask yourself whether you want to act that way.

How to Understand That They Are Applying It and How to Defend Themselves

Psychological manipulation usually breeds some form of healthy social influence, and it usually occurs between many individuals. The relationships, in this case, are usually give or take. In psychological manipulation, one person will always benefit from the other by taking advantage of them. The individual manipulating the other always does it deliberately, and they often bring about an imbalance of power since they are exploiting other people for their own self-benefit.

The characteristics of manipulative individuals are:

- They know how to detect the weaknesses of other people.
- Once they identify a person's weaknesses, they will always use these weaknesses against them.
- They will always convince the victims to give up something so that they may serve their self-centered interests.
- Once a manipulative individual manages to take advantage of another person, they will always violate the other party until the exploited person ensures that the manipulation spree has come to an end.

Some of the causes of chronic manipulation are always deep-seated and complex. However, it is not easy to identify the main drive that causes a person to be manipulative psychologically.

Also, when a person is being manipulated, they do encounter different challenges. The main question that arises, in this case, is, how people manage such a situation. Some of the best ways to handle manipulative individuals include:

Make Sure You Are Conversant With Your Human Rights

When dealing with a psychologically manipulative individual, make sure that you know more about your human rights. It would be easy to recognize when any of your rights are being violated. Also, make sure that you are not harming other individuals. Every person has a right to stand up for themselves while also defending each of their rights. If you harm other people, you may be violating each of these human rights. Some of the important rights include;

- The right to be treated with respect.
- The right to express opinions, feelings, and wants.
- The right to set your own priorities.
- The right to say no without feeling guilty.
- The right to get anything that you pay for.
- The right to have a different opinion from that of your colleagues.
- The right to protect yourself from being mistreated mentally, physically, or emotionally.

- The right to always create your own happiness while also living a healthy life.

All these human rights are meant to represent a boundary that should never be crossed by the manipulative individuals.

It is evident that our society has many people who do not respect the rights of others. Some of these psychological manipulators always want to exploit people's rights so that they may take advantage of them in every way possible. The main important thing to note is that we all have the right to declare that you have the power since most people might assume that the manipulator is the one with the power. The manipulative individual does not have any power over you whatsoever.

Keep Your Distance

One of the most effective ways to identify a person who is a manipulator is by observing how various individuals behave when they are around you and when they are around other individuals. If the individual happens to behave differently when they are around different people, then that is a character trait that symbolizes they might be manipulative. Everyone has a degree of social differentiation, and some psychological manipulators may prove to be extreme in different instances.

Or starters, they may be polite to various individuals while being extremely rude to others. They may also seem helpless, and in other instances, they will showcase some aggressiveness. When you observe such character traits regularly, you should always keep your distance. Avoid engaging with such people unless you are forced to depend on the circumstances. It was earlier mentioned that it is difficult to learn more about why people tend to be psychologically manipulative. As a result, ensure that you have kept your distance since such individuals cannot be saved from their current predicaments.

Avoid Self-blame and Personalization

In most cases, manipulative individuals tend to look for a person's weakness, and they will start exploiting them afterward. The people who are being exploited may feel inadequate. They may also indulge in some self-blame since they may have failed to satisfy the manipulator in different ways. In some of these situations, it is good to note that although you are being manipulated, you are not the problem.

The manipulator is taking advantage of you while also ensuring that you feel bad about yourself. You may surrender all your rights and power to the manipulative individuals. Always ask yourself questions such as;

- Are you being treated with the respect that you deserve?

- Are the demands of the manipulative person reasonable?

- Is the relationship beneficial to one party or both parties?

- Do you feel good about the relationship?

Focus On Asking Probing Questions

Psychological manipulators will always issue demands to each of the individuals that they are manipulating. Some of the "offers" that they may put across that seem unreasonable to some extent, but they will expect you to meet all their needs. Whenever you feel like you are being solicited unreasonably, it is good to focus on yourself by also asking the manipulator different probing questions. To look into whether each of these individuals has some self-awareness, they will recognize the inequity that is present in each of their schemes. Some of the suitable probing questions include;

- Is the relationship reasonable?
- Does what the manipulator want seem fair?
- Do you have a say in the relationship?
- Are you gaining anything?
- What are your expectations?

When you ask yourself some of these questions, you will be coming up with a mirror that is meant to show you the reality.

The questions are meant to ensure that the manipulator can see the reality about their nature. In an instance whereby the manipulator has some form of self-awareness, they will withdraw the demands that they have been putting across and they will back down. Some pathological manipulators can also be termed as narcissists, and they will dismiss each of the questions being directed to them. They will always insist they you are getting in their way. If you ever find yourself in such a scenario, always ensure that you have applied different ideas that will ensure you have outsmarted the manipulative individuals. By being creative, you can be able to bring an end to the manipulation spree.

Utilize Time to Your Advantage

Besides making some unreasonable requests, the manipulator will always ask questions and expect an immediate answer in each case. They will always exert some undue pressure while also striving to control the situation. The best example is people who are engaging in sales. Their main aim is to ensure that they have marketed different products successfully and they may be manipulative so that people may purchase each of the products that they are selling. In such an instance, the manipulative individual will expect you to answer each of their questions immediately. They will also take advantage in different ways while also distancing themselves from the immediate influence that they have brought forth. Always exercise some sense of leadership by telling the manipulative individual that you will think about it and issue them an answer at an opportune moment.

Some of these words always prove to be powerful, and since we have used an example of sales agents, the customer, in this case, is the one who is supposed to address the salesperson and tell them that they will think about it. Always take time to think about the merits and demerits that may be present depending on the current situation. Also, try to look into whether it is possible to come up with an equitable arrangement or you should say no depending on the present scenario.

Always Learn to Say "No"

It is not easy to say "no," however, you should first learn the art of communication. When you effectively learn to say "no," you will be able to stand your ground while also making sure that you have been able to maintain a workable relationship. Also, make sure that you are conversant with your human rights most importantly the area that involves making sure that you can set your own priorities while also ensuring that you have not incurred any form of guilt. After all, you have the right to choose your own happiness and a healthy life, too. Always make sure that you can resist while also ensuring that you have kept your peace.

Always Confront the Bullies

A psychological manipulator tends to become a bully at some point. They will always intimidate or harm their victims. The most important point to note is that the bullies will always prey on the individuals that they may perceive as weak. The manipulative individuals will go ahead with the exploitation whenever they come across an individual who is compliant and passive. When you make yourself a worthy target, the manipulative individuals will not hesitate to pounce on you. It is also evident that a majority of the people who enjoy bullying are also cowards. Whenever a person begins to showcase that they know their rights, the bullies will always back down. Various studies have also been carried out, and it is evident that most of the bullies have also been victims of violence at some point in their lives. Although the bullies have also been victimized at some point in their lives, it is not an excuse as to why they are bullying others. Such information is meant to ensure that you can view bullies from a different perspective.

When you confront a bully, you will be confident enough that you can protect yourself against various forms of danger. You may stand tall as an individual while also supporting other individuals when they are bullied. In an instance whereby a person has been psychically, emotionally, or verbally assaulted, always make sure that you have sought the services of a counselor and also report the matters to the legal authorities and they will take the necessary course of action. Always make sure that you can stand up to the bullies, and you may partner with some individuals who are fed up with practices such as bullying.

Set Consequences

When an individual who thrives on manipulation insists on violating your personal boundaries, always make sure that you are in a position to tell them "no." Always make sure that you are in a position to assert and also identify consequences. Possession of such knowledge can ensure that you can handle difficult people. When a bully understands the consequences that may come about as a result of their actions, always make sure that they can learn more about the value of respect.

Chapter 9: How to Defend Yourself from Manipulative Individuals

For starters, it is good to note that it is not possible to defend yourself from a manipulative individual. The best thing that you can do in this case is to make sure that you have first identified that the individual is indeed manipulative. If they happen to showcase that they are deceptive, you should ensure that you have kept a safe distance from these individuals. If they are not deceptive, you can continue being friends. It is also good to note that some people may mislead others by spreading false information. For example, you may come across some people talking about how manipulative a certain person is.

Never issue the manipulative person a warning. You should just leave and continue leading your life as usual. After leaving them, they will look for other individuals who they can manipulate into ensuring that they have heeded to their demands. If a person is unwell, you should go ahead and try to find out more about their condition. Since some people do lie, you can also go ahead and seek some expert advice from a psychologist or even a psychiatrist. If the person is unwell and they do not showcase any signs of improving, you can move on and continue living your life as usual.

If the manipulative individual is related to you, you should always be direct with them. Ensure that you have set some boundaries an always be firm such that they cannot dare to cross the set boundaries. Manipulative individuals will realize that they will be held once they tend to showcase undesirable behaviors. The manner in which such people behave towards you will also determine the manner in which you will interact with them.

If they understand some of the rules that you have set, they will be okay with that, and they will not intrude in any way. Also, ensure that you have initiated a discussion with the manipulative individual while also trying to learn more about their character and condition. Ensure that you have not lectured them in any way. Always ask questions that will help you to learn more about how they are. Never try to fix them, leave such matters to professionals such as psychiatrists or psychologists. Always ensure that you have issued them a referral to a renowned psychiatrist or any other medical practitioner who can deal with their condition accordingly. The manipulative individuals should also be issued the support that they need. Additionally, you should never interrupt a manipulative person whenever they are telling a story.

Although some of the stories issued by the manipulative individuals will appear far-fetched, you should never judge them. According to them, their story is valid, although it may appear to be made up to some extent. Ensure that you have not told them any of your stories. If anything goes wrong, they will always use the information that they have about you to fight back. Always remember that we never choose our family members; as a result, you should choose whether you will help them or ignore them. If any other people may appear to be toxic in your life, you should also avoid them.

Conclusion

Besides, this book has powerful psychological techniques that can be used to influence anyone at the manipulator's will. It provides an extensive definition of some of the general terminology used to define the traits of different people in society while disintegrating the value of understanding why people should know more about the dark secrets of psychology.

The persuasion technique is known as the strategy people use in coercing others to do as they will. For instance, are you always in a position to get everything you want from others at the expense of their happiness? If you don't, then perhaps it's time to begin to work on yourself in order to harness the power within and persuade your friends or relatives to delve into some of the projects you believe in. It's also often thought that the persuasion techniques fall under certain categories that have been highlighted in some of the chapters herein.

Using those techniques, you can easily convince your teammates or any other acquaintances to join you in the walk towards "greatness" as you may define it at the moment of need. With that said, being an excellent strategist and persuader will help you in accomplishing life's most important objectives in the long run. It's clear that persuasion is a requirement when it comes to handling different tasks not only at home but work too. Even when forming friendships, this is a requirement.

Persuasion is a vital skill that someone can develop using the right tips as well as garnered information. In this book, the initial step lies in taking the required action in order to improve a person's persuasion skills. It all starts with the important basic steps of persuasion, coupled with the ability to assess how useful you are. The second strategy lies in getting several actionable tips that can be used in enhancing your techniques and ability to get others to join you.

The rest of the chapters explore the application of manipulation. Therefore, you'll see how useful it is when it comes to learning more about the techniques of manipulation and how to use them to your advantage. The hypnosis of the book helps you to learn more about how to apply those skills to common use. It's an element that can assist you in acquiring more of what you may need from life.

Other than that, this book introduces you to the neuro-linguistic system that can be used in knowing how to garner advanced persuasion skills. It's usually followed by wanting to learn more about deception, including what should be done to improve your learning skills. You also need to master the art of administering mind games when exploring the minds of your colleagues or friends. By learning, you'll have avoided falling victim to manipulative characters in society. Eventually, you'll also get to learn more about the ability to persuade your victims to join your caliber in search of greener pastures. The techniques described in this book should provide guidance to you and anyone you consider special in your life.

Printed in Poland
by Amazon Fulfillment
Poland Sp. z o.o., Wrocław

54614884R00226